Shalom/Salaam/Peace

To Bunny —
A woman of faith
and spirit — & a
sister in the Call
of Christ.
Blessings —
Constance
March 15, 2009

Religion and Violence

Series Editors
Lisa Isherwood, University of Winchester, and Rosemary
Radford Ruether, Graduate Theological Union, Berkeley,
California

This interdisciplinary and multicultural series brings to light the ever increasing problem of religion and violence. The series will highlight how religions have a significant part to play in the creation of cultures that allow and even encourage the creation of violent conflict, domestic abuse and policies and state control that perpetuate violence to citizens.

The series will highlight the problems that are experienced by women during violent conflict and under restrictive civil policies. But not wishing to simply dwell on the problems the authors in this series will also re-examine the traditions and look for alternative and more empowering readings of doctrine and tradition. One aim of the series is to be a powerful voice against creeping fundamentalisms and their corrosive influence on the lives of women and children.

Published:

Reweaving the Relational Mat
A Christian Response to Violence against Women from Oceania
Joan Alleluia Filemoni-Tofaeono and Lydia Johnson

Weep Not for Your Children: Essays on Religion and Violence
Lisa Isherwood and Rosemary Radford Ruether

America, Amerikkka: Elect Nation and Imperial Violence
Rosemary Radford Ruether

Forthcoming:

In Search of Solutions: The Problem of Religion and Conflict
Clinton Bennett

Meditations on Religion and Violence in the United States
T. Walter Herbert

Shalom/Salaam/Peace

A Liberation Theology of Hope

Constance A. Hammond

LONDON OAKVILLE

Published by Equinox Publishing Ltd.
UK: Unit 6, The Village, 101 Amies St., London SW11 2JW
USA: DBBC, 28 Main Street, Oakville, CT 06779

www.equinoxpub.com

First published 2008

British Library Cataloguing-in-Publication Data
A catalogue record for this book is available from the British Library.

ISBN-13   978 184553 379 3   (hardback)
          978 184553 380 9   (paperback)

Library of Congress Cataloging-in-Publication Data

Hammond, Constance A.
  Shalom/salaam/peace: a liberation theology of hope/Constance A. Hammond.
    p. cm. — (Religion and violence)
Includes bibliographical references and index.
  ISBN 978-1-84553-379-3 (hb) — ISBN 978-1-84553-380-9 (pbk.)
1. Arab-Israeli conflict—Religious aspects—Judaism. 2. Arab-Israeli
conflict—Religious aspects—Christianity. 3. Arab-Israeli
conflict—Religious aspects—Islam. 4. Religion and social
problems—Israel. 5. Liberation theology—Israel. I. Title.
DS119.7.H3528 2009
201'.7273—dc22
                        2008017426

Typeset by S.J.I. Services, New Delhi
Printed and bound in Great Britain by Lightning Source UK Ltd, Milton Keynes

CONTENTS

Part 2
LIBERATION THEOLOGY

LIST OF MAPS AND PHOTOGRAPHS

THIS BOOK IS DEDICATED

To my parents William H. Hammond and C. Maxine Glover Hammond who believed in me even when they did not understand what I was doing.

To the people of Central and South America who professed the cause of Liberation Theology, lived out their faith no matter the consequences and in the process gifted the world with a new possibility for justice and peace.

To all the Christian, Jewish and Muslim people who are working to bring about peace in the suffering Holy Land, and to those who have given their lives that *shalom, salaam,* peace might be a reality.

Acknowledgments

A multitude of people—named and unnamed—have inspired or given life to this book.

From the 1960s: Sami and Badhia Burhan; Peggy and Harry Craig; Mooky Dagan; and the faculty and students at the Overseas School of Rome, Italy.

The Rev. Dr Carney Gavin, formerly Curator of the Harvard Semitic Museum, and now Curator of the Archives for Historical Documentation in Boston, Massachusetts, my gratitude for bringing me into a new understanding of the Middle East and the Holy Land in particular, as well as encouraging me through my Master of Divinity and Doctor of Ministry degrees as well as ordination as an Episcopal priest.

The Rev. Dr Canon Edmund Rodman, a fellow priest who has understood my vision and supported it, finding ways to sustain the Refugee Immigration Ministry's (RIM) early days—a person who has remained a champion of justice and equality in this country and elsewhere. My profound thanks.

The Right Rev. Thomas Shaw, Bishop of the Episcopal Diocese of Massachusetts, and former Superior of the brothers of the Society of Saint John the Evangelist, for his and for the other brothers' support of my ministry—by offering retreats and by their early volunteer work with RIM. My admiration, as well, for the work that they are presently doing leading groups to Israel/Palestine through Saint George's College, Jerusalem, and their dedication to bringing peace to the region.

Harvard Divinity School, which afforded me an opportunity to learn about and with people of different cultures and religions and to the political asylum seekers with whom I worked—many of whom were from the Middle East or of the Muslim faith. Saint George's College in Jerusalem and Sabeel, both of whom have given me new insights into Israel/Palestine through their educational programs and conferences.

The Rt. Reverends Vincent Warner and Sanford Hampton for inviting me to participate on the Bishop's Committee for Justice and Peace in Israel/Palestine and for Bishop Warner making an extensive trip I took to Israel/Palestine possible.

The Episcopal Divinity School for granting me a Proctor Fellowship so I could do the research and writing necessary for my doctoral thesis, and to San Francisco Theological Seminary (SFTS) for providing the professional and scholarly framework for my work. Faculty and students in the doctoral program, at SFTS, for their insights; Dr Cecilia Ranger, SNJM, who encouraged me to get a D.Min.; The Rev. Dr Canon Richard Toll, for advising me on my thesis project and The Rev. Dr Naim Ateek, who remains for me a model of Christian witnessing.

Dr Joan Maiers, SNJM, poet and Marylhurst faculty member, and Louise Godfrey, who proofread my thesis—Dr Maiers offering publishing suggestions and Mrs. Godfrey sustaining me with her wisdom and brownies—and The Rev. Dr Alla Bozarth, a poet, theologian and colleague, whose knowledge added much to my thesis project.

Jeff Johnson, General Manager, and Ben Eggersgluss, an employee, at the Portland MAC Store, who salvaged my manuscript when my ancient computer crashed.

My editor, Rosemary Radford Ruether, who said to 'publish' and then made the manuscript publishable by her knowledgeable and detailed editing, and Lisa Isherwood, my other editor, who guided me me through the publishing process.

Finally, to all those Palestinians, Israelis and American Christians, Muslims and Jews who have welcomed me into their homes, who have allowed me to use their experiences and for whom I hold the greatest of respect and admiration. Without the human element of 'knowing' individuals and groups, the statistics would present only a dismal cloud of profound doom.

Introduction: From the Particular to the Global and Back to the Project

In my speaking engagements and in classes I have taught, I learned that even people in university or church settings are not aware of the historical, theological and geographical lineage that threads its way from the beginning to the present day conflict between the Israelis and the Palestinians. And so, this book begins with an historical and scriptural reconstruction from which we can, hopefully, grasp more completely the difficulties the present generations face in their ongoing struggle for the ownership of the land all three religions call 'Ours'.

On the day of September 11, 2001, like the rest of America and the world, I looked for a way to bring sense out of the senseless, inhumane horror that took place in New York, Pennsylvania and Washington, DC. On that day, I searched for a way to bring some sense of center back to our stunned and deflated selves – our very souls. And so I called together the ecumenical body of Christ's churches in Aberdeen, Washington, to plan a service for that same evening. Included in our planning was a representative of the local Jewish synagogue. There was no mosque, nor anyone available from the virtually invisible Muslim community in the small town of Aberdeen. On the following Sunday, during the announcements, as I sought a way to help my parishioners – and myself – deal with the painful empty feeling of our present time, I suggested Bible study, prayer groups, meditation and then, with a sudden inspiration, I offered a class on Islam. The response was amazing! Everyone wanted a class on Islam. At our first class, the meeting room was full. The people who came were from my parish and from other local churches.

Some came uncharted, as it were. One man drove one hour each way to attend the class. All came with a desire to know this unknown religion that had seemingly spawned a terror upon us.

In the process of learning about Islam, we learned about Judaism and even more importantly, about our own roots and history as Christians. During the sixth class, as we were discussing the Christian Crusades, a woman said, 'Constance, no wonder the people hate us', and so we began to gain a more balanced, educated understanding of the situation surrounding 9/11. I was meticulous about not offering my own opinions in the class. I offered my understanding of history and scripture. The class members' opinions came from their own awareness, not mine. And, I, too got a broader understanding as the fabric of the Abrahamic religions was woven together with all of the intricacies, intrigues and endearing/ horrifying aspects of life. Yes, it is no wonder that some hate us, and it is no wonder that some resent us, and it is no credit to us that we are so self-centered and limited in our education that we do not know the history of our own selves – our own religion – our actions and inactions and the consequences they have brought throughout the millennia.

On 9/11, I personally felt a small window of opportunity open where we could respond, not in kind, but rather with an open hand, where we could offer the world a glimpse of an alternative to destruction and retaliation – an alternative that would embrace both grace and strength. The window still exists – it is always available as an option – but it has been firmly shut and barred, at this time. The world, grieving with us in our grief – horrified as we were horrified by the plane loads of people used as missiles – waited ready to join us in whatever we chose to do. We chose to go our own way – on our own – in the stance of a First Testament (Hebrew Bible) vengeful, retaliatory warrior. That stance – our response – has stacked victim upon victim, with the innocent far outnumbering the guilty.

The one thing I have learned is to preface my talks with this: 'If I say something that sounds as if it is criticizing our government's policies, that does not make me un-American. If I say something that sounds as if it is critical about Israel and its policies and actions, that does not make me anti-Semitic, which is the same for the PLO, Hamas and Palestinian peoples, for as we all know, both Jews and Muslims – Israelis and Arabs – are Semitic peoples. (Of course, many of us do not make this connection that goes back to the first peopling of the Middle East.) Wherever I speak, and whatever I say, it is with the hope that our Christian family that has been birthed as one by our common baptism – be remembered, and not forgotten, and that this remembering will not be at the expense of our Abrahamic extended family that includes Jews and Muslims. For, in my opinion, if there is no unity, no respect, no compassion, no reaching out, no bringing in, no embracing while retaining a sense of self, then there is no sense to self.

After I spoke at an Advent city-wide gathering at The Oak Tree Restaurant, in Woodland, Washington (focused on 'Bethlehem Then and Bethlehem Now'), a woman said to her pastor, 'She [meaning me] made me think, and I didn't want to!' Well, if people think, reflect, are opened to more than they presently think they know, then I feel my goal has been reached in a small way, a person-by-person, small community-by-small-community way. Many speak in the large cities, where often we reinforce one another's opinions at our own, liberal – or conservative – gatherings of like-minded folk. In the byways, off the major highways, exist people open to knowledge and understanding that may jar their preconceived opinions. No, all people anywhere are not open to new learning, but I have been impressed by the receptivity of those in places thought to be peopled by close-minded souls. Perhaps we too quickly judge and criticize those not of our kind, in our 'club', in our tribe, in our church, neighborhood, school, or framework of reference. Perhaps, we judge when we might better listen and learn from those outside our places of the usual. Perhaps we judge, and in the judging lose the opportunity to learn and understand more deeply. Perhaps – just perhaps – we judge in order to insulate ourselves from having to face something potentially disruptive to our own personal world view. Perhaps – just perhaps – we are all like the woman who did not want to think, for if we really think we may change and if we change the ripple effects can go beyond our imaginings. 'Judging' allows one to remain within a rigidly secure perimeter of the known. But what is faith? What is God? What is life, if not entering into the mystical unknown with an open mind and an open heart?

My own personal experiences from my years in Rome, meeting with Bishop Lawrence and his friends, during Vatican II, spending long hours in theological discussions with a class of seminarians attending the Irish College, developing close friendships with a Muslim from Syria and an Israeli Jew – both peace-loving yet neither willing to be in the same room with the other – all these relationships informed me and gave me understandings for my later work in New England where I developed programs related to Central America, was a leader in the Sanctuary Movement and worked with women and men who were political asylum seekers.

Invited to go with Witness for Peace on their first trip to Nicaragua, and another group that went later, I was unable go because of seminary commitments. I did go, however, as part of the first Peace Delegation to El Salvador, returning to the area several times, spending time as well in Honduras and Guatemala. From the people, struggling to survive, I learned the soul-restoring reality of Liberation Theology. This knowledge and practice carried into my ordained ministry as a chaplain and my subsequent work as a rector and interim priest.

And Israel/Palestine – ever since time spent in Egypt in the 1970s, I have felt a link to the Middle East. Classes in Boston and work at the Harvard Semitic Museum, led me to become more informed. My first trip to Israel/Palestine was to St. George's College, the Anglican Episcopal center in Jerusalem. I took one of their classes as a part of my own continuing adult education program. Subsequent trips, with Sabeel and on my own, were to better inform myself, with the goal of helping others in the United States be better informed. I was doing what I had done in Central America, which many are doing, presently, in groups and on their own. Out of these trips I have developed a study program for churches, and teach a university class, to better help people understand the history and the present reality in Israel/Palestine. As a Christian, whose ministry has often been interfaith and ecumenical, I feel it is my obligation to be a voice for my brother and sister Christians in Israel/Palestine – not to the disadvantage of other faiths, but to speak for those who have little or no voice in our nation. Those of us who have seen and heard, I feel, must then speak for those who are unseen and unheard. As a baptized person, that is my obligation. As a priest, that is my ordained responsibility. Social justice and peace issues are at the core of my being and my ministry. Israel/Palestine is an issue that speaks to the lack of both, with the United States' involvement residing at the core of the problems and the possibilities.

My M.Div. thesis was on Sanctuary. My D.Min. thesis was on Israel/Palestine. My life seems to circle in experiencing, studying, witnessing, teaching and experiencing again. It is my desire that this book should offer some insights to others about the situation in Israel/Palestine that will challenge them to question more, learn more, think more and act upon these new understandings. If enough of us speak out and if enough of us demand action from our elected representatives, then we the people can bring an end to this quagmire in Israel/Palestine. No one – Jew, Christian or Muslim – benefits from an ongoing occupation with the continued threat of an escalation of violence. May the spirit of truth lead us all so that the peace of God may rest upon all of us, in Israel, in Palestine, in the United States and in the rest of the world.

PART 1

THE LAND AS PLACE

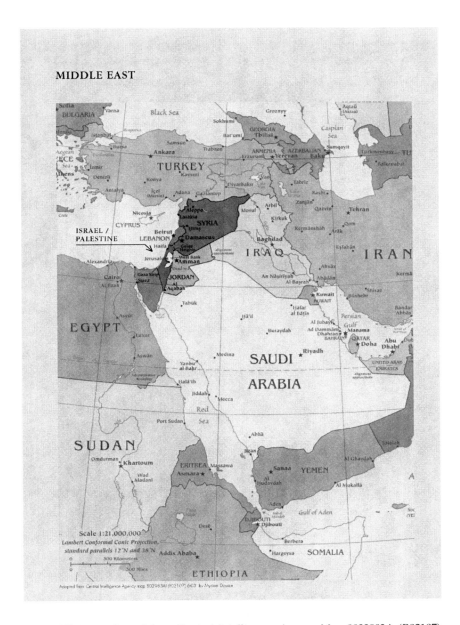

The Middle East, adapted from Central Intelligence Agency Map 8022983A (R02107) 603 by Miriam Dousse, permission kindly granted by Anna Baltzer.

Palestinian/Jewish Owned Land 1946, and *Land Designated for Palestinian/Jewish States,* UN Plan 1947, original version by NAD-PLO. Adapted from Oren Medicks 1999, permission kindly granted by Anna Baltzer.

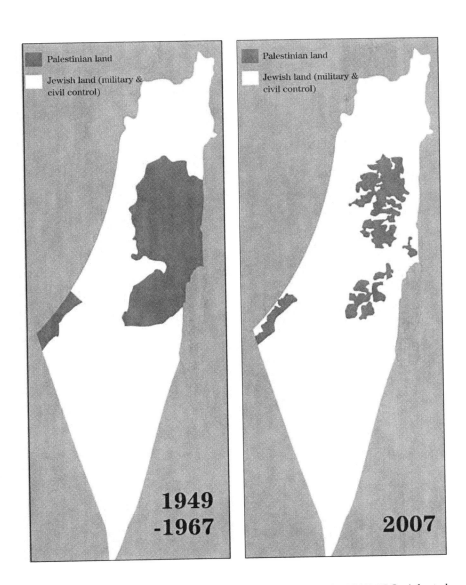

Palestinian/Jewish Land 1949–1967 and 2007, original version by NAD-PLO. Adapted from Oren Medicks 1999, as published in *Occupation Magazine*, modified by Engin Coban, permission kindly granted by Anna Baltzer.

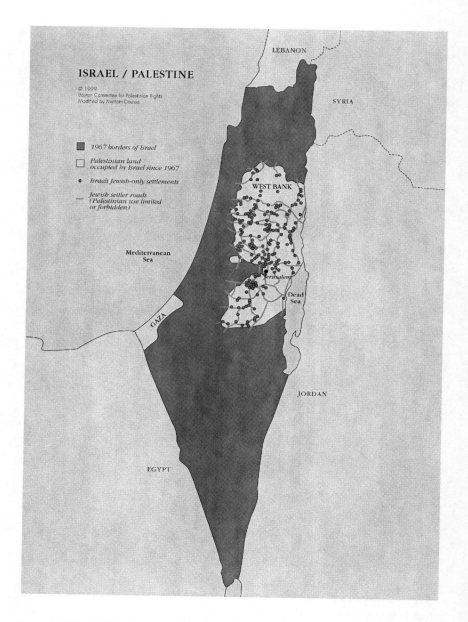

Israel/Palestine, © 1999, Boston Committee for Palestinian Rights. Modified by Myriam Dousse, permission kindly granted by Anna Baltzer.

The Land of Israel/Palestine

'The Palestine of Jesus' Times', reads the heading on a map in a Sunday School room at St. Andrew's Episcopal Church in Aberdeen, Washington. The map, like many maps in many churches throughout America, has been there for generations – not as a political statement, simply as a defining label on a map of the world of Jesus as it was in the days of Jesus. I was in the classroom to tell the children a little bit about Christians in Israel/Palestine (This was to enable them to prepare a Peace Candle for our sanctuary – a candle lit at all services in remembrance of our baptismal brothers and sisters in Israel/Palestine.) As I talked, one child said, 'Constance, why does it say, "Palestine", on the map, and not Israel?' I, frankly had not noticed the wording on the map. And so I began a brief explanation of the 'Why' of Palestine in Jesus' time and the 'Why' of Palestine in our time. Her question, brought into focus the greater question of today: 'Why is Palestine no longer a politically recognized entity – a nation or a state?' Certainly the name *Philistine* or *Palestine* has been on record for centuries.

The name *Palestine* comes from the Philistines, who arrived in about the fourteenth century, BCE (Before the Common Era/Pre-Christ). These early Palestinians lived in an area that extended along the eastern Mediterranean coast west to the Jordan Valley, south to the Negev desert and north to the Galilean region. It is believed these early arrivals came from Asia Minor and areas of Greece. Variations on the name *Philistine* are thought to have appeared in Egyptian texts at the temple of Medint Havu and in the Annals of the Assyrian Emperor Saragon II. They occupied a land that has been shared and defined and ruled over at various times by the Canaanites, Philistines, Hebrews, Nabateans, Byzantines, Arabs, Turks, British and more recently the Israeli Jews. During the Roman Empire's rule, *Palestine* was the name used for the region.

The problem with available source material concerning the Philistines' origins and history is the actual origins of the source material itself. For the most part, until recently, the material about the Philistines has been written from a western or Hebrew/Judaic perspective. As Palestinian scholar, author and educator Edward Said wrote in his article, 'Blaming the Victims: Spurious Scholarship and the Palestinian Question', 'Palestine has been the home to a remarkable civilization centuries before the first Hebrew tribes migrated to the area' (Whitelam 1996: 8) This doesn't sound like the biblical stories Christians and Jews have been brought up on. Wasn't Abraham the father of all the Hebrew/Canaanite tribes? Could it be that the Philistines predated the Hebrew people in the area now referred to as the Holy Land? As Keith Whitelam writes in his book, *The Invention of Ancient Israel, The Silencing of Palestinian History*, Palestine's history has been framed within the context of the Hebrew Bible. 'The history of the region has long been seen as neatly compartmentalized into Patriarchal, Exodus, Conquest or Settlement periods followed by the United Monarchy of David and Solomon, the Divided Kingdoms of Israel and Judah, Exile, and then Restoration…Palestinian history is effectively silenced by this tyranny of biblical time which has been perpetuated by Western scholarship' (Whitelam 1996: 60-61).

And so who came first? In some ways it depends on who is recording the event. As for the Philistine people, we do know that they came and settled on the coast. And we know, as well, that at a time in history, after being considered a great threat by the Hebrew ruler Saul, the Palestinians were evidently defeated by the Hebrew ruler David. After that the Philistines seem to have disappeared from our Western historical records (Whitelam 1996: 136).

Looking at the area of Palestine/Canaan and the East Bank of the Jordan River there were cave dwelling hunting and gathering peoples as early as 100,000 BCE. This was a land lived on by a peoples destined to be occupied by other peoples over the centuries. By 2,800 BCE, Egypt had dominated the area, then Syria took control in 1,700 BCE and back the land went to Egypt in 1,430 BCE and 1,154 BCE, with brief losses of control in between. In the midst of this, during the 1,800s BCE, Abraham first settled a section of the countryside of Canaan/Palestine that ranged from approximately Shechem (Nablus) to Beersheba (Ruether 1989: 4).

In 1,000 BCE the Hebrew people formed a United Kingdom of Judah and Israel, which split in 927 BCE. Then we see the Assyrians, the Babylonians (present day Iraqis), the Persians (now Iranians) and finally Alexander the Great ruling this parcel of land for 175 years, from 330 BCE until it became a Jewish Kingdom in 142 BCE. The Greeks are the ones, from the fifth century, BCE, who called the area Syria of the Philistines. In 63 BCE Canaan/Palestine was ruled by Rome. This lasted through and beyond the life of Christ. The Romans, perhaps from as early as 70 CE (Common Era/Post-Christ) (Wagner 2000: 33) – certainly from the Bar Kochba Jewish revolt against Rome in 135 CE – called the area the Province of Palestine or the *Provincia Syria Palaestine*, which became *Palaestinia*, from which the anglicized *Palestine* of today is derived. This name remained through the Islamic period, the Crusades and into the British Mandate of Palestine. Roman occupation was followed by Byzantium Christian rule (324–614 CE), followed by Arab Muslim rulers (638 CE), who were intruded upon by Christian Crusaders (1099-1191 CE). Mamelukes (1244–1517 CE) preceded the Ottoman Empire's rule, which lasted from 1517–1918 CE (Ruether 1989: 5).

It is interesting to note that during these times, when rulers shifted, the attitude of Jews to Christians, Christians to Jews, and 500 years later, Muslims to Christians to Jews and each to one another often retained an attitude of tolerance, although there were times of incredible destruction, persecution and death. One begins to see how the land of Israel – the land of Palestine – has been the land of many peoples, who have at many earlier times lived in peaceful coexistence. It is also important to note, as Rosemary Radford Ruether said at a Sabeel Conference in Berkeley in August, 2007, that in ancient times the land was never referred to as Israel. *Israel* was the name given to the ten northern tribes who disappeared in Assyrian times. In the Hebrew Bible this area is called the land of Canaan. The two southern Hebrew tribes that remained, and their area of land, was called Judah. Only when the modern state of Israel came into being, was the land called Israel.

On my first trip to Israel/Palestine, in 1993, I was walking toward the Damascus Gate (the earliest and main gate into the Old City), from the West Bank, when I caught my first glimpse of the inclusivity and exclusivity surrounding the ownership of place. Outside the walls of the city extended a bazaar of international treasures, ranging from CDs to scarves to socks to sunglasses. There was both the traditional and modern basics, as well as the beautiful and the desired. Among these items were sprinkled sweets and treats of exotic looking origins. The people were as varied as the offerings. Some were robed in traditional jalabas, some were covered in traditional veils (hijab), some wore western clothing, some were dressed in the black clothing of the Orthodox Jew, with ringlets hanging by the ears of the bearded men. It was a glorious, festive seeming combination of Jew and Muslim and Christian and nonbelievers living out their secular lives as if in a mosaic of harmony.

As I entered, through the gate, I was struck at first by darkness – a quick refocusing and then, once again, I was stunned by the brilliant sunlight of Jerusalem within the walls of the Old City. This time, however, I had entered into the open market – full of light and full of life that defies description. Colors and smells and sounds all assaulted my senses. The movement of people, of carts and animals, of fish and chicken and vegetables, fruit, bread and meat – the movement of life as it is lived today and life as it has been lived and moved all the days of Jerusalem – all this seemed to bounce across the great cobble stoned street, lifting me up and carrying me forward. Shops, doorless, with clothing, electronics, toys, household goods – all things necessary for life – welcomed me – invited me in – as I wandered by in this flow beyond time. Suddenly, in a widening of the street – a space where several streets intersected creating a small piazzeta – the movement, the mood the bubbling, babbling ceased. Before me were Palestinian school children sitting in their wooden, one-armed chairs in the street outside their school. Pictures of a fellow schoolmate were hanging on their desks. They were sitting in silent protest against the shooting of one of their own by the Israeli Defense Force (IDF), the day before. There was a tension. There was a silence. Where before there had been the sounds of the routine, there was now the soundless voice of protest, of pain, of fear. When the Israeli soldiers came, as they did, the students were forced back in to their school. This demonstration, by a handful, ended without incident. This incident, however, underscored the ongoing tension, struggle and conflict that exists in the city and in the area as a whole.

Jerusalem

Jerusalem is a city divided. That seems clear enough even to someone not conversant with the political geography of the city. Jerusalem is divided. Although the United Nations (UN) in its first act as a body, on 29 November 1947, established Resolution (II), which was a plan for the governing of Jerusalem that would make, as Naim Ateek states in *Justice and Only Justice*, 'Jerusalem as a corpus separatum, internationalized' (Ateek 1989: 173), belonging to and serving both Arabs and Jews as a common capital city of the Holy Land. The reality of this hoped for act has never been realized, enforced or enacted. Just looking within the walled city of Old Jerusalem one can see an intricate, tightly compressed, overlapping and intermingling of sacred and historical places that are divided, though one, within the walls of the Old City.

The Old City of Jerusalem is a walled city, enclosed and divided into sections or quarters. The present day walls and gates were built between 1537 and 1542 BCE, during the reign of the Turkish ruler, Suleyman the Magnificent. They have been modified in ensuing centuries, but in essence remain the same. Within the Jewish Quarter, which is found in the southeast sector, there are six synagogues and many areas of archaeological interest including a Hasmonean Walk, left from the time of the Hasmonean Kingdom (167–63 BCE, when Pompey took control of the region). The Hasmonean family and other devout Jews fled Jerusalem in opposition to what they saw as Greek and Olympian cults' influence on their Jewish faith. Judah Maccabee led his people back to regain control of the city and region. After restoring and purifying the Temple buildings in Jerusalem, they lit the lamps of the menorah and stated that this day of dedication would be called Chanukah (Hanukah). Also in the Jewish Quarter is the Cardo Maximus (the ancient main street that ran from the Damascus Gate into the city and was equivalent in width to a modern eight lane highway); The Burnt House (a basement with charred pots and debris and an archeological story that speaks to the Roman destruction of Jerusalem in 70 CE); the Herodian Houses (remains of wealthy Jewish mansions and a seminary, with frescoes, mosaic floors and household items of great value from the same era) and the Column and the Apse of the Nea (the remains of what had been a complex containing the Orthodox Church of Mary Theotokos – the mother of God/the God-

Bearer – unique in that it represented a doctrine of the church and not an event in Jesus' life) (Murphy-O'Connor 1992: 72).

In this quarter, as well, is located the Western Wall (the Wailing Wall) of the former Jewish Temple – the wall that stands as a symbol for Jews for what was lost in the destruction of the temple in 70 CE and what is to be regained – the wall that stands as a buttress under the plaza on which Haram esh-Sharif (the Dome of the Rock) stands. It is at this wall that religious Jews come to pray, to poke tiny papers of prayers into the crevasses of the wall, to remember and to honor the past, the people, those loved ones being placed in God's loving hands. It is at this wall that Orthodox religious Jews come to bend and to bow in their prayers. All this is happening, below, while above the Muslims are kneeling in their prayer, facing Mecca, calling forth their faith and their hopes and their desires to God. In the mix are the Christians who come to wonder at the history, at the architecture, at the archeological and religious importance of the place. For it is for us, in our shared Abrahamic faith, as well, a wall of our faith's foundation. We all are praying, in our own way, to the One God, even though the presence of machine guns at the ready in the hands of the soldiers of the IDF belies that commonality of our faith.

Unfortunately, it is also at this wall that Palestinians come to grieve the loss of their homes. Before the 1967 Six Day War (when Israel attacked Egypt, Syria and Jordan, taking control of Syria's Golan Heights, Egypt's Sinai Desert and Gaza Strip and Jordan's West Bank and East Jerusalem), the area in front of the wall was full of urban life. There was not a plaza or open area, rather there existed the usual urban mix of homes and shops that extended out from the wall, with a narrow passageway next to the wall for those who wished to pray at the wall. In 1948, the area in which the Western Wall stands was under the control of Jordan and Jews were denied access. In 1967, when Israeli paratroopers took control of the Old City, they bulldozed the Arab neighborhood to create the plaza that one visits today. I, personally, was not aware of this until the Archives for Historical Documentation had the photo exhibit, 'Journey to Jerusalem: Hospitable Memories, An Exhibit of the Earliest Photographs of Jerusalem', taken by a resident photographer, Mindel Diness in the mid-1800s. The exhibit was sponsored by the Austrian government and the Austrian Hospice of the Holy Family (which is located in the center of the Old City of

Jerusalem), in celebration of the hospice's 150th anniversary. Local Palestinian archeologists, patriarchs, Israeli politicians and diplomats, shopkeepers and television personalities, religious persons – old and young and in between – all sorts of people – came to the exhibit. Many came as families to describe to the younger generation where their home or business or relative or some object of particular interest had been in the days before the division of the land. It was not only a learning experience for me as a staff member, but a personal opportunity for both Israeli Jews and Israeli Palestinians – Christians and Muslims – to hear one another's stories. It was a reminder of how sacred a place may be to one, and how, at the same time, it may exist as a desecration of place or a place of painful memories, to another.

Within the Old City of Jerusalem there are two Christian areas: the Christian Quarter and the Armenian Quarter. The Armenians have had a presence in Jerusalem since their king's conversion in 303 CE, when Armenia became the first Christian nation. Since the end of the Kingdom of Armenia, at the conclusion of the fourth century, the Armenians have considered Jerusalem their spiritual home. They have had an enclosed section of the Old City since the early fifth century. This enclave was originally designed for religious purposes, but expanded to include secular parts of the culture during the persecution of the Armenian people by Turkey – a time of persecution which ended in a 1915 genocide, in which over 1.5 million Armenians were killed. Today, about 1,500 Armenians live in the compound. The Armenian Quarter has been called by Jerome Murphy-O'Connor 'a city in miniature', as the quarter contains within its boundaries an Armenian Monastery, Armenian schools, a library, an Armenian Museum (that was formerly a seminary), residential quarters, and the great Orthodox Cathedral of St. James (Murphy-O'Connor 1992: 64). In contrast, the confines of the Christian Quarter, a 45-acre area found within the northwest section of the city, houses 4,500 people, where there is a mix of historic and active sites: the Jaffa Gate leads into the Christian Quarter which includes, among many sites, two mosques, the Lutheran Church of the Redeemer (built in 1898 on the site of the eleventh century church of St. Mary la Latine), the Church of St. John the Baptist (Greek Orthodox, it is the oldest church in Jerusalem) and Christ Church (built in 1849, it is the first Protestant church built in the Holy Land). This is where the Church of the Holy Sepulchre (where Christ is purported to have died, been buried and was resurrected) is located. The Church of the Holy Sepulchre is jointly occupied by the Latin Catholics, Greek Orthodox, Armenians, Syrians, Copts and the Ethiopians (Murphy-O'Connor 1992: 48).

The first time I went to the Church of the Holy Sepulchre, in 1993, we were taken in a group by the Dean of St. George's College. His way (the very best way in my opinion), is to approach the church from the roof, entering from the top, where the Coptic Orthodox Church's quarters have grown like organic blossoms, sculpted and stuccoed onto the roof (The Coptic Orthodox Church comes from Egypt and is based on the teachings described in the Gospel of Mark in the Christian Bible.) From this rooftop vista, one wanders down through the various layers of churchdom, to the ultimate, most earth-bound chapel, the Chapel of St. Helena, the mother of Constantine the Great, Emperor of Rome. Named Helena Augusta by her son, she was given full honors as the mother of the King. She was a devout Christian and Christian legends attribute the building of Christian churches throughout the West to Helena, as well as the discovery of the true cross of Christ's crucifixion and the tomb of Christ. She commissioned the basilicas in Bethlehem (the place said to be the site of Christ's birth) and on the Mount of Olives. From there, in the Chapel of St. Helena, through a closet in the wall of the chapel, we entered into what scholars believe was the quarry – the place – of Jesus' death, entombment and resurrection. There, the stones are unblemished by the pollution of the centuries. There is most likely the place – the there – on which Christian pilgrimages focus.

While the quarry area remains pristine in its enclosed purity, the upper levels of the Church of the Holy Sepulchre are full of the scent of incense and sacred oils – centuries and centuries of incense and oils – of soot smudges and the wax from candles, of prayers, of memories of conflict within and conflict that has entered from without. And now, this holiest of Christian sites is looked down upon by a Jewish settlement. On a trip to Jerusalem, in 2002, while everyone was oohing and aahing about the roof, I looked over and up and saw something new: a rooftop barbed wired enclave, with housing and a children's playground, all guarded by elevated machine gun turrets and soldiers high on platforms looking down on us, as we walked the roof of the Church of the Holy Sepulchre. It was a chilling reminder of the reality of the settlements – those communities built upon confiscated land. Built overlooking the place of the resurrection, this settlement casts a shadow upon a place seen by Christians as holding The Light of the World.

In the Muslim Quarter, which covers 76 acres in the northeast section of the Old City and houses 14,000 people, there exist many places of Christian interest. Among them are: St. Anne's Crusader Church (the possible site of the home of Jesus' mother Mary and her parents Joachim and Anne); Pool of Bethesda (where Jesus is purported to have healed a sick man); St. Stephen's Gate, also called Lion's Gate (this leads from the Old City toward the Mount of Olives and Gethsemane (the garden where Jesus is believed to have been arrested). It is named after the first Christian martyr, Stephen); Ecce Homo Arch (believed at one time to be where Pontius Pilate called out, 'Behold the man': Ecce *Homo*, in reference to Jesus. It is most likely a triumphal arch built by Hadrian); The arch crosses Via Dolorosa and becomes part of the wall of the Convent of the Sisters of Zion, within which a stone pavement is etched with Roman games; Site of the Flagellation Monastery (where it is believed Jesus was flogged); Via Dolorosa (the 'Way of the Cross' where tradition holds that Jesus walked carrying his cross on the way to his crucifixion). On Via Dolorosa there are fourteen stations of the cross, each one venerating a moment related to Christ's final walk. The Via Dolorosa weaves through the busy streets of the Muslim and Christian Quarters from an area near Ecce Homo Arch to the Church of the Holy Sepulchre. In addition to these, there are twenty-three other Muslim sites of interest within the confines of the Muslim Quarter, including six monuments and the Marmluk Buildings (which housed bond servants of former Islamic rulers).

It was in the Muslim Quarter that the Archives for Historical Documentation held its photo exhibit at the Austrian Hospice. The guest house (or Bed and Breakfast) was originally the only hospital in the area, therefore it is called a 'hospice'. It is mentioned in guide books for having the best roof-top view of Old Jerusalem, nice accommodations, good toilets and the best apple strudel in Israel/Palestine. I can personally attest to these guidebook declarations as being accurate. Having been in Israel/Palestine several times before, I had walked past the hospice many times but I had never really noticed the place. Jewish tour groups, however, had read the guide books – or their tour guides had – and every day groups would come to the hospice to see the rooftop view, use the toilets and eat apple strudel in the comforts of the hospice's garden area. Perhaps good toilet facilities and apple strudel provide the common ground upon which we can bring together Jews, Muslims and Christians and build a new peace plan!

Haram esh-Sharif (the 'Noble Sanctuary', called the 'Temple Mount' by Jews) sits atop the ruins of the Second Temple. The original temple buildings were built on a rock protruding from Mt. Moriah. The Jewish legend is that this rock was the foundation stone of the world – providing the earth of Adam's making and the site of sacrifices made by Adam, Cain, Abel, Noah and Abraham. It was here, in actuality, that Solomon built the First Temple almost 3,000 years ago (in c. 950 BCE). The First Temple was destroyed by Nebuchadnezzar and the Babylonians in 586 BCE. When the Jews returned from their Babylonian exile, seventy years later, they built the Second Temple on the same site. King Herod enhanced the edifice. In 70 CE, the Roman Emperor Titus had Jerusalem and the Second Temple destroyed. In 638 CE, following the Muslim conquest of Jerusalem, Turkish Caliph (ruler) Omar ibn al-Khattab removed the rubble at the site of the first two temples and began building a house of prayer. The Dome of the Rock was completed fifty years later. As legend has it, The Dome of the Rock houses what is supposed to be the rock upon which the earlier mentioned sacrifices were made. This is the third holiest shrine for Muslims. This Dome of the Rock stands on or near the original Jewish temple site. The al-Masjid al-Aqsa Mosque (the first Muslim mosque) is located as well on the Temple Mount. It was built in the early eighth century. Following destruction by two earthquakes, it was rebuilt in 1035 CE.

When Haram esh-Sharif was built (685–705 CE), it was meant to 'symbolize the fulfillment of the Jewish and Christian prophecies of a rebuilt Temple' (Ruether 1989: 37). It is here – on this site that Abraham is said to have been ready to sacrifice his son, Isaac (although some Muslims feel the rock of sacrifice is in the area where the Hajj – pilgrimage to Mecca – takes place, in Saudi Arabia). It is upon this site, as well, that Muhammad is said to have come on his night journey to heaven. The night journey – considered by some Islamic scholars to be a physical journey but by others to be a dream – is purported to have begun with the archangel Jibra'il (Gabriel) coming to Muhammad with the winged steed Buraq – a spirit horse. According to the story, Muhammad rode from Mecca to Jerusalem on the back of Buraq. In heaven he visited the former prophets, including Abraham, Moses and Jesus, and Allah (God). Allah gave Muhammad messages for the Islamic people – not unlike our Judaic/ Christian story of when Moses received the Decalogue (Ten Commandments) from God on top of Mt. Sinai. Upon his return to Mecca, the people rejected Muhammad's story. His friend, Abu Bakr, supported the truthfulness of Muhammad. This story of the night journey is celebrated each year in the Muslim community as *Lailat al Miraj*. The al-Masjid al-Aqsa Mosque is named for this event.

As with all the quarters – all the parts – of the old city of Jerusalem, the Abrahamic religions share the very stones and the very earth of their common faith. And yet, each has been quite intent on controlling and withholding from the others its precious share of the city. It has not always been so. It has become more so in recent years. When I first went, in 1993, we were allowed into Haram esh-Sharif, leaving our shoes in the provided shoe shelves, covering our heads (if we were women) and showing the respect one should show in any place of sacred nature. In fact, it seemed that people were glad to see our interest. Our presence was welcomed.

More recently even Muslims trying to enter have had to go through stringent security (although the Waqf – Muslim custodians of Haram esh-Sharif – have been given control of the area, the IDF still control who enters from the outside). Many, coming long distances for holy days, have been turned away. I observed this, when I went myself, in 2002, to find that I could not enter. It was not because of Muslim restrictions; it was because of restrictions imposed by the Israeli government following Prime Minister Ariel Sharon's 28 September 2002 visit to the Temple Mount. The purpose of Sharon's visit to the holy site was to proclaim Israel's permanent control of the Temple Mount. Arriving, as he did, with several hundred Israeli policemen, his presence was considered challenging as well as offensive to the Palestinian Muslim community (Carter 2006: 149). It also did not help, that at the time of his visit to Haram esh-Sharif, Sharon was also the Likud Party Chair. Because of his previous history with the Palestinian people, that included a 1953 raid on a Palestinian refugee camp in Jordan (which killed 69 people), a 1982 Israeli invasion of Lebanon, and involvement in the Sabra-Shatila massacre (where 2,000-4,000 Palestinians were killed), his presence at one of the holiest of Muslim sites sparked a series of Islamic responses. Four Palestinians were killed and over a hundred were wounded. By December, 325 Palestinians had been killed and over 9,000 were wounded.

These attacks against the Palestinian Muslims brought more violent attacks against the population in the Israeli Jewish sector of Jerusalem. This resistance by the Palestinians grew into the second Intifada (uprising) – called the Al-Azsa Intifada (the first Intifada began on 7 December 1987, when an Israeli military vehicle drove into a line of Gaza workers waiting to be assigned their employment for the day. Eight workers were killed. Others were injured). By 2006, even though the region was not stable, visitors were once again allowed entrance to Haram-esh-Sharif. From what we were told, entrance is dictated by the times and is not all that predictable for worshipers or for visitors (These restrictions are still imposed, at times, upon all young Muslim males, who are denied access without cause because they are seen as a potential threat to security by the Israeli government.)

In 1993, on our last day in Israel/Palestine, a recent acquaintance and I decided to walk along the top of the wall of the Old City. For one not so enthralled by heights it was a bit of an adventure, of course, it was also one I instigated because I had read that it was a great way to see the city, and so it was. (Unfortunately, in later trips I found this option is no longer available, due to claims of security concerns.) And so we picked our way along the path built into the top of the wall. Some places were rough and ruinous, others smoother and easier to walk. One could imagine defenders – in the ancient past – standing on the wall, watching as the invaders came.

And, then, as we ruminated on the past, Israeli soldiers appeared, challenging us. Since we were obviously 'tourists', simply walking the ramparts of the wall, we were allowed to proceed until the walkable part of the wall ended. What a view of the rooftops! Ever since my years living in Rome, I have loved the vistas of rooftops. These rooftops are among the world's greatest and most amazing in their beauty. The very earth seems to have erupted in glorious gilded splendor, in colorful domes and knobs of stone and minarets reaching high into the sky, all in an organic homage to the intertwined and interconnected reality of our humanity, be we willing or not to recognize this commonality that we share. Looking from the Mount of Olives, containing an olive grove and gardens commemorating where Jesus went with his friends to pray the night prior to his capture, looking past the many churches, the world's oldest continually used cemetery, past the marvelous onion-domed tribute to Mary Magdalene, the Haram-esh-Sharif, the Church of the Holy Sepulchre and all the other rooftops, it seems as if they all meld into one another, religious and secular together as they mingle in the maze that is the story of the city of light.

The Ownership of Land

So who owns the land, in modern day terms? Jews, Christians and Muslims each have their own reasons and rationales, be they based on a religious, historical or emotional basis. To make the ownership issue even more complex, among each religion there are tectonic plates of differing viewpoints and beliefs that rub against one another, bringing about outbursts as disastrous as any earthquakes. In this twenty-first century, we have witnessed the polarization *between* religions and the polarization *within* religions. This polarization has impacted the ongoing discussions of ownership of land in Israel/Palestine. For who can speak on behalf of any one religion? Who will listen or follow any representative of any one faction or subgroup within a given religion? There may be dominant voices, but no unity of thinking or believing. The ownership of a given religion is becoming a key factor in the struggle for ownership of the land.

For Jewish people, the rebuilding of the Jewish temple in Jerusalem and the restoration of the land to the Jewish people are two separate issues. This presumption of 'restoration of the land' relies on a Jewish understanding that the land was theirs to begin with. This understanding is in contrast to the belief of the Palestinians that the land was, and still should be, theirs.

The first issue is that the ancient and traditional beliefs of the Jews is that their temple will be rebuilt in Jerusalem. 'The Jewish Prayer Book is full of requests for God to return to His/Her dwelling place in Zion', said Linda Shivers, Cantor at the Conservative Synagogue, Neveh Shalom, in Portland, Oregon. It is the Orthodox Jews, today, who have held onto this ancient idea of having the temple restored. For non-orthodox and secular Jews the restoration of the temple is not their concern. Their concern is that the land be 'restored' to the Jewish people, according to Linda Shivers. For these people, the focus is not on the rebuilding of the temple, rather it is on the rebuilding and reoccupying of a place –

of the place they have clung to either as people living on the land or as people wishing to return to the land. While it is true, as Shivers pointed out to me, that there are people in Israel/Palestine with all the Hebrew Bible scriptural references (and building materials) ready to rebuild the temple – including reinstituting animal sacrifice – they are in the minority of the minorities. The last thing the non-orthodox Jews would want, Cantor Shivers said, is for the temple to be restored with all of the animal sacrifice and rituals entailed from the ancient time when the temple was in place!

The second issue is that religious Jews feel they own the land, because it is the land of their religious heritage – the land upon which they moved in and moved out as they grappled with God's promises, God's wrath and the human-to-human encounters they experienced with those native to the land – upon their arrival – or to those moving into the land as later occupiers of both the Hebrew and Canaanite/Palestinian people. The Jewish religious observances of Yom Kippur (the Jewish Day of Atonement) and the Seder (the feast of Passover) both end with the words, 'Next year in Jerusalem' – a phrase said with much meaning by many. There is an historic link as well as a spiritual and scriptural link to the land for religious Jews.

The religious rationale for the return of the land to the Jews is, according to the *Jewish Prayer Book*, that God will gather the people of Israel 'in peace from the four corners of the world and lead (them) with (their) heads held high to (their) land'. This land would be Israel, a 'place where the Jewish people would have sovereignty and be able to worship God in peace', said Shivers. Be they pre- or post-World War II Holocaust rememberers, many secular and religious Jews at the heart of it desire a homeland where their own government, let alone other governments, can not persecute them. The secular Jews, without the underpinnings of religion, look at Israel as a place that belongs to them for more modern day reasons. They believe, according to Shivers, that the land was purchased by them – rightly or wrongly – from the Turkish overseers, pre-1947, given to them by the British Petition in 1948, won back after the Israeli/Arab War (fought with neighboring Arab nations) in May, 1948, and won, again, by the Israelis in the Six Day War of 1967. For religious Jews, there is the underlying sense of being the 'Chosen People' of God. For the secular Jews, there is a pragmatism that underlies their belief that the land of Israel is meant to be theirs. It appears that ownership and possession of the land, for the Jewish people, are inherent in the concept of Israel for the Liberal Orthodox, Reformed, Conservative, Constructionist and secular Jews.

After the horrors of World War II, after the displacement and the loss of ownership of land in their European homelands – the loss of lives and sense of security of self – it is understandable how the religious and secular Jews both might want a place – a land – and yet, repeating the cycle of taking, rather than sharing – of seizing, rather than negotiating – does nothing for the land or the peoples who live on the land. It does not bring security to any, rather it brings more fear and a greater sense of insecurity.

The Muslims feel they have a relationship to the land, at least the parts held holiest to them, as part of their shared Semitic heritage, their shared Abrahamic faith and their own history that revolves around the life and writings of Muhammad – the Word of God as received by Muhammad from the Angel Gabriel. Muslims would not say they own the land, as they believe that the land is owned, as it were, by Allah. They would acknowledge, however, those who have a historical title to the land. Before 1900, the titled land was held primarily by Arabs.

We, Christians worldwide, feel an identification with the land because of the places and significant scriptural references that relate to our faith. For within the very confines of Israel/Palestine exist the book ends of Jesus' life – his birthplace, his death place and the place of his resurrection. Held within the beginnings and the endings of the life of Jesus are the years of his adult ministry – the footsteps of his adult life – paced out, today, in the liturgy and liturgical calendars of our Western and our Eastern Christian calendars. While we Christians may have a sense of place, unless we have been born to the land of that place like our Palestinian Christian brothers and sisters, most of us do not have the same sense of ownership – the same sense of possessiveness – as do those rooted in the earth of Israel/Palestine. This rooted earthiness – this sense of belonging – is felt most deeply by those who are of the soil of the Suffering Land, this Land of Israel/Palestine which we call the Holy Land. These links to the land build upon one another through the religious heritage of the religious Jews, the Christians and the Muslims. These links to the land build upon one another, equally strongly, through people simply having lived upon the land, having felt an ownership of and a sense of being part of the land for lifetimes. Many feel a birthright, a place of ancestors, a connection that is human from earth and human to earth. These people can trace their heritage – their family – their place of being – back many centuries. The passions such a connection to place creates can be seen in our modern day eruptions of violence – on both the Israeli and the Palestinian sides.

And what is the sense of ownership – this sense of possession – that binds and breaks the peoples of the Abrahamic faith? For religious persons, be they Jewish, Christian or Muslim, their understanding of scripture and their sense of belonging to – of owning – being identified with – is determined by the particular filter they use when they hear the word of God – when they see the land which God has made. The extreme, reactionary sides of all of the religions view the world differently than the centrist religious position. The following understandings are taken from a centrist position. By centrist, I mean a position that is not extremist, not radically skewed to the right or the left, but held in place in the center by a sense of our having a God of love – not of hate, a God of forgiveness – not of unredeemable judgment, a God of reconciliation – not unending division. The two extreme positions presently held, as I see them, are Zionist – be they Jewish or Christian – and 'terrorists' – be they Jewish or Muslim. These two viewpoints or groups so named will be dealt with later.

According to Naim Ateek (an Anglican/Episcopal priest, founder and director of Sabeel, both to be discussed in later chapters) in looking at the situation from a Christian perspective, 'The land of Israel/Palestine is part of God's world. It belongs to God...today. God has placed on it both Palestinians and Jews. They must share it under God and become good stewards of it. It does not belong to any of them exclusively. They must share it equitably and live as good neighbors with one another' (Ateek 1989: 5-6). Certainly the Palestinian people understand most immediately the concepts of land as owned and then lost – of land cultivated and then destroyed – of land being the promise of the all, versus land being the promise of the one.

Since the Zionist (militant supporters of an establishment of the State of Israel) destruction of Palestinian villages, removal of Palestinian people from their land and the establishment of the State of Israel in 1948 and the following occupation of additional Palestinian land following the Six Day War in 1967, Palestinian land is now 22% of its original size, being limited to the West Bank and Gaza; the State of Israel actually holding 98% of the entire land of Israel/Palestine in the Jewish Trust System through an involved legal procedure that, among other things, does not allow for restitution of Palestinian land (still titled with Palestinian ownership). In addition, since the fifth Zionist Congress in 1901, the Jewish National Fund has existed as a privately owned charitable organization. This Fund was founded to buy and develop Palestinian land for Jewish settlements. Since its inception, it has planted 220 million trees, created 120 dams and reservoirs, developed 250,000 acres of land, created 400 parks, developed 120 water projects and in the next five years has plans to increase Israel's water supply over 6% by building 100 more reservoirs, to provide 53 billion additional gallons of water for Israel. By 2001, the Jewish National Fund owned 14% of the land in Israel. On the surface this sounds laudable, but one must ask upon whose land were these projects completed and from whose source of water are these gallons of water to come? In addition, further incursions into occupied Palestinian land continue to be made by the Israelis – onto land which has been declared by international and United Nations' decisions to be Palestinian.

Both the religious Jews and the Muslim and Christian Palestinians have their own similar history of persecution, loss and reprisal. Is it not time for all sides to change their understandings of earth – of land – of ownership – to look, once again, at who the owner really is? The sense many Palestinians have about Israel's understanding of 'ownership' of the land is, according to what The Rev. Dr Richard Toll (retired Episcopal priest and Chair of Friends of Sabeel-North America) has been told in his many travels to the area: 'What is mine is mine, and what is yours is mine to share'. The converse sense many Israeli Jews have about Palestine's understanding of ownership of the land is that only the Palestinians may own the land – that Israel has no right to exist in this modern setting or in these modern times. These attitudes – these impressions – these images – these realities – must change if the present day cycle of violence, deprivation and injustice is to end.

According to a Muslim friend (a former political asylum seeker who must remain anonymous for his own personal safety) and his iman (minister), all is gifted by God, to be managed, to be cared for, ultimately, to be released. According to him, the Qur'an (the

Muslim holy book) states that we own nothing. God is the owner of all things; we can only possess them – on loan, so to speak – during our lifetime or during the time of our life when we are, in fact, the possessors, holders, caretakers and stewards of the moment. If this belief of caretaking the land could replace the belief of possessing the land, perhaps there would be hope. But as we presently watch the multi-storied security fence – The Wall – the Israeli government is building to separate Israel and Palestine (about which more will be said later), and buses being bombed and extremists from all sides doing what they can to seemingly destabilize, rather than stabilize the region, one wonders if 'place' can ever be seen through a lens that encompasses more than the particular and personal? Yes, land is to be cared for, shared by the ones on it, but this land, with all the religious overlays that have been placed upon it, seems destined to remain a place – a land – under siege, occupied by Jewish, Christian and Muslim peoples at different times, in different ways, always emphasizing the difference between them, not the sameness of their relationship to the land, to the place, to one another.

The Theology of the Land

The land I hold sacred – my place of refuge – my homeland, is on the Little North Fork of the Santiam River, in the state of Oregon. My parents bought it when I was about eight years old. From that time – wherever I lived – The Cabin has been my point of reference. The ground is familiar ground, trod by barefooted feet, raced about on bikes, explored, loved, known for almost a lifetime. The river has held me – in summer times and mentally in feverish times. The Vine Maple, Oak, Cottonwood, Dogwood and Fir have graced me into a green land of multi-wooded hues. I know where the deer rest in the heat of day and where they walk in the cool of night. Each step of the dirt road speaks to me of some aspect of my life – the baby bunnies darting into the ferns, the deer, 'George', who adopted me, the roosting of Turkey Buzzards – there is no nook, no cranny, no spring nor stream nor nestling of trees that I have not known and explored and learned from. I am possessive of this sacred land that has come to me from my parents. I am possessive, and in my possessiveness I realize that this land will not always be my land. Before my parents purchased it, it belonged to another.

And before that, it was lived on by Native Americans, unowned by any person, free land wandered at will by all kinds of creatures. I am grateful for this place – this space – this river-fed, green oasis Eden separate from the life of city. I am grateful, but I remain possessive. How much more so those who can relate back to Christ's time – and before – on their land? How much more so those who can remember God's promise to Abraham and to Moses, in their land of promise that has been in and out of their hands over the millenniums? My years as an owner – a holder – of earth are nothing compared to the Palestinian and Israeli claims to the land they both hold as holy.

Generations of God Gifting the Land

To understand the intensity of feelings, today, in Israel/Palestine, I feel that one must have an understanding of the historical, scriptural and theological links the people of the region have had over the centuries regarding the land of their promise. It is one thing to feel a personal ownership to land – to place. It is an entirely different thing to feel a personal God-given ownership to land – to place. While most of us brought up in a church, synagogue or mosque, and even in the non-religious secular world, have a memory of stories recalling the lineage of God's land-blessing given and land-blessing taken, as mentioned earlier, it has been my experience speaking to church groups and to universities that the supposed background is not always in place, or if in place, not as clear as it might be. For that reason, I offer an overview of God's scriptural promises to those who are the offspring of the original Semitic peoples, the Israeli and the Palestinian peoples of today, remembering that these scriptural promises are as 'true' to history and scripture as was the writer of that time and as is the interpreter of today. These stories are offered because they have shaped our consciousness and our identities, not because they are historical or factual, but because – whether we are religious or secular – these stories have informed our cultures and our understandings of one another. It should be remembered, as well, that these stories have come to us from the Hebrew people. If they had been written by Palestinian or another peoples, the stories might be different.

As the creation story tells it, it all began with Adam and Eve, those mythical, scriptural, legendary figures of our human beginnings. After the apple episode, 'the Lord God sent him (Adam) forth from the garden of Eden, to till the ground from which he was taken. He drove out the man' (Gen. 3:23-24a). Adam and Eve produced two sons, '…Abel a keeper of sheep, and Cain a tiller of the ground' (Gen. 4:2b) Out of a jealous, sibling rivalry rage, Cain killed Abel. His blood spilled upon the ground, drenching the very earth of their origins and seeping into the consciousness of all to come. God came and said, 'And now you are cursed from the ground, which has opened its mouth to receive your brother's blood from your hand…you will be a fugitive and a wanderer on the earth… And the Lord put a mark on Cain, so that no one who came upon him would kill him. Then Cain went away from the presence of the Lord, and settled in the land of Nod, east of Eden' (Gen. 4:11, 12b, 15b-16).

In the scriptural story, Cain and his wife had a son, Enoch, who married and the lineage of Adam and Eve and Cain continued to grow and to flourish and to expand upon the face of the earth – sons and daughters, grandsons and granddaughters great and great-great generations spinning off from the first parents of humankind. Unfortunately, though, the people who grew numerically did not grow in grace, humility, kindness, godliness and generosity of spirit. Instead, they became corrupt, violent and disruptive inhabiters of earth. 'The Lord saw that the wickedness of humankind was great in the earth, and that every inclination of the thoughts of their hearts was only evil continually. And the Lord was sorry that he had made humankind on the earth, and it grieved him to his heart. So, the Lord said, 'I will blot out from the earth the human beings I have created – people together with animals and creeping things and birds of the air, for I am sorry that I have made them. But Noah found favor in the sight of the Lord' (Gen. 6:5-8). Noah and his family and two of every kind of creature were saved, by God, from the flood that ravaged the earth. For forty days and forty nights the family of humankind and creature-kind floated above the earth's surface. And when the waters had subsided, the ark had landed and an altar had been built by Noah, in order for them to give thanks for their safe deliverance from the ravages of the flood, 'the Lord said in his heart, "I will never again curse the ground because of humankind, for the inclination of the human heart is evil from youth: nor will I ever again destroy every living creature as I have done" ' (Gen. 8:21b).

And so Noah, with his sons Shem, Ham and Japheth, began tilling the soil in order to reestablish the plants of the earth upon which they depended for their food. In doing so, it is said that they planted the first vineyard. And from this vineyard came the first wine which Noah drank. One evening, while Noah lay naked in a state of drunkenness, Ham (the father of Canaan) came by and saw his father's naked body. The other two sons, realizing that Ham had broken a taboo by seeing their father's naked body, covered Noah, without viewing him themselves. When Noah discovered what had happened, he said, 'Cursed be Canaan' (Gen. 9:25a) and declared that Canaan would be a slave to his other two sons Shem and Japheth. Thus begins – or one could say continues – the curse of Adam and Eve through the generations of the descendants to follow.

From this second branch of the Tree of Eden, according to the biblical story, spread the peoples of the world speaking the same language, yet bearing the same brokenness of their original parents. As they migrated they came to the plain of Shinar and they built a city which they named Babel. And, because of their behavior and their willfulness, God made it so that there was no longer a common language and God dispersed the people of Babel all over the earth. For many generations and decades and centuries the peoples of the world multiplied and expanded.

> Abram, a descendant of Shem who was a son of Noah, was visited by God, who said, Go from your country and your kindred and your father's house to the land that I will show you. I will make of you a great nation, and I will bless you, and make your name great, so that you will be a blessing. I will bless those who bless you, and the one who curses you I will curse, and in you all the families of the earth shall be blessed...and they set forth to go to the land of Canaan. When they had come to the land of Canaan, Abram passed through the land to the place at Shechem, to the oak of Moreh at Hebron. At that time the Canaanites were in the land. Then the Lord appeared to Abram, and said, 'To your offspring I will give this land'... (Gen. 12:1-3, 5b-7a) from the place where you are, northward and southward and eastward and westward...all the land that you see I will give to you and to your offspring forever (Gen. 13:14b-15).

And here is where the scriptural origin of the present day problems over the ownership of the land begins. According to the story, the Canaanites were in the land that God gave to Abram and his offspring. The descendants of Shem were told they could take what was, now, the land of the descendants of Ham, the father of Canaan

– the one cursed to be a slave for and to his brothers and their descendants. From the nakedness of Adam and Eve to the nakedness of Noah came the conflict of the ages. The naked truth is that Arabs and Jews – Semites both, be they Muslims or religious Jews or Christians – the whole mix and match of the Middle East goes back theologically to God's judgmental intervention – one could say meddling – in the lives of God's children of earth.

The underlying theological rational for our present day dilemmas, feuding hatreds and killings go back to the original reactions, responses and ways of being of the children of earth. A promise broken, in the eating of the apple – a taboo broken, in the son's viewing of his father's naked body – linked and led the descendants into an ongoing conflict over the landscape of our common ground. Born out of the very earth of our existence, the Shemites, the Canaanites, the Japhethites continued to live out the disinheritance of those cursed from the land, citing God as the one granting the land, as the one giving authority and legitimacy to the land's deeds which gave credibility for their own deeds. All this was, and is, done in the name of 'The Lord'.

The touch point of pain for present day Israeli Jews and Palestinians comes from this place of understanding of blessedness and cursedness. The sins of the fathers are indeed passed down from generation to generation! Through Abram and Hagar (Sarai's Egyptian slave-girl) came Abram's first born son, Ishmael, and from Abram and his wife Sarai – fourteen years later – came Abram's second born son, Isaac. The year before Isaac's birth, God appeared to Abram and said:

> your name shall be Abraham, for I have made you the ancestor of a multitude of nations. I will make you exceedingly fruitful; and I will make nations of you, and kings shall come from you…and I will give to you, and to your offspring after you, the land where you are now an alien, all the land of Canaan, for a perpetual holding; and I will be their God. As for Sarah your wife, you shall not call her Sarai, but Sarah shall be her name. I will bless her, and moreover I will give you a son by her. I will bless her, and she shall give rise to nations; kings of peoples shall come from her (Gen. 17:5b-6, 8, 15b-16).

Both Sarah and Abraham laughed, when they were told that Sarah – who was ninety – and Abraham – who was one hundred – would parent a child. The laughter of joy has been suppressed by the ensuing centuries of malevolence and violence.

As recorded in scripture, God promised Abraham that out of the lineage of Ishmael would come twelve princes and a great nation, but God also promised to bless God's covenant upon Isaac. And so, as both sons grew together, Sarah began to fear Ishmael's position in the family. She demanded that Hagar be cast out into the wilderness, with her son, Ishmael. In spite of Abraham's distress over the banishment, Hagar and Ishmael were forced to wander in the wilderness of Beer-sheba. Waterless and without nourishment, God appeared to them and provided them with a miraculous welling up of water (The purported site of this wilderness water is one of the holiest of places, today, in the Islamic religion). The two settled in the area of Paran and, eventually, Ishmael married an unnamed woman from Egypt and they had many children. Ishmael's brother, Isaac, married Rebekah, who, after being unable to conceive, found herself pregnant with twins who battled one another while still in her womb. Distressed by this situation, she called upon God to tell her why this was happening. God responded by saying, 'Two nations are in your womb, and two peoples born of you shall be divided; the one shall be stronger than the other, the elder shall serve the younger' (Gen. 25:23). And so it continued: Esau – the first-born – sold his birthright to Jacob for a meal. Jacob – the second-born – proceeded to, also, deceitfully obtain the blessing of their father at Isaac's deathbed, leaving Esau with only an inheritance of hatred for his brother. To save Jacob from the wrath of his brother, Esau, their mother, Rebekah, sent Jacob away to relatives in Haran. She sent Jacob with her own blessing and a charge to not marry a Canaanite woman. Jacob was given the blessing of Abraham: the land in which they still lived as aliens. God blessed Jacob and changed his name to Israel. Here we have the Canaanite (Palestinian) and Israeli split named, as it continues to be named in our modern day usage.

And so the lineage of intrigue, deception, sibling rivalry and incredible faithfulness, as well as faithlessness, has continued throughout all generations of our commonly held scripture. Jacob/Israel married Rachel and had two children by her as well as six children by her sister Leah and two by Leah's maid. Esau married Canaanite women and had one child each by Adah and Basemath, and three by Oholibamah. Esau and his family moved to the hill country of Seir (known as Edon), while Jacob/Israel and his family settled in the land of their father, the land of Canaan. From this intermarriage and this settlement – this pioneering – this intrusion into a land and people settled, came about a force that eventually rocked Egypt and surrounding areas. Into Egypt, out of Egypt – land owners then slaves, free then seeking freedom – the people that became known as the Hebrew people, the Israelites, moved and were moved. Always, at the core of the people, or at the core of one of the people, remained the seed of prophetic promise. Through treachery and through times of obedience to the word of God, the people followed, or were dragged onward to fulfill the prophetic promise that their leader put forth.

According to the biblical story, Joseph, who was the son of Jacob/Israel, had been despised by his brothers, who attacked him and left him to die in the wilderness only to be found and taken by people passing by to Egypt, where he subsequently became a great leader and confidant to the Pharaoh. This very Joseph later, rescued his own family from a famine in Canaan and brought them to Egypt. Before Joseph died, he gathered his sons and related to them the lineage of their birth, naming them each as one of the twelve tribes of his father, Jacob/Israel, blessing them and commanding them to bury him with his/their ancestors, 'in the cave in the field at Machpelah, near Mamre in the land of Canaan, in the field that Abraham bought from Ephron the Hittite as a burial site' (Gen. 49:29b-30). In this place, Jacob/Israel joined Abraham, Sarah, Isaac, Rebekah and Leah. And so we have the twelve tribes of Ishmael (Canaanite/Palestinian) and the twelve tribes of Israel named and in place for the historical struggles to come.

This holy burial place, now in the city of Hebron, is a pilgrimage site for Jews, Christians and Muslims. The place that houses the tombs of the Patriarchs is part of the Ibrahimi Mosque (the Cave of Machpelah/the Mosque of Abraham). The tombs, or cenotaphs, are built over what is thought to have been the actual tomb of Abraham and his family (Some traditions believe it to be the burial place of the biblical couples Adam and Eve, Abraham and Sarah, Isaac and Rebekah and Jacob and Leah). The tombs are large tent-like structures, symbolic tombs honoring those represented, somewhat like a house without windows, doors or details of any kind, side by side in a large vaulted room. Fabric covers the individual tombs and gold glistens upon them, with decorations that embellish and emphasize the grandeur of the space and the memory of those who are the Abrahamic ancestors of the Jewish and Christian and Muslim religions. The tombs are impressive in their enormity, regal and revered. Built in the time of Herod, the enclosure was made part of a church in the sixth century, becoming a mosque in the seventh century, a church, again, in the twelfth century and a mosque and church under Saladin's rule in 1188. Following the Six Day War in 1967, the Israelis took control of the area, dividing the structure into a mosque and a synagogue.

On 25 February 1994, Dr Baruch Goldstein an American-born doctor and settler, who had lived at the Kiryat Arba settlement outside of Hebron for eleven years, entered the Ibrahimi Mosque as eight hundred people were praying. He started shooting with an Israeli-made Galil automatic rifle, wounding over 125 and killing at least 30 Palestinian Muslims who were there as part of their religious observance of the holy month of Ramadan. Dr Goldstein, who died in the shooting – either shot by the Israeli guards or by himself – is considered a hero by the ultra conservative Jewish element. His actions have been denounced by moderate Israeli and American Jews. When I was in Hebron – during a period of increased tension between the Palestinian and Jewish parts of the city – there was a large poster with Dr Goldstein's picture and words in Hebrew which declared him a 'hero'. While this was posted on the Jewish side of the city, it still sent an inflammatory message to all who passed by. An earlier memorial site to Dr Goldstein has been outlawed by the Israeli government, but to some he is still revered as a martyr.

After the Goldstein Massacre the Wye River Accords in 1995 restricted access for both Jews and Muslims, giving the Muslims control over 81% of the building. However, the Israeli Defense Force maintains control over who enters the structure and the Wye River agreements were not implemented (Carter 2006: 149). Hebron, once a predominantly Muslim city, presently with an estimated population of 120,000, has within the center of the city an Israeli Jewish settlement (Gush Emunim) with 500 heavily guarded settlers. Two other settlements, or colonies, are on the outskirts of Hebron (Kiryat Arba and Givat Harsina) housing some 7,000 settlers or colonists. Recently, four new Jewish settlements (Beit Hadassah, Beit Romano, Avraham Avino and Tel Rumeida) have also taken land in the center of Hebron, according to the Human Rights Watch, expanding the presence of both Jewish settlers and the Israeli military who are there to protect the settlements. Hebron, the second largest city in the West Bank, has been a manufacturing center as well as a place of pilgrimage. While the military presence in Hebron can be sobering – even frightening – it is also an irritant to those Palestinians who have been in Hebron for decades and decades, many of whom no longer are able to get to their former places of employment due to the Israeli military restrictions on their movement.

This ongoing military presence has infected and continues to infect the population with resentment and a resulting anger that has produced resistance of both a nonviolent and a violent nature. Underlying the present day feelings on both sides of the division are not only the massacre at the mosque, but memories of a 1929 massacre where sixty-seven Jews were killed by Palestinian Arabs. In contrast, four hundred and thirty-five Jews were given safe haven in twenty-eight Palestinian Arab homes in the city of Hebron. Until this time, Palestinian resistance had been nonviolent for the most part. Frustration and anger over the increase in Zionist settlements (they had tripled in size) and the British mandates and policies imposed upon the people of Hebron brought about this anti-Jewish riot. It was after this, in 1935, that Sheik Izzad-Din al-Qassem (a local Palestinian chief) led a group into the Galilean hills to fight the Zionist presence. Captured and killed on 12 November 1935, al-Qassem's final words were, 'Die as martyrs' (Bonds *et al* 1977: 44). The Palestinian uprising began after this.

Both sides have suffered in this place that houses the patriarchs of their uniquely shared history. Both sides are still subject to the fears that are present when the ongoing possibilities for violence are such a reality. In the place of their beginnings, it is particularly sad that their differences have become so emphasized that their similarities can not be recognized and used as a way of returning to a place of separate but equal and peaceful existence.

Going back to the biblical story that led us to Hebron, following the death of Joseph, a new Egyptian king came into power. As the Israelite people continued to flourish in Egypt, they grew in numbers and in prosperity. This very wealth was seen as a powerful threat to the new Egyptian king and to the Egyptian people. As a result, an edict came out from the king of Egypt that Israelite boy babies should be killed (while girl babies were spared). In this atmosphere, the baby later to be known as Moses (born from the Israeli tribe of Levi), was placed in a papyrus basket among reeds in the river and discovered by the daughter of Pharaoh, who took the child as her own. It was this Moses baby boy, saved by a royal daughter of Egypt, raised by the royal family, who fled, as a young man, into the land of Midian to escape being discovered and killed as an Hebrew. It was also this same Moses who became a shepherd and married Zipporah, the daughter of the priest of Midian.

After the king of Egypt died, liberation of the Israelites was brought about by an initial encounter of Moses with a self-emoliating, Godly-sparked burning bush. The voice of God called out to Moses from this bush, aflame with divine fire. This voice said,

> I am the God of your father, the God of Abraham, the God of Isaac, and the God of Jacob... I have observed the misery of my people who are in Egypt; I have heard their cry on account of their taskmasters. Indeed, I know their sufferings, and I have come down to deliver them from the Egyptians, and to bring them up out of that land to a good and broad land, a land flowing with milk and honey, to the country of the Canaanites, the Hittites, the Amorites, the Perizzites, the Hivites, and the Jebusites. The cry of the Israelites has now come to me; I have also seen how the Egyptians oppress them. So come, I will send you to Pharaoh to bring my people, the Israelites, out of Egypt (Exod. 3:6b-10).

This is the story of the exodus – The Exodus – the movement of the Israelite people of God out of Egypt. Six hundred thousand men, with women and children and a 'mixed crowd' (Exod. 12:37-38) walked from slavery toward and into a land of freedom. This is the story that has inspired and that has intimidated – a story that has given hope and promise and has raised up fear and resentment. For those being led from servitude, this is a great story of release. For those already living in the land of promise – the land of the prize – the land of hope, this is a story of impending loss and sorrow. One land owned, promised, given, taken from a peoples named the Canaanites, the Hittites, the Amorites, the Perizzites, the Hivites and the Jebusites, becomes a land contested in our time. The Exodus story with its celebration of leave-taking and land-taking is a rich part of our modern day Liberation Theology, and as such will be examined more fully in Part 2.

These decrees of God run counter to our present day moral and ethical understandings of how we should treat one another in a 'civilized' world. If God says it is not only approved behavior to kill those in our way – on our path – but that it is a god-given justifiable right – and if both sides use God as their rationale to leave no remnants – no remains – only ruins of who and what had been – if God decrees all this, and more, then where does this leave us on our human journey toward enlightenment and wholeness of self and community? Whether a person be Jew or Muslim or Christian, at the very center of that person's faith and self, I believe, exists a God-sense of connection – connection to all that is, was and will be. Inherent in our own personal very human cellular makeup exists a microcosm of universal beauty and balance.

If God made us reflective of an interaction with the whole of creation, why then would this same God at the Great Beginning – the God of the I AM, the God of the Word before time, authorize us to destroy what has been made? Human-to-human, we are all made in God's image. Human-to-human, we are all made as God's own. Human-to-human, we are born blessed – each – with a soul – a conscience – and the potential to become more than flesh and blood earthlings – to become more than we are – to become reconnected to the source of our being and the other images of God among us, our sisters and brothers on earth.

After making these reflections, I came upon this quote from the Chinese Christian theologian Kwok Pui-lan, who said, 'Where is the promised land now?... Can I believe in a God who killed the Canaanites and who seems not to have listened to the cry of the Palestinians now for some forty years?' (Prior 1999: 40). Where indeed is the promised land, and for whom is it promised and from whom will it be taken? In the name of God, how much more carnage will take place, how many more lives will be lost, how much more of our environment will be destroyed in the warring and wrestling for power among the various peoples of this small planet of earthly origins and godly grace?

As the Israelites killed and dispersed the Canaanites, so too the later Christians killed and dispersed the Jewish and Muslim peoples during the Crusades (1095–1464). The battles between the Englishman Baldwin – self-proclaimed Christian King of Jerusalem – and the Arab army between 1100–1118 CE exemplify this. Baldwin, offering safe passage to the Arabs garrisoned at Acre, massacred the people as they left the fortress. Later Islamic forces killed and dispersed some of the Christian and Jewish peoples, during the Ottoman Empire's reign in the Holy Land (1453–1566). However in general, their reign was more one of accommodation than of warfare. In our 'holy' Christian Crusades (1095–1464) (which President

George W. Bush brought to Islamic minds by using the word 'Crusade' in his speeches following 9/11), Christians were guaranteed, by the Council of Clermont in 1115 CE, a remission of sins if they went out to reclaim the Holy Land. During this time of Christian pilgrimages, the Monks of War, men dedicated to protecting these same pilgrims, took vows of poverty, chastity and obedience as they took on the role of protector, 'killing for Christ' as it was deemed necessary (Prior 1999: 35). The individual Muslims who consider themselves 'martyrs' in this present day era of 'terrorism', how different is their understanding and their passion and their focus from the Christian Crusaders who saw death for Christ – death in battle – as a highly desired form of martyrdom? (During a two-year period of the Crusades, 20,000 men became martyrs (Prior 1999: 36) something even the jihads of today have not yet produced).

Conquering in the Name of God

As Michael Prior writes in *The Bible and Colonialism*, 'The commandment that, 'You shall devour all the peoples that Yahweh your God is giving over to you, showing them no pity' (Deut. 7:6) is seen in a new light, when one recalls how such texts were used in support of colonialism in several regions and periods, in which the native peoples were the counterparts of the Hittites, the Girgashites and others' (Prior 1999: 34). Arnold Toynbee continues this thought, when he says, 'It was the same biblically recorded conviction of the Israelites that God had instigated them to exterminate the Canaanites that sanctioned the British conquest of North America, Ireland and Australia, the Dutch conquest of South Africa, the Prussian conquest of Poland and the Zionist conquest of Palestine' (Prior 1999:39).

In addition, I would say these views of Prior and Toynbee are seen in our own United State's past history of conquest of the Native American peoples, our paternal protective and overseeing relationship with Puerto Rico, Guam and most recently our 'conquest' of Afghanistan and Iraq. In these one sided and biased relationships, power is uneven and out of balance. Goodness and godliness and righteousness are claimed – at the core – of the conquestor's rationale, yet are not necessarily present in godly, goodly action.

In these scenarios ancient and present, the battle scenes – the brutality – the horror plays out, replays and continues in what I feel is a dishonoring of God, not an honoring of God. The God who made us did not make us to kill, to maim, to torture in the name of all that God conceived and birthed into being; the God who made us did not do so to create machines of martyrdom, bodies of self-sacrifice, robots of destruction. Why would a God of all being desire the ruination of a people – any people – rather than the restoration, reconciliation and renewal of those who are part of the human family?

It seems to me, as I read and reread the scriptural story of God among us, that the God of vengeance is more a God of man's making – not woman's – man's hearing and writing and transmitting and speaking and interpreting of God, rather than a history of God's real being. I say, 'of man's making', because throughout scripture – Hebrew and Christian and Islamic – the actions of war and the acts of vengeance have been wrought by men, and men almost exclusively. The recording of these storied acts in scripture has been done by men. There is an imbalance of power evidenced in these stories, where power is not shared between individuals or a peoples, rather power is used by one over another. An example of the possibilities of shared power is modeled by Jesus – a man – in our Christian Bible. It appears to me that we humans need more such modeling of power that allows for a balance of power, a power-sharing that allows all – male or female – to live in a place respectful of self and others, with a dignity that affords safety and security for all – be it in Israel/Palestine or any other place in the world. In contrast to the male prophetic models in scripture, scripture's women prophets, such as Sara, Elizabeth and Mary – to name a few – are recipients of God's Word blessed upon them, bringing them new hope, new life and new joy to share with the world.

In the scriptural stories, men, it appears, hear the voice of God as a challenge to overpower, to seize, to destroy, to plunder and to make as their own, in the Name of God. Women, it appears, hear the voice of God as a prophetic shattering of the human reality of their known life – their human expectations. They birth new life – new understanding of scripture, new ways of be-ing in the word. This is, perhaps, more a part of the story or the myth, than the reality of how men and women have been or can be. The modeling and expectations of behavior for boys and girls – in our own United

States – has changed in recent decades. One hopes the modeling of behavior in both men and women can also change and be redefined and held to a new interpretation, a new definition of God's compassion and charity that will allow for strength in accommodation and strength in sharing rather than our previously seen strength in overpowering and overwhelming of the other.

So who is this God who promises? So what is this power that gives – takes – rebukes – restores? Is God a phantom of our hopes – a figment of our desires – a rationale for our actions? Or, is God – a liberating God – an active participant in the creation of all time – the before-now-after-time of human consciousness and the before-now-after-time that is beyond our comprehension? The solid scriptural reasoning – by all sides – for ownership of the land comes from and comes through the voices, lives and words of a few. If God were not in the midst of our present mix, would the issues of land be any less or any more complex, emotional or convoluted?

The question rises out of the present day's wreckage of scriptural words that have been tossed back and forth – piled upon one another as kindling for a bonfire of righteousness – used, abused, defined, redefined and gilded gold as God's self. The question arises, would the Palestinians (Muslim or Christian) or the religious Jews be any less or any more humane if the word of God were removed and compassion, as the very Heart of God, were restored to the center of the conflicts?

'God' is a word, a word that has come from human imaging, human linguistic skills and human limitations. I believe the force – the power – the breath of beauty that birthed our universe surpasses our abilities to image, speak or define. Mentally, we skirmish with, we try to contain – or retain – a sense of the divine. Hope comes, for me, in the intuitive emotional knowing of God. That we can share, be we Jewish, be we Muslim, be we Christian, be we of other faith and belief systems. Hope comes, for me, in the Great 'Aha!' that shocks and stuns us into a new reality. Hope comes in the utterly simplistic, yet all encompassing utterance of the Great I Am.

Some years ago, when I was chaplain to political asylum seekers in the Immigration Naturalization Service (INS) Detention Center, in Boston, Massachusetts, I found this center, this core, this meeting place that exists in the midst of the many of faith. At our Sunday service, as we sat in a circle with the altar as part of the circle, with the gospel and Qur'an and Psalm and the unique myths and epic stories of the various cultures in the circle, we found God in the circle. We found reconciliation, hope, compassion, love and a very restructuring of our being, in the circle. An Iraqi, sitting next to an Iranian, both former soldiers, both former enemies, both of this same Semitic land which still rocks, shifts, splits and catches the blood of so many – so very many – both suddenly realized they were brothers before they became enemies. This happened over and over again, not always as dramatically, but it happened and we – all of the wee, humbled we of the circle – saw and felt and knew that the God of our faith is a God great enough to contain all of our faiths – our futures – our families – our foundations, our fumbling and frail selves. I learned that all of the great religions have, God-worded or not God-worded, a sense of love, compassion and heart from which evolve their moral and ethical values, laws and edicts.

One God: Three Faiths

What we – Jews, Christians and Muslims – forget is that we are all of the Abrahamic faith, united in the same beginning and revering the same places. As a former detainee said, who recently returned from the Hajj (an Islamic pilgrimage to Mecca), 'Constance, while I was there, we had time to read various books and I found out that Christians also have the story of Ibrahim (Abraham). When we went to the rock upon which Ibrahim was going to sacrifice his son, it is the same Ibrahim – the same rock – for you!' I agreed, and explained to him, that yes, we are both from the Abrahamic tradition, as are the Jews who preceded us (That point may have caused a bit of a pause in our conversation, but our common connection is what will cause a greater pause, I believe, in the ever escalating battles for sacred land and sacred places.) We talked a bit about our common religious history. We discussed the frailty of our humanity and the hope, as he put it, that in this land (the United States) perhaps we can put the fighting and warring aside.

I hope his hope is well placed. But the amazing thing to me was his focus upon Islam, without seeing the relationship between Judaism, Christianity and Islam. And why, I ask, was I surprised? After all, most of us (and I include myself in this generalization) – if we know anything about our own religion – do not see beyond the borders and the time lines of our own faith. To see the stream, the family tree, the blood lines of our common lineage, means looking at the before our time and after our time to the ones who preceded us and to the ones who will follow. It goes against our established human cultures to extend ourselves out of our comfortable context, but that is what God is all about, stretching us out of our comfortableness into an uncommon context.

For those of us of the Abrahamic faith tradition, we have a range of names for God, each revealing in a personal, definitive way our relationship with God. From 'HWY', The Passionate One' (in Arabic); or 'YHWH', the 'Sustainer, Maintainer or Establisher' (in Hebrew), we can trace our historical relationship with God through places and experiences and concepts and challenges. Throughout the prophetic period between the eleventh and the ninth centuries BCE, when Samuel, Nathan, Ahijah, Elijah, Micaiah and Elisha were prophesying, the name of God was crucial to the being and the meaning of God: 'For all the people walk, each in the name of its god, but we will walk in the name of the Lord our God forever and ever' (Mic. 4:5).

To walk in the name of God, is, in more recent Native American tradition, to 'Walk the walk and to talk the talk'. To walk in the name of God, implies the importance of the name of god and the willingness of the individual or culture to emulate that god's being through actions as well as professions of belief. In earlier times, in the name of the individual god lay the power and the inherent nature of that god, for, 'As his name is, so is he' (1 Sam. 25:25), for better or for worse, named in the being of the god's reality.

In the past, the naming of humans has held that same sense of naming the reality of the person. On a minor, yet personal note, when I lived in Italy, I was asked my name. I said, 'Connie'. The people would not accept that as my name. Finally, I said, 'Constance', and 'Costansa' it was! (I found out 'Connie' was close sounding to 'Cane', the Italian word for 'dog'.) In seminary, 'Constance' again became my name, this time a naming of my own choice, as I grew more into the persona of my calling. In changing my name, I joined many others, in seminary and before, whose names changed as their lives changed when God entered into the 'normal' and created a new 'norm' of existence out of the old being of self.

Part of the theology of god and land is associated with names of god and land. The ancient Canaanites called the god at Beer-sheba, El Olam (Elyon), 'God Everlasting One/God of Eternity'. At the shrine at Bethel, the god was called El Bethel. And El Roi, the 'God who sees me/God of Vision/God of Divining' protected Hagar during her time in the wilderness. El Berith, 'God of the Covenant/ God of the Shechem Covenant' and El Elohe-Israel, are names related to the altar at Shechem, first by the Canaanites and later by Jacob. Like modern day occupiers of the land, the sacred places remained sacred, while the old traditions were incorporated into the new religion's rites and traditions. The sacred places were renamed, rededicated to God, to Yahweh, to Jesus and to ensuing places and names associated with Islam.

In Mexico, The Church of Our Lady of Guadalupe is built upon a place held to be sacred by the indigenous people who preceded the Christians and their vision of Mary. The Earth Mother of earlier times became The Virgin Mother, and various accommodations ensured that those who had worshipped there before would continue in the new vein of religion. Of course, what the Christian overseers did not know, as the story goes, is that the workers who built the cathedral placed within the walls figures of their Earth Mother! Whether it is true or simply a legend people pass on from generation to generation, all worship together, each in his and her own way, with the results floating like incense up to the heavens – out to the ends of the earth – blessings upon blessings, weaving and interweaving in ways none of the god-namers totally comprehends or perceives. God the all seeing, all merciful, receives the prayers and the desires and the petitions and the thanksgivings with, one hopes, a sense of divine humor and pleasure at the fumblings about of God's earthly creatures.

And so the name of god can also be the name of place, or of vision or of action. That incarnation of the name, seen in Jesus The Christ, gives added power and weight to the name. When God proclaims to Moses, that God is, 'The Lord, a God merciful and gracious, slow to anger, and abounding in steadfast love and faithfulness, keeping steadfast love for the thousandth generation, forgiving iniquity and transgressions and sin, yet by no means clearing the guilty' (Exod. 34:6b-7), God is proclaiming a new reality that is all encompassing. This is a god of caring and a god to whom humans are beholden, a god to whom the fourth generation will be held accountable for the previous generations' sins. For the religious Hebrew/Jewish people throughout the world, it is this personal knowing of the name of God – the knowing of the self of God –

that has both personalized and problematized the Jewish faith as it has moved from exilic to the present day times.

For the Christian people, it is this same sense of knowing and being connected to Jesus as the word made manifest, that has brought about factions, schisms and conflicts within the faith throughout these last two millennia.

For the Islamic people, it is another, newer, sense of knowing and being connected to Allah, the Beneficent, the Merciful, the One God – the God of Muhammad's prophetic message – while remaining a part of the historic lineage of the Jewish and Christian scripture, that has caused, at times, a sense of separation from the other two Abrahamic religions. By 'separation' I mean the almost billion worldwide Muslim people are often misunderstood or not heard clearly by their Abrahamic sisters and brothers, which leads to a sense of being apart from, rather than a part of the shared Abrahamic tradition.

Be the name of Hebrew origin, Arabic, Aramaic or Greek origin, the name of God speaks to God's people and through them to the rest of the world. I Am (I bring into being what is), Jesus, Abba, Isa, Prophet, Creator, King of Kings, Allah, All Compassionate One, the still small voice or the God is Great that is shouted from the top of the minaret – all these, and more, words and phrases come through the prophets – come through the voices of those humans who name God or testify to hearing God speak God's name. We, the recipients, are left to live out the call the voice has for us. We, the recipients, are left to be the word lived out – defining the very essence of God's word in our words and in our actions and in our lives. 'In the beginning was the Word…' (Jn 1:1a). For us, Christians, it's quite a responsibility to be people of the word, but no more or no less so than for our Jewish and Muslim sisters and brothers.

Rosemary Ruether said in *The Wrath of Jonah*, 'Rabbinic Judaism, Christianity, and Islam each saw itself as an elect people in relation to a monotheistic God, a God who had elevated each of them to unique chosen status as a historical community' (Ruether 1989: 106) The phrase, 'In the name of God', however named, has been a battle cry, a defining cry, an elite cry for a people against another people – for a cause against another cause – for a belief system against another belief system. When one invokes the name of God – as a being on one's side, there is an immediate assumption that one person or group is better than another. When the Israelis refer to themselves as the 'Chosen People' and the Christians refer to themselves as 'Saved' and the Muslims refer to themselves as the 'True Followers' of Allah, there is a definite sense of an in group and an out group. Rosemary Ruether says, 'God creates, loves, and seeks to save the other peoples equally with Israel' (Ruether 1989: 13). God wants all – not one group – to be saved, to be solaced, to be wholly in relationship with God and with one another. 'There is no single, coherent view of 'the land' in the bible, but rather a variety of perspectives from periods when 'the land' was evaluated variously' (Prior 1999: 17). If only we believed what the Bible teaches, what God reveals and what our heart's self knows. If only we believed in love enough, in something other than ourselves, enough, to truly live out our scriptural edicts in a new way, a bold way, a way that would ensure peace for all on our way.

The Word of God as Seen in Scripture

When one looks at scripture, the word of God as it has been given, translated and interpreted by humans (and for the most part by males), one can see how not only the individual writer, but the peoples and the politics of the historical setting and times, have affected the meaning of the word. We all see through the lens of our particular understanding. We understand through the lens of our education – our culture and our personal, spiritual and life experience. In other words, scripture does not come to us clean, unadulterated and pure. It comes to us filtered through people and cultures. The word chosen to be in the canons and holy books of scripture comes as selected pieces, some of many, hopefully picked for their known veracity, truth and authenticity.

But many such writings were not chosen and therein lies a whole other topic for discussion. This is not to dismiss the voice of God among us. This is not to dismiss the reality of the experience of those who heard the voice and remembered the voice and told of their experience with the voice of God. This is not to dismiss, but rather to remind us all, that the experience did not happen in front of cameras with recorders in place; rather this happened over time in cultures that were based on oral tradition, not written tradition. The Hebrew Bible was held in the mind and heart much longer than the Christian Bible. The Qur'an was written some five hundred years after Jesus' life, by Muhammad, as a recording of a series of revelations given to him by the Angel Gabriel. And so one could argue that the written recording done closest to the origin of the story is most likely to be a more accurate rendition of the story itself, going back from the Qu'ran through the Christian Bible to the Hebrew Bible. At the same time, the intermingling of stories and visions and God's word flows through the Hebrew Bible into the Christian Bible, some finally being referred to in the Qur'an. Each holy book reveals, to a certain extent, the former writings – the former experiences – in their own way.

And so the word of God, be it spoken by a religious Jew, a Christian or a Muslim is the word as seen, as heard, as experienced by that individual and by that particular subdivision of his or her religion. How we discern and understand the word is dependent on how we have learned the meaning of the word. We Episcopalians like to say our faith balances on the three legged stool of scripture, tradition and reason – with a fourth leg thrown in, by some, to balance the stool with experience. But how one hears – how one incorporates – how one truly sees the word of God in the world really determines how that word is used. One word has many meanings, coming from many translations, and one word can be and is used by the many for their own purposes.

Whether one is Jewish, Christian or Muslim – ultra conservative, liberal or moderate – at the core and the center of God's word and the human soul is, in my opinion, love, peace, grace, justice, forgiveness and reconciliation. Anything else is not of God's nature, rather it is of our human interpretation and not of God's intention. Genesis, Exodus and Deuteronomy – the most often referred to books of the Bible in Liberation Theology circles and in Israel/ Palestine land discussions – are seen in different lights by people with different visions and desires or goals. First of all, we should remember there is a disconnect between the word of God as it was passed on in oral tradition and the word of God as it was passed on in written tradition. Second, we should remember that 'the word of God' comes from our human construction – our human intellectual grappling with the concept of 'god'. The Hebrew Bible and the Christian Bible were canonized, selected and in-booked at about the same time. The Hebrew Bible, in 400 BCE to the second century, CE and the Christian Bible, in the second century, CE. James Scott, in *Exile, Old Testament, Jewish and Christian Conceptions*, says, '...some historical texts were intended for recitation in cultic settings (e.g.

Deut. 26:1-15) and within the family (e.g. Deut. 5:21) and it is likely that authors who feel that their stories are important will have the good sense to offer them in a pleasing form, so that they will be listened to, remembered and transmitted further'. Scott further points out that, '…biblical texts continued to be transformed, sometimes in a radical way in ancient Israel. Embellishments could have taken place, slantings of the story fashioned, even after they began to be transmitted in written form, as various copyists took on the role of editors, partaking in the continual creative transformation of the text' (Brettler 1995: 139-40).

The creation of history often emphasizes one's side versus the other's, intentionally or unintentionally, which has created misconceptions and misunderstandings. We all know, even today, how several people at a given event – hearing a given account – will come away with nuances and differences that through the passage of time become our own apocryphal individualized versions of a shared reality. It is also true that text books have been written in this nation, and in others, to favorably show one side to the detriment of the other (In the United States, historically, omissions of women, African Americans, other nonwhite and indigenous peoples' contributions to society have been largely ignored.)

While the Jewish and Christian believers both have the Hebrew Bible – the Christians having in addition their own Christian Bible – and the Muslims have references to ideas in both the Hebrew and Christian Bibles in their own Qu'ran – each sees God-with-them differently, according to their theology and their world view. For the religious Jews, the Exile made them the people of God – the Chosen People of Israel. But Edward Said wrote, 'There exists, then, what we might term a discourse of biblical studies which is a powerful, interlocking network of ideas and assertions believed by its practitioners to be the reasonable results of objective scholarship while masking the realities of an exercise of power. We are faced with the paradox of the invention of 'ancient Israel'…an entity that has been given substance and power as a scholarly construct, while Palestinian history lacks substance or even existence in terms of our academic institutions. Attempts to challenge this powerful narrative are likely to be dismissed as politically or ideologically motivated and therefore unreasonable' (Whitelam 1996: 4). One might ask, what is more political than Israel/Palestine – than Zionist Judaism and Christianity – than Muslim Jihads – than all the sundry interpretations of holy scripture as lived out in our world, today?

We three share Abraham, but we relate to Abraham in our own unique and different ways. While Abraham remains the linchpin of our shared beginnings, the ways and means and directions out from Abraham have varied as much as our theologies. For the religious Jews, Abraham, Moses and the prophets of the Hebrew Bible are the lens through which they look at today's world. For the Christians, Christ is the revealing persona and the lens of our faith. For the Muslims, the revelations given by the Angel Jibra'il to and through Muhammad have become the lens of their understanding. Abraham, the father of all nations, is seen by Muslims, according to M.S. Seale, as the progenitor of the Arabs and 'a Hanafite: one who has yielded to God and become his friend' (Lueders 1950: 119). According to Seale, this understanding of Abraham as a Hanafite was an important revelation for Muhammad. 'Without it, a pagan Arab repudiating idols and turning to God would have had to become a Jew and take upon himself the double yoke of the written and the oral law; or alternatively, to become a Christian and accept the gospel and with it the accretions which had come to be associated with it in the course of the centuries' (Lueders 1950: 118).

The Muslims, in their understanding of the Qur'an, use and interpret both the Hebrew Bible and the Christian Bible, according to G.R. Haling and Abdul-Kader A. Shareef, in their book, *Approaches to the Qur'an*. The Muslim exegesis, or study of the Hebrew Bible and the Christian Bible, is done through, '...the use of biblical material in the Qur'an itself, its use in the tafsir material (late seventeenth to early eighteenth century Shi'i interpretations) and its use in polemical literature' (Haling 1993: 26).

Some may be surprised that material from the Hebrew Bible and the Christian Bible are referred to within the context of the Qur'an, but it is no more startling than the fact that the Hebrew Bible is contained in the Christian Bible. In fact, we Christians tend to know little or nothing about our Judaic roots or Muslim connections that are part of our later history. As Said says, 'Most people, if asked to name a modern Islamic writer, would probably be able to pick only Khalil Gibran (who wasn't Islamic). The academic experts whose specialty is Islam have generally treated the religion and its various cultures within an invented or culturally determined ideological framework filled with passion, defensive prejudice, sometimes even revulsion; because of this framework, understanding of Islam has been a very difficult thing to achieve' (Said 1997: 6-7). It is my sense that we know – we religious Christians – even less about the historical, theological writings that have come from Islam. Perhaps in the United States that is why, after 9/11, the bookstores ran out of any books related to Islam and the Muslim world.

Scripture from a Palestinian Christian Perspective

Looking at a Palestinian Christian perspective, The Rev. Dr Naim Ateek has written in his paper on the theology of the land, 'The Earth is the Lord's': 'The concept of the kingdom in the (Christian Bible) is the counterpart to the concept of the land in the (Hebrew Bible) with one major difference, namely, a consistent stress on the inclusive nature of God's kingdom. It does not differentiate between gender, race or ethnicity. It is for all the world and all peoples' ('The Earth is the Lord's': 3). Centrist Muslims believe the land – the earth in its entirety – is God's for us to care for, to use as stewards and to pass on to those who follow. For the religious Jews, who believe in the 'land of Israel' (sixteen times in Ezekiel), the 'Holy Land' and the 'Promised Land', they may be surprised to learn there is no word in Hebrew for 'promise'. The land is holy, only if God is present. The land is theirs, only if they follow the Laws of God. The land was, is and will ever be possessed by God, not by humans.

In the 'promises' – in the covenants – in the offerings of God – there was no contracted sale of the land, no deed handed over for the land. The land remained possessed by God. This is equally true for the religious Jews, the Christians and the Muslims. And so 'the land of Judah' (Deut. 34:2) and 'the whole land' (Gen. 13:9) are for the moment, for the time, and for the people who respect and honor the Law of God, the One God who truly remains the real owner of the land. From Adam, the keeper and tiller of the soil (Gen. 2:15) we have moved out as humans living upon different places of earth. How we live and what we believe and how we act upon that interactive relational faith stance with God has determined how holy the place – the land – would be. Jerusalem, the mythical navel, the mystical birthplace of life is only as holy a place as we allow it to be. At the moment, at this shattering, splintering, fragmenting moment in Israel/Palestine's time, it is hard to see the 'holy' in the land. While there always remains the potential for peace, at the moment the place of holiness to so many is not whole; rather it is being wrenched asunder by extremist believers of the Abrahamic faith. That same sense of brokenness of body and spirit happened on the cross of our Christian Good Friday, and then came the resurrection. One can only hope that this present day time of ripping apart all that is humane and sane can be the forerunner of a new day's 'resurrection' – a new way – a restoration of what is truly holy.

Certainly the old ways have passed away and a new way is upon us, like it or not. As Naim Ateek has written, 'At every point and turn, the focus now is not on one land (the land of Israel) or one people (The Jewish people) but on what God will do or, indeed, is doing for the whole world...the land of Palestine is only the launching pad for God's activity in and for the world' ('The Earth is the Lord's': 3). Ateek continues, 'God never limited himself to one land. No one land as such was holy. It is not the land nor the temple, it is Christ' ('The Earth is the Lord's': 4). For many of the religious Jews it is, strangely enough, not the temple either, for since the fall of the Second Temple, when Rabbinic Judaism replaced the Pharisaical temple priests, the temple has gone with the Jews – in their home rituals, in their synagogue services, in their customs wherever they might be. The holy scripture, the Mishnah and, the reality of their life in thought word and deed, became for religious Jews the 'temple' of their existence.

We Christians hold Christ as our Son of God, remaining with us in Spirit, given to be with us as we move about. We are the temples of the soul – our very bodies, the living witness to Christ's presence among us. Elias Chacour (a newly consecrated Archbishop in the Melkite Church in Israel/Palestine), of whom I will speak about in more length later, refers frequently to the 'living stones of Galilee', refers to the people as holy, not the sites, which are kept precious in their 'holiness' by the church universal, while the presence of Christ – the people of Christ – are persecuted, dismissed, pushed out and often forgotten and forsaken (Chacour 2001: 203). And for the Muslim, the often-mentioned coming apocalyptic restoration of the temple has already taken place. For them the Dome of the Rock is the temple restored, in even more grandeur than the other sites of holiness held within the walls of the Old City of Jerusalem. What if the Muslims, calling themselves to prayer five times a day, observing the laws of God as passed on through Judaism and

Christianity and Muhammad to Islam – what if in our midst, the temple is present and we, human as we are, are missing the entire happening? It's a 'What if?' for us to ponder, as we consider what it is that makes holy holy – a temple – a land – a place – or a particular people feel that they are uniquely God's holy own.

Scripture from a Muslim Perspective

In the Shakir translation of the Qur'an, the author writes: 'It is accurate to maintain that translations of the Holy Qur'an, however faithful to the original Arabic, cannot be regarded as more than an interpretive translation of the word of God into a language in which it was not revealed in the first place. Moreover, the translation is bound to be conditioned by the understanding of the Qur'anic message in its entirety by the translator, who, if he or she happens to be a Muslim, will represent one or the other school of thought within the Islamic community in the translation' (Qur'an: Preface).

This is to be remembered by religious Jews and Christians alike, as well as our Muslim brothers and sisters. A fondness for a particular translation – say *The King James Version* for us Christians – may speak to us of poetic familiarity, the 'language of God' as we learned it – but it does not speak to the authenticity of the translation. As dear as the word may be to us – all of us who are members of the Abrahamic faith – we must never allow ourselves to replace the God of our being with the God of the word we have learned. When it comes to a potentially explosive topic, such as land, the importance of understanding in a critical exegetical way the meaning of our individual scriptures is crucial. Speaking as a Christian, none of us, Muslim, Jews or Christians, can no longer afford to have wars and persecutions carried out in the name of God, using The Word of God as our cause celebre.

Scripture from a Jewish Perspective

As in Christianity, there are a variety of ways for a Jewish person to approach scripture. On one end of the spectrum are the traditionalists who believe that the entire Torah (the body of Hebrew scriptures, the Pentateuch), its laws and its narratives, is the direct word of God. 'However', according to Rabbi Aryeh Hirschfield of Congregation P'nai Or in Portland, Oregon, 'it should be noted that even among those who hold this view it has been considered acceptable for rabbinic authorities to interpret some of the more draconic laws of the Torah in such a way as to effectively make them inoperative. It is also important to note that, among traditionalists, allowing for multiple interpretations of the narrative portions of the Torah is considered praiseworthy'. On the other end of the spectrum are those who view the Torah and all the biblical scriptures purely as works created by human beings – at times inspired, at times relics of a bygone era. According to Rabbi Hirschfield, these people's relationship to and acceptance of the laws of the Torah is one of personal choice. There are also those, said Hershfield, who like himself, have an intermediate or moderate view of scripture as being the record of the people of Israel in their long encounter with the Divine. For them the scriptures speak, at times, with the voice and consciousness of people, at other times with the voice of God. Images such as Jacob's ladder or the burning bush are archetypal, to Hirschfield, and seem to emerge from the deep unconscious. For Hirschfield, passages such as Isaiah 6, where the prophet is transported to the very 'throne room' of God, or the first chapter of Ezekiel describing the prophet's mystical view of the divine chariot, are transcendent experiences. This intermediate view of the interpretation of scripture demands a willingness to live with a high degree of uncertainty and ambiguity, said Rabbi Hirschfield.

And so some have a scholarly approach to the study of the Hebrew Bible, some a mystical approach and others see scripture as a historical record. Many, when interpreting scripture, use a combination of approaches, depending on the given passage. In doing a critical analysis of Hebrew scripture, there are two generally accepted approaches. The older, source criticism, looks at the underlying sources in the biblical documents – what were the scripture's origins, where was it found, what is its authenticity? Norman C. Habel's 1971 book, *Literary Criticism of the Old Testament*, is one book used in source criticism. The newer approach, sometimes called new literary criticism, looks at the literary aspects of the scriptural passage, as one would any piece of literature, examining the plot the structure, etc. Robert Alter's 1981 book, *The Art of Biblical Narrative*, is an example of this literary criticism genre.

W. Davies, who wrote a critique on Jewish critical analysis of Hebrew scripture, has said that, '...what Jews believe to have happened constitutes a fact of undeniable historical and theological significance. The belief itself, he claims, has become a historical datum: "Its reality as an undeniable aspect of Judaism cannot be ignored"' (Prior 1999: 54) He additionally feels Krister Stendahl (a Lutheran Bishop, New Testament scholar and former Dean of Harvard Divinity School) saw Zionism as a liberation movement, and the State of Israel as the fulfillment of biblical promise' (Prior 1999: 256). Michael Prior feels, 'The failure to distinguish between the biblical narratives as story and as history in the sense of informing about the past is no longer acceptable' (Prior 1999: 259). And these are the limitations he lists as roadblocks between 'scholastic treatment of the land' and 'sensitivity to the moral questions involved in one people dispossessing others' (Prior 1999: 258). In the following statements, Prior is referring to religious Zionist Jewish interpretation.

1. Its writers settle for a synchronic reading of the biblical text that does not address the significance of its provenance and literary evolution.
2. They appear to accept on this one issue that the literary genre of the biblical treatment of the origins of Israel is history – a view which runs in the face of all serious scholarship.
3. They assume in most cases that one is dealing with a homogeneous people of Israel, ethnically, culturally and religiously one at all periods.
4. They consider the biblical attitudes towards the land to be above moral reproach, and make no value judgment on them.
5. They assume that the attitudes to land portrayed at one biblical period have an automatic currency for quite a different one; particular, that they automatically transfer to that specific form of attachment to land which we know as Zionism (Prior 1999: 259).

With these things in mind, one can see the need for all sides to revision their individual understandings of god and to integrate these understandings in a way that will allow all believers within the Abrahamic faith tradition to live together in god's peace, rather than apart as adversaries using scripture against one another. Interpretations of scripture that call for displacement, removal or eradication of a peoples are not interpretations any of us can continue to condone. God gave us – all of us – one another to learn from, to grow with, to be with in an ongoing, ever expanding interrelationship with God. God gave us – all of us – a responsibility for all of creation. With that responsibility came an implicit requirement that we ensure dignity for all things as we delight in all things. From the smallest speck of sand to the greatest most vast creature on earth, we are called to care for all in awe and reverence.

If we religious Jews, Christians and Muslims believe any of what we say we hold dear to us in our scriptures, then we must trust in our faith and turn from our present day sense of possessiveness and ownership of God's land to a living, breathing, acting-out of a new day sense of stewardship of God's land. If we believe what has been scripturally recorded as coming from God, then we must trust enough to hear what God is really saying, and move from the past ways of being into the future open to the potential for new ways of living that will bring life and not death – that will bring Shalom, Salaam, Peace and not discord. If we are to live – in Israel/Palestine or anywhere in the world – beyond the now of this moment, then we had best let our heart beat a new rhythm and our ears tune themselves to a new sound, for the old ways and the old interpretations of the words are no longer applicable.

A Timeline from 1840 to 1967

To understand better how we as the world, got to this place in Israel/Palestine, I offer a timeline of some dates and events of importance that led up to the establishment of the present State of Israel and the expansion of Israel's borders. These dates lead from the beginnings of what would become the Zionist Movement to the 1967 Six Day War when Israel expanded its boundaries following an invasion of Egypt, Syria and Jordan by Israel.

1840: Lord Palmerston, the British foreign secretary, according to an article written by Daniel Pipes in the New York Post on July 15, 2003, ' "strongly" recommended that the Ottoman government (then ruling Palestine) "hold out every just encouragement to the Jews of Europe to return to Palestine" '.

1881–1882: Following years of Jews being accepted in the wider European and worldwide community, and then being forced into Jewish ghettos (a section of a city to which Jews (or any specific group) are restricted) – back and forth from acceptance to rejection and/or persecution – the assassination of Russian Tsar (emperor) Alexander II opened the door for newer and even harsher persecutions and restrictions to be imposed upon Jews. 'In 1891, over ten thousand Jews were expelled from Moscow, and there were massive expulsions from other regions between 1893 and 1895. There were also pogroms (attacks)...culminating in the pogrom at Kishinev (1905) where fifty Jews died and five hundred were injured' (Armstrong 2001: 147).

Jews fled Russia, migrating to the United States, western Europe and Palestine in the 1880s. Large numbers of these Jewish immigrants arrived in Palestine, fleeing continuing pogroms and persecution in Russia and Romania (Lacquer 1987: 4). There were anti-Semitic attacks in Europe following the influx of these immigrating Jews whose presence stirred, among some Europeans, earlier biases against Jews. It was at this time that a Russian Jew, Dr Leo Pinsker, became a strong supporter for creating a Jewish state. He suggested Palestine or Argentina as possible locations for a state of Israel. He wrote, 'The anomaly of the Jews consists in their lack of a homeland...Let the Jews acquire a homeland of their own and become like all other nations' (Ateek 1989: 23). He was one of many, then and later, who assumed that Palestine was uninhabited or not a place – a homeland – for others, already.

1891: Baron de Hirsh donated two million pounds to establish the Jewish Colonnial Association, with the intent of resettling three million Russian Jews in other countries, including Palestine. As the influx of Jewish people began to arrive in Palestine, a Petition was sent to the Ottoman Government (The Ottoman Empire oversaw Palestine until the British Mandate took place in 1922) by Palestinian leaders, demanding an end of Jewish immigration and land purchases in Palestine (Friedman 1991: xi). Some Palestinian Arabs, and other non-Arabs who visited the region, wrote similar letters and articles to various governments and newspapers trying to stench the immigration flow.

There were also attempts to help educate people outside of Palestine to see that there were people already in Palestine – Palestinians. However, this was a time, in the United States, when there was great support for a Jewish state. A petition, 'The Blackstone Memorial', was signed by four hundred and thirteen highly recognized American legal, political and religious citizens requesting that the President of the United States and the Secretary of State do what they could to bring about an international conference designed to discuss establishing a Jewish State in

Palestine. It was as if no one could see that establishing a state upon a 'state' was a problem. Could it be that we, Americans, who come from a heritage of conquering and overtaking a peoples in order to establish our own nation had not – and have not yet – learned from our own earlier actions of occupation?

1895: On 5 January Colonel Alfred Dreyfus, the only Jewish officer on the general staff of the French Army, was falsely accused and found guilty of spying for Germany. Upon learning of the guilty verdict, people shouted, 'Death to Dreyfus! Death to the Jews!' (Armstrong 2001: 148). He was later found innocent and pardoned. Following Dreyfus' trial, further outbursts and anti-Semitic attacks took place in Paris, where Theodor Herzl was working as a newspaper correspondent for a paper in Vienna. These violent incidents following Dreyfus' hearing, provided the inspiration for Herzl's initial thoughts regarding Zionism (Ateek 1989: 23). A secular Jew, Herzl began thinking and planning about ways to create a Jewish state where Jews would be free of anti-Semitic attacks like those he had witnessed in Paris.

Theodor Herzl wrote in his diary on 12 June concerning the people who would already be present in whatever land was chosen for the Jewish state, '…when we occupy the land…we must expropriate gently the private property on the estates assigned to us (and) try to spirit the penniless population across the border' (Ateek 1989: 23). There was no specific geographic place in mind for the State of Israel. There was, however, a total disregard for the non-Jewish people Herzl planned to displace, as well as an eerie similarity to Germany's future Nazi policy of confiscating Jewish goods, art work and estates and the Nazi's disregard for the humanity of Jewish people (as well as gypsies, homosexuals and other 'non-Aryan' peoples).

1896: Theodor Herzl wrote *Der Juden Staat* (the Jewish State), which called for the establishment of a Jewish state in a non-specified location, Palestine being one suggestion among others, including Argentina, Uganda, Cyprus and El-Arish in the northern Sinai Peninsula.

On 10 March 1896, The Revd William Hechler, Anglican Chaplain of the English Embassy in Vienna, came to visit Theodor Herzl to offer his help in what he saw as Herzl's ' "prophetic role…" (He saw Herzl) leading the Chosen People (Jews) to the Promised Land (Israel). Heckler was a dispensationalist Christian and as such believed in the literal fulfillment of certain prophetic biblical texts...and (he) understood that the hour of the Jews had come' (Wagner 2000: 78). Because Hechler was well connected politically, he was able to introduce Herzl to people who would be important to him as he more fully worked out the concepts and coming actions of the newly formed Zionist Movement. Herzl, a secular Jew, and Hechler, a religious evangelical, formed the first such Zionist union between secular Judaism and evangelical Christianity.

August, 1897: The first World Zionist Congress took place in Basle, Switzerland. Out of this congress came the beginnings of the privately owned charitable organization, the Jewish National Fund, officially founded in 1901 with a mandate to buy and develop land for settlements in Palestine (This organization was mentioned in detail earlier.) Also, out of the first World Zionist Congress came the following: a flag (blue and white, reminiscent of the Jewish prayer shawl (the tallith) and a national anthem 'Hatikvah' (The Hope) (Ellis 1997: 21) All this was done in preparation for a State of Israel, before such a state existed. The plans were in place – the place was yet to be established. This first World Zionist Congress – begun by a secularist socialist – provided the venue that brought forth what has become the present day political, secular and religious Zionist Movement. Herzl had accomplished, in three years, the creation of a Zionist cause that is still affecting the present day situation in Israel/Palestine – one that continues to have a profound effect in the religious and political world within the United States.

As the world moved toward the First World War, and then into and through the Second World War, these benchmarks in Israel/ Palestine's history took place:

1915–1916: The British McMahon papers were written, promising independence to the Arabs, if they would join in the war against the Ottoman Empire. The papers, held in secrecy, were released in the 1930s, a move which 'greatly assisted the British goal of gaining access to Arab oil reserves for the war effort' (Wagner 2000: 119).

Britain and France signed the Sykes-Picot Agreement on 15-16 May 1916, which Russia approved, in principle. In this secret agreement, Britain was to obtain control over Palestine and France was to obtain control over Lebanon and Syria. This was dependent on the fall of the Ottoman Empire. The Ottoman Empire was not included in the discussions.

November, 1917: Lord Arthur Balfour, the British Secretary for Foreign Affairs, authored the Balfour Declaration, following a meeting with Chaim Weizmann, leader of the World Zionist Movement. The British statement said, 'His Majesty's government views with favour the establishment in Palestine of a national home for the Jewish people and will use their best endeavors to facilitate the achievement of this object, it being clearly understood that nothing shall be done which may prejudice the civil and religious rights of existing non-Jewish communities in Palestine or the rights and political status enjoyed by Jews in any other country' (Ruether 1989: 81). 'The declaration was…incorporated into the laws of the British Mandate for Palestine, approved by the League of Nations in 1922, and thus assumed the legal status of a treaty' (Ruether 1989: 79). This document promised the fledgling Zionist group a national home in Palestine (Ateek 1989: 27).

1922–1929: During this time frame, British commissions produced eighteen policy statements (or papers and letters). None were accepted by the conflicted Jewish and Palestinian parties. In 1925 Chaim Weizmann stated that, 'Palestine is not Rhodesia and 600,000 Arabs live there who…have exactly the same rights to their homes as we have to our National Home' (Ellis 1997: 25) Following World War One, in 1929, Britain was granted a mandate to rule over Palestine: 'A nation receiving a mandate would control the land and resources of another people until that people had 'progressed far enough along the road to self-government'. The nation given the mandate had the right to decide when enough progress had been made' (Bonds *et al*: 31). The British Mandate gave Britain supervision of what is now 'Israel, the West Bank, Gaza and Jordan. After Jordan was separated from the Mandate in 1922, the remaining territory between the Jordan River and the Mediterranean Sea became known as Palestine' (Carter 2006: 56).

1933: Adolph Hitler became the dictator of Germany under the Nazi party (German Fascist Political Party). Under his leadership, which lasted from 1933–1945, the Nazi Holocaust took place, resulting in the extermination of millions of Jews. Large numbers of Jews fled Germany and other European countries at this time. Because many countries that might have been considered as places of refuge for the Jews had established immigration limitations, including the United States, the majority of the Jewish refugees were forced to immigrate to Palestine.

1939: The Second World War (W.W.II) began. Britain put forth the White Paper on Palestine, which limited Jewish immigration to Palestine and land purchase in Palestine as well as protection of the Jewish, Christian and Muslim holy sites. There was included, also, a somewhat vague statement that indicated that Palestine would be independent in ten years (Ateek 1989: 30).

1942–1946: The Zionist organizing base shifted to New York City, where the Biltmore Program was declared, calling for a Jewish State in Palestine. An Anglo-American Committee of Inquiry was established, as well, to look into a Jewish State in Palestine. The U.S. position on partition was, '…unrestricted immigration of displaced Jews into Palestine'. In 1946, the U.S. Congress recommended that one-quarter million Jewish immigrants go to Palestine, where 1.2 million Palestinian Arabs presently lived. Only 4,767 Jewish refugees were allowed into the U.S. (Ellis 1997: 27). Armed warfare took place between the incoming Zionists and the British, who still had a mandate to govern Palestine.

14 February 1947: Britain referred the Palestinian situation to the United Nations. The United Nations established an United Nations Special Committee on Palestine (UNSCOP). On 29 November 1947, The United Nations passed Resolution 181 calling for the Partition of Palestine into two states, Jewish and Palestinian, leaving Jerusalem as an internationally shared city. At that time Palestine 'still owned approximately 93% of the land and constituted a clear majority (66%) of the population. However, the partition vote granted the Zionists a decisive political, economic and strategic advantage, as they would receive 54% of Palestine including the prime coastal and agricultural areas. The partition also gave the Zionist leadership the political opportunity they had been awaiting…the entire land of Palestine would eventually become the Jewish state' (Wagner 2000: 163). Following this partition, Jewish Zionists and Palestinians engaged in armed battle, but the Palestinians were not armed or prepared for a battle and were easily outmaneuvered and overpowered.

1948–1950: A Proclamation of Independence for the State of Israel, was made by the Provisional State Council in Tel Aviv on 14 May 1948. On 15 May 1948, Britain withdrew from Palestine. The State of Israel was declared. By May of 1948, 800,000 of the resident Palestinians had left as a result of being driven out by Zionist Jews entering the land, who destroyed or occupied their villages and towns. Some of these Palestinians left out of fear, expecting to return to their homes when it was safe to do so. As a result, Palestinians became displaced within their own country or refugees in surrounding Arab nations and other parts of the world (Ateek 1989: 31). An estimated 150,000 Palestinians remained in Israel. Of these, 30,000 were displaced persons (Ateek 1989: 32).

The Absentee Property Regulations were established: Palestinian land was confiscated that belonged to persons living within and without the boundaries of Palestine. '...approximately one-half of the Arab population of Israel was subject to the categorization as "absentee" ' (Ateek 1989: 35). These regulations became the Absentee Property Law in 1950. This law allowed for the confiscation of land belonging to Palestinian refugees (who lived out of the country) and the land belonging to Palestinians removed from their land by displacement or, as with the Wall, by separation – even sometimes by mere meters.

On 11 December 1948, UN Resolution 194 was passed establishing a Conciliation Commission. This UN Resolution, in paragraph eleven, addressed the Palestinian refugee problem: 'Resolved that the refugees wishing to return to their homes and live in peace with their neighbours should be permitted to do so at the earliest practicable date, and that compensation should be paid for the property of those choosing not to return and for the loss of or damage to property which, under principles of incarnational law or in equity, should be made good by the government or authorities responsible' (Wagner 2000: 153). By January, 1949 Israel had occupied 80% of Palestine, 1,000,000 Palestinians were made refugees. This figure of refugees grew to 2,000,000 by 1982 (Ruether 1989: 103).

UN Resolution 194 was violated in 1950 by Israel's passing a Law of Return which gave 'every Jew (born of a Jewish mother) the right to immigrate to the country' (Lacquer 1987: 87). 'This law of racial exclusivity was a direct response to the claims of Palestinians for compensation or the right of return' (Wagner 2000: 153). It was a law of racial exclusivity, as only Jews could purchase property, which meant that the Palestinian land – confiscated – was then sold to Jews at a price established by the Knesset. The Palestinians were left out of this process entirely. '...Property was stolen through these means from Palestinians and handed over to the Jewish

National Fund, who sold it only to Jews...(this) brought additional revenue to the government of Israel' (Wagner 2000: 154).

Lod (an Arab Palestinian village) situated between Jerusalem and Tel Aviv was entered by Israeli troops. Twenty-five Muslim worshipers were killed inside the mosque. Eight Palestinian survivors who surrendered, were forced to go into the mosque to remove the bodies and blood from the walls and floors of the mosque. The survivors were executed to ensure that the story did not get out (Ellis 1997: 4). For many Palestinians, this is where today's cycle of violence began.

On 9 December 1949: UN Resolution 303 passed concerning the internationalization of Jerusalem and for the protection of all holy sites within and outside of Jerusalem. The United Nations was to oversee this internationalization of Jerusalem which has yet to be implemented.

1956: The Suez/Sinai War took place in which Israel, Britain and France invaded Egypt, occupying the Sinai Peninsula and taking over the Suez Canal. (Egypt having only recently been declared a free Arab nation.) The President of Egypt, Gamal Abdel Nasser, freed of the domination that Europe (Britain and France) had held over the area, declared the nationalization of the Suez Canal zone – which the British and the French still owned – and blocked the Straits of Tiran (Israel's outlet to the Red Sea). Prior to this, Egypt had asked Britain and the United States for assistance in building the Aswan Dam on the Nile River. Both declined and the Soviet Union agreed to partner with Egypt in this project. When Britain, France and Israel invaded Egypt, The Soviets threatened to join Egypt in defending itself. U.S. President Dwight D. Eisenhower intervened, getting the British, French and Israelis to agree to a cease-fire and withdrawal, thus averting the Soviets entering into the battle. The Russians later withdrew. The war lasted a week.

1958: The Palestinian Liberation Movement (Fateh) was founded, whose meaning in Arabic is 'victory'. Yasser Arafat, a Palestinian leader born in Cairo, Egypt, related to the Husseini clan of Jerusalem and working in Kuwait as an engineer, founded Fateh. The Husseini clan was part of the Palestinian nationalist movement that, in Jerusalem, had Christians and Muslim members, with Muslims being in the majority. The Palestinian nationalists, '...were concerned about the emergence of any ethno-religious nationalism whether it be Muslim, Jewish, or Christian as it would inevitably relegate minorities to a second class status' (Wagner 2000: 196). Fateh became the militaristic arm of the Palestinian resistance, attempting to organize the West Bank into rebellion.

May, 1964: Twenty-two Arab countries comprising the Arab League met in Cairo, Egypt and established the Palestinian Liberation Organization (PLO). The intent of the PLO was to deal with the Palestinian Arabs, however a Palestinian was not in charge of the PLO, rather Ahmed Shuqairy, an Egyptian, was the first Head of the PLO. It is from him that the phrase, 'driving the Jews into the Sea' came, perhaps understandable given the recent intrusions, at that time, into Egypt by the Israelis, but unfortunately still in use in politics in 2007. After the 1967 war, in 1969, Palestinian Yasser Arafat, took control of the PLO. He was able to do this by means of Fateh, which he had organized in 1958.

5-11 June 1967: The Israeli-initiated Six Day War took place. As a result, Israel occupied the remaining Palestinian land (including the Gaza Strip, East Jerusalem and the West Bank) and Egypt's Sinai Peninsula and Syria's Golan Heights (This has been discussed in an earlier chapter).

The Land and Population in Modern Day Israel/Palestine

The Jewish population has increased dramatically in the last two centuries. In 1832, there were 1,500 Jews in Palestine. In 1860 the Jewish population had grown to 15,000 and in 1881 the Jewish population was 22,000. By 1944 there were 614,229 Jews and 1,363,387 Arab Palestinians (These figures are from the Palestinian Society of Demographic Education). At the time of the Balfour Declaration, in November, 1917, when the secular Zionist Movement was officially recognized, 92% of the population in Palestine were Arab Muslims and Christians (Ellis 1999: 19). Four years later, in 1921, there were 590,000 Muslims, 85,000 Jews and 89,000 Christians (Ateek 1989: 29). As we have seen, by May of 1948, when the State of Israel was declared, as was noted in a preceding paragraph, 800,000 of the resident Palestinians had left Israel as a result of being driven out by Zionist Jews entering the land. As of 2003–2004, the combined population in Israel and the West Bank, Gaza Strip and Golan Heights was 51% Jewish and 49% Palestinian Arabs (Population Statistics/Demographics of Israel-Palestine).

In 2006, the Bishop's Committee on Justice and Peace in Israel/
Palestine, in the Episcopal Diocese, in the western part of the State
of Washington, published a fact sheet stating that the population in
Israel/Palestine, at that time, was comprised of 18% Arab
Palestinians Muslims, 72% Israeli Jews and 10% Arab Palestinian
Christians. Several years later the Arab Palestinian Muslim
population in Israel/Palestine is growing. At the same time, the
Arab Palestinian Christian population is on a steady decline, making
up only between 1- 2% of the population. This dramatic decline is
due to the Israeli government's restrictive practices, which include
the occupation and colonization of Palestinian land either by creating
settlements upon the land or by building a wall that is meant to
separate Palestinians and Israelis, but in reality extends into
Palestinian land, beyond the border previously accepted as the
'Green Line'. The 'Green Line' is the border between Israel and
Palestine as established in 1967 in United Nations Resolution 242,
and further agreed to at the 1978 Camp David Accords, in the 1993
Oslo Agreements and the 2005 Roadmap of the International Quartet
(Britain, France, Russia and the United States) – all of which will be
discussed later. Israel also restricts Palestinian movement within
the occupied territory of Palestine to such an extent that Palestinian
people are forced to leave in order to work and survive. Some
projected that by the year 2005 there would be more Israeli Jewish
settlers in East Jerusalem alone, than Palestinians (Wagner 2000:
179) but there was, also, a projection that the Palestinians – Muslim
and Christian combined – could be in a majority within the next
decade. At this point, the evidence shows that the population is in
flux, as Jewish people are brought in to settle and colonize
Palestinian land and Palestinian Muslims and Christians are forced
out to make room for the new members of Israel's population.

In March, 2007, the Israeli Census showed that the population of
Israel was 6.4 million. The population of the West Bank and Gaza
was estimated at 3.8 million. Of those people, in Israel, 76% were
Jewish, 16% were Muslim, less than 2% were Christian, 1.6% were
Druze (a Muslim-derived sect) and 3.9% were unspecified. In the
Palestinian Territories of the West Bank and Gaza, 95% were Muslim
and 5% were Christian.

Settlers and Settlements

When one says the word 'settlers', a variety of images come to mind. Depending on one's experience, education and ethnicity, the word may have a positive or a negative connotation. In Israel/Palestine, 'settlers' are Jewish people who have moved onto confiscated Palestinian land and have established settlements, or communities upon that land. In American terms, they could be seen as 'squatters', however they are in reality colonialists who are on the land through the invitation of the Israeli government. As Dr Jeff Halper (American Jewish Professor of Anthropology at Israel's Ben Gurion University and Coordinator of the Israeli Committee Against House Demolitions) explained to us at the International Sabeel Conference in 2002, some settlers are religious Jews, many from the United States. Religious Jews are those who not only identify themselves as having an ethnic link to Judaism – through birth or through adoption or through conversion – but religious Jews are called such or are self-named because they are believers and practitioners of Judaism. Others are secular Jews, with no theology or idolatry driving them to take the land; rather they are simply Israeli Jews who have been offered low cost or free housing outside of the city – housing far better than they could afford on their wages, with the luxuries of community swimming pools, green lawns, lush gardens, all, by the way, draining water from the aquifers of the Palestinians. Bethlehem, for example, now has to ration its water because the nearby settlements routinely overuse their common water supply.

How did these settlements begin? In 1948, much of the State of Israel was settled on confiscated Palestinian Arab land. In 1960, the Greek Orthodox Church began selling or leasing Palestinian land to Israel. Following the 1967 War, Israel began taking, occupying and confiscating land without compensation and without providing housing for those displaced. The people removed became refugees or persons displaced within their own country. The land became Israel's land – legally by Israeli law by right of possession. This is counter to the decision made by the Hague Convention of 1907, which said: 'The property of municipalities, that of institutions dedicated to religion, charity and education, the arts and sciences, even when State property, shall be treated as private property. All seizure or destruction of, or willful damage to, institutions of this character, historic monuments, works of art and science, is forbidden, and should be made subject of legal proceedings' (Wagner 2000: 174). In addition, The Hague Convention stated that, 'private property cannot be confiscated or unilaterally declared state property and transferred or annexed by the occupying power' (Wagner 2000: 174).

The United Nations has criticized Israel for its confiscation of land and for the settlements it has built. According to former President Jimmy Carter, 'The Israeli Supreme Court has chosen not to accept the International Court's decision (concerning the building of Israel's security wall into Palestinian territory) but acknowledged that Israel holds the West Bank 'in belligerent occupation' and that 'the law of belligerent occupation...imposes conditions' on the authority of the military, even in areas related to security' (Carter 2006: 194). To this date there have been no sanctions of, or consequences to, Israel's actions. The United States has occasionally asked Israel to stop building settlements, yet our government continues to provide the money and means to expand the settlements. Israel has continued to ignore international 'law', or standards which are not enforceable under Israeli law. In response to criticism of Israel, Donald Wagner pointed out, in *Dying In The Land of Promise*, that the Likud Government of Menachem Begin issued this statement: 'Settlement throughout the entire Land of Israel (Eretz Yisrael) (which to Likud included the West Bank, East Jerusalem, Golan Heights, and Gaza Strip) is for security and by right. A strip of settlements at strategic sites enhances both internal and external security alike, as well as making concrete and realizing our right to Eretz-Yisrael' (Wagner 2000: 175). As one can see, the international standards and policies may exist, but the actual practices of Israel remain the same – counter to these standards – as the settlements continue to grow and expand.

I saw the settlement reality for myself on my first trip to the region in 1993, as a long, wide ranging modern community built atop a hill overlooking Jerusalem. It was strategically placed, it was massive, it was overwhelming in its place and size. It was anything but subtle. On a trip in 2002, the reality of the settlements was as a string of communities, some quite large cities, others smaller, all surrounded by barbed wire fences, protected by armed military, guard dogs and machine gun turrets. At one stop, in the middle of a no-where-wilderness area, we found road signs to a shopping center, a gas station and other 'city sites', none of which existed. There was a large area, the size of a small town, surrounded by barbed wire cyclone fencing, gun turrets and prison-style yard lighting. Within the enclosure was nothing. The area had been marked – tagged – set aside for future building. The land was on the West Bank. The land is Palestinian. This pattern of seizure, setting the perimeters and later building/peopling the settlements had been set in place – in this place – as it has been in place throughout Israel/Palestine for sixty years.

In spite of United Nation's resolutions, in spite of worldwide condemnation, in spite of all the criticisms and pleas that have been made, the Israeli government has continued to expand its settlements and the United States' government has continued to fund these same settlements. As a tax-paying American citizen, I am personally appalled and disgusted by our behavior as a nation. As the only nation who primarily funds Israel through our financial and military governmental aid programs, we have an obligation to Israel, and to Israel's neighbors and to our own citizens, to see that the money we give is used for those purposes which are clearly within the laws and the best interests of the international and Israeli/Palestinian communities.

The settlements continue to expand and the settlers grow more openly assertive in their demands. Witness the dismantling of the small settlements in Gaza and on the West Bank in 2006. It took IDF's military force to remove the settlers, whose ferocious and often violent refusal to leave their confiscated land was seen on international television. In 2006, the worsening of the situation was exemplified, for me, by an incident that took place outside our hospice, on the Via Dolorosa (The Way of the Cross). During a concert, at the Austrian Hospice, shouting was heard in the street. People thought it was related to the ongoing soccer games, which had captivated both the Palestinian and Israeli citizens. Unfortunately, it turned out to be other than jubilation over a soccer match; instead it was Jewish settlers protesting the presence of Christians in Jerusalem. The settlers were marching and shouting their way down the via Dolorosa, calling for Christians to leave both the city and Israel in general. They shouted that the land is their land. They shouted blasphemous things against Christians and Christ. Then they set upon a young man, Matthias, who was walking toward the hospice. He was, at the time, a deacon in the Melkite

Church (originating in Syria and Egypt, now part of the Byzantine rite of the Catholic Church) dressed as always in his ankle length black sutan, wearing a cross. The crowd circled him, spat in his face, spat at him from all directions. As one man came toward him, Matthias put out a hand to restrain him, while three other men came at Matthias from behind. They hit at him. They cursed him. They continued to spit upon him. Meanwhile, three IDF soldiers stood at the side of the street watching, but not intervening. Eventually, Matthias escaped into the hospice, where we learned of his ordeal. Fortunately, he was not badly injured, physically, but he was stunned by his encounter with such hatred and prejudice aimed at him as a representative of something those particular Christian-hating settlers resented.

Ironically, Matthias had recently joined an ecumenical and interfaith choir, to be with people in a way that would allow him to know people, as he said, for themselves, not for what they believed. He wanted to interact with all the various kinds of people who populate the city of Jerusalem. The people who set upon him did not know him. They only hated what he represented. Matthias filed a formal complaint with his embassy and the Israeli government, neither of whom ever responded. During the following days, other settler protests took place on the Via Dolorosa which, as was mentioned earlier, is in the Muslim Quarter of the Old City of Jerusalem. These protests took place during regular shopping hours. As the wave of protesters came down the street, the Palestinian shopkeepers moved out of the street, back into the shadows of their places of business, or simply brought in their merchandise (traditionally exhibited outside the shops) and pulled down their metal shutters. The normally busy streets of the souk (market place) were empty of shoppers. The atmosphere, instead, was electric with the fierce demands being shouted by the settlers – demands for the return of the Temple Mount and the removal of all but Jewish persons. These demands were being made in English by mostly American Jewish settlers.

In that same time period, looking out my bedroom window at the Austrian Hospice, I had a panoramic view extending from before the Dome of the Rock past the location of the Church of the Holy Sepulchre. This Christian hospice, located as it is in the Muslim Quarter is part of the historic Palestinian part of the city – first Christian, then Muslim, now mixed. Across from my room, on the flat rooftop of the adjacent building, was an armed tower, armed guards, barbed wire and Israeli flags. Other Israeli flags were dotted about on rooftops. To the far right, on the main Palestinian shopping street that leads to the Damascus Gate, were Israeli flags – one large one hanging down in the center of an arch that spanned the street. This particular flag is about a story or more high in length. This one identified the house owned – some say seized – by Ariel Sharon. These flags, planted as they are in the Palestinian Arab Muslim section of the Old City are a constant affront – a reminder of what is happening with the permission of the State of Israel, although not acceptable under international law.

Palestinians, incidentally, under Israeli law, are not allowed to fly their own flags on their own homes or on their own land. To this date, the settlements are present – to an unknowing visitor – in the placement of an Israeli flag on a city wall or roof top, on a hill, ever expanding, engulfing and encroaching upon Palestinian soil. It is in this way that Bethlehem has become an isolated city. Ringed by a Jewish Israeli wall, which dips into Palestinian land, through the middle of Palestinian properties, orchards and even homes, Bethlehem is also becoming ever more the center of an encirclement of settlements.

Since the Lyndon Baines Johnson Administration, which took place between 1963–1969 – before, during and after the Six Day War – presidents of the United States and their representatives have made critical comments in regard to the Israeli settlements. Listed below are selected statements, taken from the Churches for Middle East Peace's information sheet, 'Quotes From U.S. Government Officials on Israeli Settlements'.

Department of State to the Embassy in Israel, under Johnson:

> 'Although we have expressed our views to the Foreign Ministry and are confident there can be little doubt among GOI leaders as to your continuing opposition to any Israeli settlements in the occupied areas, we believe it would be timely and useful for the Embassy to restate in strongest terms the U.S. position on this question... By setting up civilian or quasi-civilian outposts in the occupied areas the GOI adds serious complications to the eventual task of drawing up a peace settlement...' (Undated).

Charles Yost, U.S. Permanent Representative to the U.N., under Nixon:

'...an occupier may not confiscate or destroy private property. The pattern of behavior authorized under the Geneva Convention and international law is clear: the occupier must maintain the occupied area as intact and unaltered as possible, without interfering with the customary life of the area, and changes must be necessitated by the immediate needs of the occupation' (1 July 1969).

William Scranton, U.S. Ambassador to the UN, under Ford:

'Substantial resettlement of the Israeli civilian population in occupied territories, including East Jerusalem, is illegal under the convention...the presence of these settlements is seen by my government as an obstacle to the success of the negotiations for a just and final peace between Israel and its neighbors' (23 March 1976).

President Jimmy Carter:

'Our position on the settlements is very clear. We do not think they are legal' (April, 1980).

The Reagan Plan:

'The Reagan plan states that 'the United States will not support the use of any additional land for the purpose of settlements during the transition period (5 years after Palestinian election for a self-governing authority). Indeed, the immediate adoption of a settlements freeze by Israel, more than any other action, could create the confidence needed for wider participation in these talks' (September, 1982).

James Baker, Secretary of State under George H.W. Bush:

'Every time I have gone to Israel in connection with the peace process... I have met with the announcement of new settlement activity. This does violate United States policy...I don't think there is any greater obstacle to peace than settlement activity that continues not only unabated but at an advanced pace' (22 May 1991).

President Bill Clinton:

'The Israeli people also must understand that...the settlement enterprise and building bypass roads in the heart of what they already will know one day be part of a Palestinian state is inconsistent with the Oslo commitment that both sides negotiate a compromise' (7 January 2001).

President George W. Bush:

'Consistent with the Mitchell Plan, Israeli settlement activity in occupied territories must stop, and the occupation must end through withdrawal to secure and recognized boundaries, consistent with United Nations Resolutions 242 and 338' (4 April 2002).

Richard Boucher, U.S. Department of State under George W. Bush:

> 'Our position on settlements, I think, has been very consistent, very
> clear. The secretary expressed it not too long ago. He said settlement
> activity has severely undermined Palestinian trust and hope, preempts
> and prejudges the outcome of negotiations, and in doing so, cripples
> chances for real peace and prosperity. The U.S. has long opposed
> settlement activity and, consistent with the report of the Mitchell
> Committee, settlement activity must stop' (25 November 2002).

So there are many pretexts for taking land. We have land taken, as a means of restoring 'Israel' as a place, and we have land lived upon by people with a zealot's Zionistic intention to restore Israel and the temple, and we have people living on land as settlers, not knowing or not willing to see the reality of their situation. Since the Six Day War, in 1967, a religious crusade has taken over what began as a secular socialist movement. From the outside, looking in, some might think this is a simple scenario for a very complex situation, but the most complex can still be reduced to the most basic of issues: To whom does the land belong, legally, morally and ethically? Everyone thinks they know the answer. But for each side of the issue there exists a different answer. And when international legal or humanitarian organizations offer an opinion or a judgment, no one is willing to enforce that answer. The United States and Israel are seen as the power brokers of the region, inseparable in their strength. But, it should be remembered that even Goliath was brought down by David. In such a land of biblical proportions, humility is called for. Peace and justice are not to be played with. We must hope that in time right will overcome wrong and justice will prevail over injustice. It behooves us to ensure that justice is done – justice for both Israel and Palestine and the entire Middle East.

The tragedy for the Palestinian people is that, following the Second World War, those Jews fleeing their own tragedy of the Holocaust were imposed upon the Palestinians, a people innocent of any responsibility for the evils of that war. As Collins and LaPierre write, 'The Christian nations of Europe were responsible for the horrors of WW II, not the Arabs' (Ellis 1999: 2). I have heard this sentiment expressed by others, in Israel/Palestine, the feeling that the Arab peoples – the Palestinians in particular – were made to pay for the sins of Europe. A sort of out of sight/out of mind mentality took place, in removing the survivors of the horrors of the Holocaust and placing them in a land 'unpeopled' and virtually unseen by the non-Arab world. Unfortunately, the modern day history of Israel/Palestine is no less complex than the ancient history of this area and these peoples.

What is the answer to the Israeli/Palestinian situation? For each side the answer is different, but for each side the possibilities are becoming more limited by the daily and weekly escalations of violence that are perpetrated one against the other. Perhaps the 2003 Geneva Accord (or Initiative), defining borders and providing for an equitable exchange of land between the Israeli Jews and the Palestinians, as well as addressing Jerusalem and the return of Palestinian refugees – or some leaders who can inspire the people of all sides, or the United Nations, who are not a part of either of the governments of either people – will find a way to shift the reality as it is now, to a new reality, offering new, creative and acceptable results for all. Perhaps – but for the now, the perhaps seems far, far away.

Zionism: Secular and Religious

Zionism is, according to *Webster's New World Dictionary*, 'a movement that reestablished, and now supports, the state of Israel'. From that succinct beginning, Zionism has evolved and expanded to embrace not only Jewish supporters but Christian supporters – both secular and religious.

The beginning of Zionism was primarily secular and socialist, as Herzl led the Jewish people to think of reestablishing a homeland. The geographic location was in question, as was mentioned previously. Israel, as it is today, was not necessarily where it might have been, in those beginning modern day discussions. The temple was not the focus. The religious Zionists, today, however are focused on the restoration of the temple. In the 1890s the land was being settled by Jews. It was partitioned in 1946 by the United Nations and in 1948 the land was officially reclaimed and part of it was declared to be the State of Israel.

In 1967, following the Six Day War, the occupation of the West Bank and East Jerusalem turned what had been in the majority a secular Zionist movement into an increasingly religious Zionist tendency. Out of this post-1967 war came thinking among the Jewish Israelis – and Jews around the world – that the land had been 'liberated...(that) the religious claim to the land (had) become...very prominent and dominant' (Ateek 1992: 2). It became a religious prerogative to hold onto the land, reclaiming what the fundamentalists felt had been given to them – once again – by God. The land of Israel was expanded and the part of the Old City of Jerusalem that was Palestinian was occupied by Israeli forces. Some Israeli Jews and Palestinians feel that Jerusalem should be restored as their individual capital city, that is, Jerusalem should be only for the Israeli Jews or for the Palestinians. Other Israeli Jews and Palestinians believe that Jerusalem should exist as a city shared as a capital for both. At this time, Israel's occupation has closed the former PLO headquarters, the Orient House, and forced the center of Palestinian government to move to Ramallah and Jericho. Israel has built a center of government for itself in Jerusalem.

At this time there is no temple – only a wall. For these Zionists, be they Christian or Jewish, the desire to restore the temple is central to their faith. For some Zionist Jews, the temple must be restored in order for the Israeli people to regain total control of the land to await the coming of the Messiah. For these Zionist Christians, the temple must be restored in order for Christ to return and take those believers – those righteous Christians – up to heaven in the long awaited rapture that is, for Christians, the Second Coming of Christ. It is important to remember that for these believers, for the temple to be restored, the Dome of the Rock and the additional mosque on the Temple Mount must be destroyed and removed.

Among the leading Zionist Christians are such leaders as Derek Prince, Jerry Falwell, Pat Robertson, Hal Lindsey, Mike Evans, Charles Dyer, John Walvoord and Dave Hunt. A wide-ranging number of Christian Zionist groups, with various intentions and hopes for Israel, include Bridges for Peace; the International Christian Embassy, Jerusalem; Jews for Jesus; the Church's Ministry among Jewish People (CMJ); Exodus and the Ebenezer Trust; and Christian Friends of Israel Communities (Sizer 2003: 6). According to Stephen Sizer, 'Christian Zionism is pervasive within mainline evangelical, charismatic and independent denominations including the Assemblies of God, Pentecostal and Southern Baptists, as well as many of the independent mega-churches. Crowley claims they are led by 80,000 fundamentalist pastors, their views disseminated by 1,000 Christian radio stations, as well as 100 Christian TV stations.

Doug Kreiger lists over 250 pro-Israeli organizations founded in the 1980s alone' (Sitzer 2003: 7).

I asked Donald Wagner, a leading authority on today's Christian Zionist Movement, 'What ever is going on? Don't the Jews get it? If Christ comes to take up the Christians, the Jews must convert to get to heaven, or they will be left behind with all the rest of humanity for the proverbial 1,000 years of suffering and pain?' Dr Wagner agreed with my premise. It seems obvious, to me, that the Christian Zionists are using the Jewish Zionists, who in turn are using the Christian Zionists, or as a person attending a Sabeel conference in Berkeley, California, in August 2007 said she had been told by a Jewish Zionist, 'We (the Jews) are simply sitting back, watching the Christians do our work for us in reclaiming the land of Israel'. And so I ask, why would such a coalition between Jewish and Christian groups ever happen? Each seems to feel the other will assist them in meeting their desired goal. It still confounds me that these two Zionist groups with such dissimilar outcomes of their temple restoration goal are working together. But it is happening and the Zionist Movement is growing in a way that is only beginning to be seen by the greater worldwide public.

Stephen Sizer, in an article in *Cornerstone* magazine, puts forth Colin Chapman's alternative idea to the usually held Zionist Christian position. Chapman may offer a solution to this present schism between Zionists and non-Zionists that exists within the Christian churches. In Sizer's article, 'The Origins of Christian Zionism', he states that '...a form of Biblical Zionism which accepts the existence of the State of Israel, can work and pray for the peace and security of the Jewish people alongside a Palestinian state on political and humanitarian grounds without needing to justify or sacralise Israel through biblical or theological arguments' (Sizer 2003: 8). Certainly no one need be against Israel – or against Palestine – to be for a peaceful resolution. It is the theology and scriptural referencing that appear to stand in the way of God's peace.

When I was in Israel/Palestine, in the spring of 2002, I joined two Christian Peacemaking Team (CPT) members and the Peace Now group at Peace Now's vigil across the street from Ariel Sharon's house. (Peace Now, a Jewish peace organization, had a twenty-four hour peace vigil at this location which included a sign showing the current number of Israeli and Palestinian deaths). While we were standing facing the street, a group of young Israeli men formed an ever growing protest, facing us across the street – an ever louder protest to our silent protest. As their group grew, they seemed at first like fraternity brothers, singing, smiling, enjoying themselves. But then they got louder and bolder, standing on each others' shoulders, swinging large Israeli flags, shouting – moving from the friendly appearing to the obviously angry and hostile. I felt as if I were witnessing a Nazi Youth rally, and I do not use that image lightly. The Israeli police officer, posted by the Peace Now group, left his position and moved across the street to stand by the demonstrators. At the same time, people were driving by, making obscene gestures, shouting and cocking their fingers at us, as if they had a gun in their hand. It was the eve of a visit to Israel by the United States' Secretary of State, Colin Powell.

As it turned out, a large – an enormous – gathering of thousands of ultra conservative Zionist believers were gathering to protest what they expected would be, at the very least, strong demands for change or punitive measures exerted by the U.S. government against Israel. This expectation came from both Israeli's and Palestinian's awareness of international criticism that came about following violent, restrictive actions the Israeli government had taken against the towns of Bethlehem, Jenin and Ramallah, and the recent shooting, by the IDF, of International Solidarity Movement (ISM) members, who had been standing in a nonviolent, peaceful vigil in the town of Bethlehem before the town was encircled and cut off from the rest of the world. The Zionist group, made up of Christians and Israeli Jews, rallied around banners blood-red, the height of at least a one story building, the length of half a football field – banners that said, 'Bush Don't Push'. As an American citizen, I was particularly offended at what I perceived as an arrogant hand raised in defiance toward the United States by a people supported financially and militarily by the United States.

Powell came the next day, Bush did not push, and the Israeli newspapers noted that the people of Israel, who had expected Secretary Powell to come out of strength, 'came without teeth' – came without power or authority or the ability to constrain or reframe the continually escalating tension that is today's reality in Israel/Palestine.

In *Our Roots Are Still Alive*, Joy Bonds states that, '...the aim of Zionism is to create for the Jewish people a home in Palestine secured by public law' (Bonds *et al* 1977: 17). On the surface that reads well, but 'in Palestine' is where the otherwise reasonable sounding statement gets into trouble, for Israel had no modern day place of 'home' prior to 1948. It is the changing of positions as possessors on the one land that has sparked and continues to spark the controversy, the pain, the suffering and indeed, the war between the Israelis and the Palestinians.

In March 1977, when then President Jimmy Carter used the words, 'Palestinian homeland', in a speech, the American Christian evangelical fundamentalists and charismatics responded with a full-page advertisement that was printed throughout the United States: 'The time has come for evangelicals to affirm their belief in biblical prophecy and Israel's divine right to the Holy Land' (Prior 1999: 41). This early affirmation of divine right to the Holy Land – the land held holy by religious Jews, Christians and Muslims alike, has become, today, a holy alliance of Zionist Christians and Zionist religious Jews (or unholy alliance, depending upon one's point of view).

And so we entered a new era where the political Zionist Movement began to garner a religious element. This was not only a topic and passion for the religious, but the general public's interest was captured through such offerings as Leon Urus' *Exodus* – the movie and the book. Who could not feel for the new Israel, especially with Paul Newman in a leading role?

As Christian fundamentalism grew in the United States and elsewhere, these fundamental Christians joined with the Zionist Jews as seemingly a similar theologically believing body. They both felt, as they still feel, that the 1967 war was God's victory for Israel over the Palestinians and other Arabs who, in their opinion, should not own the land of the Holy One – be it Yahweh or Christ. From the 1948 return of large numbers of Jews to Palestine (soon to become, in part, Israel), it took only nineteen years for this unification of thought and belief to formulate. In 1967 there were sixty million Christian fundamentalists in the United States. As of 2007 the number has multiplied and the movement has become more visible and powerful in the United States in religious and political arenas. A large number of these fundamental Christians support the Zionist Jews in Israel, through their prayers, their presence and through their financial support. Obviously this has created a schism between the moderate or centrist Christians and Jews and the fundamentalists, particularly those Christians and Israeli Jews living in the very midst – the center – of the focus of Zionism: Israel/Palestine. To respond to this escalating Christian conflict, the Patriarch and Local Heads of Churches in Jerusalem published a paper on 22 August 2006, 'The Jerusalem Declaration on Christian Zionism'. In this paper they state:

> Christian Zionism is a modern theological and political movement that embraces the most extreme ideological positions of Zionism, thereby becoming detrimental to a just peace within Palestine and Israel. The Christian Zionist programme provides a world view where the Gospel is identified with the ideology of empire, colonialism and militarism. In its extreme form, it places an emphasis on apocalyptic events leading to the end of history rather than living Christ's love and justice today.
>
> We categorically reject Christian Zionist doctrines as false teaching that corrupts the biblical message of love, justice and reconciliation. We further reject the contemporary alliance of Christian Zionist leaders and organizations with elements in the governments of Israel and the United States that are presently imposing their unilateral preemptive borders and domination over Palestine. This inevitably leads to unending cycles of violence that undermine the security of all peoples of the Middle East and the rest of the world.

The Patriarchs further commit themselves to nonviolent resistance and affirm the unity of all Palestinians, be they Christian or Muslim. It is this commitment to nonviolence and this reclaiming of a common religious origin that holds out hope, in my opinion. It is this kind of ecumenical and interfaith reaffirmation of self that offers a unifying and whole solution to the lands and peoples of Israel/Palestine, counter as these offerings may be to the desires and/or solutions offered by many Zionist political and religious groups inside or outside of the area.

In 2006, I had a first-hand experience with American Zionist Christians in Israel/Palestine. In Jerusalem, with the 'Journey to Jerusalem' exhibit staff, I discovered that three of the staff either had not been to Jerusalem before, or were not familiar with Jerusalem and various of the holy sites of the city. And so I volunteered – or was commandeered – to lead the group through the various places of importance on the Mount of Olives. As we descended down the Mount of Olives, we passed a tour group, and I thought I heard the leader say something derogatory about Roman Catholic nuns. Later, as we came out of the area of the Tombs of the Prophets (where fifth century BCE Haggai, Zachariah and

Malachi are buried), I overheard the same guide saying something against the mainline Christian Churches. Curious, I told my colleagues that I would just be a moment, as I went over to the tour group's leader and asked what his denomination was. He responded, 'Presbyterian'.

I, thinking I had misunderstood the previous statements, responded by saying, 'I am an Episcopal priest. Are you going to visit Sabeel?' (Sabeel is an ecumenical organization dedicated to bringing about peace and justice in Israel/Palestine. Founded by Naim Ateek, an Anglican/Episcopal priest, its members include all the indigenous Christian Churches of the Holy Land, as well as churches and organizations worldwide. Retired Archbishop Desmond Tutu is the Patron of Sabeel). Well, the gates of hell evidently opened before the man. He proceeded to tell me that the Episcopal Church in Florida was leaving to be under a bishop in Brazil. (In fact a church was, not the entire diocese.) He then went into an Alpha Male tirade against me and all that I seemed to represent – obviously playing to his tour group audience as he recited to me the need for the temple to be restored, for salvation to play out in the redemption of the Chosen People. He insisted that I listen to a particular conservative radio program that he named, and I suggested that I would, if he would consider visiting Sabeel so that both of us could have the experience of hearing all viewpoints on the Christian subject of 'salvation', the 'temple', 'Armageddon' and related topics. My suggestion didn't sell. He was full of anger and accusations and unchristian sounding epitaphs. Oddly, I felt totally grounded and peaceful, the more he became irate. Nonviolent resistance seemed to be appropriate on the Mount of Olives. I left, wishing him and the group a peaceful time in Jerusalem.

I hope they did find some of Christ's peace as they walked in the footsteps of the Son of God. The staff members with me said, after we had left the area, they felt they had witnessed a cursing of Christ take place, again, on the Mount of Olives. Later, when I told Naim Ateek, the founder and director of Sabeel, about my encounter, he laughed. He laughed, not because it was funny, rather he laughed because he receives this kind of reaction frequently to his own ministry and pronouncements of peace and justice. Back in the United States, talking with Presbyterian friends, I found out that there are – within the Presbyterian Church, as well as the Episcopal

Church and other denominations – schismatic groups, break away churches and a polarization of extremes taking place over the theology and the reality of being a person baptized into Christ. The body is fragmented, but Christ's message of wholeness still offers our faith a way of hope and reconciliation.

Politics, Wars and New Beginnings

The years since 1967 read like a modern testament version of the Hebrew Bible's story – uprisings, civil war, agreements, condemnations, resolutions, invasions, people made homeless, people given a home, retaliation and suffering on all sides, with the ultimate stated goal – for all sides – being peace. Throughout, there has been a decidedly one-sided Western view of the activities, the actions, the movements within the Palestinian and what has become Israeli or Israeli occupied land. The 'myth' that the land that was to become Israel's land was unoccupied, was fed by such statements as the following, written on 15 June 1969, by Golda Meir, Israel's Prime Minister: 'It was not as though there was a Palestinian people in Palestine…and we came and threw them out and took their country away from them. They did not exist' (Ateek 1989: 36).

In the spring of 1967, before the Six Day War took place, I had to return to the United States from Rome, Italy, where I lived. Before I left, an Israeli friend, Mooky Dagan (nephew of General Moishe Dayan) took me aside. He wanted me to know that an as yet unknown, but upcoming war would be taking place. He was excited, as I recall, as he told me of the plans Israel was making for this attack. His story varied completely from the story as I heard it and read it in the western part of the U.S. following the Israeli invasion. In San Francisco, it came off as the attacked, fighting back and winning. But the attacked were not the Israelis, they were the Palestinians, the Egyptians and the Syrians! Our – the United State's – complicity in overlooking the reality of Israel's actions struck me, even then, as duplicitous and dangerous. As Donald Wagner writes in, *Dying in the Land of Promise*, 'Israel's preemptive attack destroyed the Egyptian air force before a single plane lifted-off the runway, making the remainder of this abbreviated 'six day war' not so much a miracle as the success of Israel's first strike ability' (Wagner 2000: 179). In 1967, before the Six Day War, in the West Bank and the Gaza Strip, there were virtually no Jewish members of the population. At that time, East Jerusalem had 5,000 Jews, in contrast to 70,000-75,000 Palestinian Christians and Muslims (Wagner: 189) Today, as noted earlier, the balance has changed dramatically.

Yasser Arafat was elected Chairman of the Palestinian Liberation Organization's (PLO) Executive Committee, in 1969. In 1974, the PLO was named the 'sole and legitimate representative' of Palestine at an Arab summit held in Rabat, Morocco. This gave the PLO – and Arafat – the recognition and prestige needed to promote the Palestinian cause. From 1969, until his death in November 2004, Arafat retained his position, even though others were elected to serve as Chairman of the PLO. Prior to Arafat's death, Palestine's attempts to provide new leadership were contested for a variety of reasons. In the years just prior to his death, it appeared clear that Yasser Arafat was not willing to step down or to allow another to accede to his place as leader of the Palestinian people. While the Palestinian people were beginning to verbalize their discontent with the corruption and lack of order of Arafat's administration, all criticism of Arafat stopped when the Israelis held him a virtual prisoner in his offices in Ramallah. The televised images of him in a tight, dark space damaged by artillery fire and bashed in by tanks – with no electricity, water or sewage – turned the man into an instant martyr, no longer a Palestinian problem, but a man seen as suffering for his people.

The question when Arafat was alive, and the question remaining now: is there anyone strong enough, charismatic enough, willing enough to be the voice of reason and clarity in what has become an incredibly tense and explosive situation? Following the 2006 Palestinian elections, Mahmoud Abbas (known as Abu Mazen), the previously duly elected chairman of the PLO, and the newly elected Palestinian Prime Minister, Dr Ismail Haniyeh, a member of Hamas (an Islamic movement with the intent of establishing a Palestinian state, with Jerusalem as the capital, on the land that was formerly Palestine), were faced with a challenge from the Palestinian voters to bring together a non-corrupt, functioning Palestinian government. Hamas had won the elections in what was a surprise to many observers. But to the many who voted, a change was declared necessary. Hamas was seen, by at least some of those who voted for Hamas' leadership, as a provider of humanitarian assistance, education and as a means of restoring the very underpinnings of the crumbling infrastructure of the marginalized Palestinian society.

We in the West saw Hamas as it was portrayed in the media – as masked terrorists. Some – a voting majority – in the Palestinian Territory – saw under Hamas' mask something Fateh and the PLO had not provided. In some ways I relate this to the Black Muslim movement of the 1960s, where efforts to support, sustain, uphold and uplift a section of the American society was seen within and without the African American community through different lenses of understanding. This is not to equate Hamas' violence with the Black Muslims, it is rather to say that the humanitarian aspects of each was not dissimilar one from the other.

Unfortunately in Palestine, as with many shifts in political realms elsewhere, splinter groups broke away – power struggles ensued and what may have begun to a certain extent as an idealistic, patriotic Palestinian movement began to erode. This erosion or deterioration was exacerbated, in my opinion, by the fearful unwillingness of the West to let the democratic process we cherish be a democratic reality in Palestine. Hamas, voted into office, was rejected by some within the Palestinian community, certainly by those in the Israeli government, and even more importantly, the fledgling Hamas leadership was condemned by the U.S. and European Community. We, as a nation, tend to forget we were forged out of conflict and resistance to a presence upon our land by the Spanish and in particular the British. I do not condone the rash of kidnappings, murders and violence on either or any side of the political spectrum in Israel/Palestine, be it Israeli or Palestinian, but I do believe that an election overseen by various international observers – an election found to be honest – should have been allowed to become what it had promised its people to be. There existed the possibility that Hamas' refusal to recognize Israel or Israel's right to exist could have become less radicalized and could have changed once discussions had begun concerning what Hamas meant by such statements. There could have been discussions of what it wanted in regard to the boundaries of Israel and Palestine and where these boundaries might be established so each could exist in safety upon its own land.

At the moment, with Israel occupying Palestinian land, it is unlikely that Hamas would have taken a political stand in opposition to its known stance, which calls for a defined Palestinian State and the ousting of Israel from Palestinian land. Following Hamas' Izzidin al-Qassam Brigade's takeover of Gaza in June 2007, Fateh's armed militia, Al-Aqsa, burned, looted and turned against followers of Hamas. The underlying 'rule' that no Palestinian would kill or harm another Palestinian has been lost in the post-2006 elections. And yet there are still six West Bank cities where Hamas retains or shares political power with Fateh. Will the two parties be able to work together, in spite of their disaffection for one another and their different approaches to freeing Palestine from Israeli occupation?

When the West (and Israel) cut off aid and taxes due to the Palestinian people, following Hamas' win in the elections, it destroyed for the time being the fragile link between the Palestinians – those in Gaza and those on the West Bank. But there is the common cause of a free Palestine that could still unite the Palestinians in both camps. With 178 Fateh militiamen being released by the Israelis (to join Palestinian security forces) it is always possible to hope that other Palestinians being held without due process might also be released – those in Fateh or the PLO or Hamas. Such a humanitarian act might take the edge off of the sword of Hamas.

At the same time that Hamas and Fateh were struggling for leadership, Israel found itself no longer under the leadership of Sharon (who was removed from his role as Prime Minister by a devastating stroke). Ehud Olmert, the former Mayor of Jerusalem, became acting and then elected Prime Minister of Israel (Israel is governed by a prime minister, with a 120-member national legislature, the Knesset. There is a President of Israel, but that position is largely ceremonial). At the time Olmert became Prime Minister, the Israeli Knesset, with a twenty-five member cabinet, found itself, also, divided with twenty-nine seats in the Kadima Party, twenty seats in Labor, twelve in Likud, twelve in Shas and forty-seven in minor parties (Carter 2006: 188). The infighting and power struggles in both Israel/Palestine continue, even after the 2007 ouster of Hamas from its duly elected position in the Palestinian government in 2006. With the Palestinian National Authority near bankruptcy, the West seemingly brokered a buy-out of Palestinian politics. Secretary of State Condoleezza Rice met with Abbas and Olmert (not recognizing, as well, the legitimately elected officials of the Hamas Party). This meeting, and subsequent negotiations – supported by new attacks by the Israeli military on Gaza – led to more serious fighting in Gaza. This left Hamas with Gaza and the PLO and Fateh in charge of the West Bank, creating the ongoing skirmishes as the legitimacy of leadership – on all sides – is critiqued and challenged. The peace process, perhaps, will resurface and become a viable topic. This may be more as a reaction to the extreme, 'terrorist', presence, than to a desire to seriously resolve an issue that has been ongoing since at least the 1948 Proclamation of Independence and the establishment of Israel as a state.

Peacemakers: Jewish, Christian and Muslim

This modern history is one full of hope and despair. The promise of the 1993 'Handshake' between Israeli Prime Minister Yitzhak Rabin and PLO Prime Minister and Chairman Yasser Arafat was followed by the assassination of Rabin and the election of a right wing, conservative ruling body in Israel. One can only imagine how Israeli and Palestinian emotions rose and fell – plummeted – in the aftermath of the killing of the peace process, which essentially was seen in the aftermath of the killing of Rabin.

Some people have kept the faith on all sides of the conflict, notable among the Christians are: Elias Chacour, a recently consecrated Melkite archbishop; Naim Ateek, an Anglican/Episcopalian priest – both Palestinian Israeli citizens – Jean Zaru, a Palestinian Quaker; Mitri Raheb, a Palestinian Christian Lutheran pastor; and Hanan Mikhail Ashrawi, an Anglican herself, previously the sole female Palestinian Cabinet Member and spokesperson for the Palestinians in the occupied territories. These people are more fully addressed in the chapter on 'Peacemakers in Israel/Palestine'.

According to Muslim and Jewish persons with whom I spoke, Yossi Beilin and Ehud Barak are two individuals who stand out for them as Israeli Jewish peacemakers. I would add Itzhak Rabin as a man who worked for peace and became a martyr for peace. Mahmoud Abbas (Abu Mazen) and Abu Jihad remain examples of Palestinian Muslims who worked, or continue to work for a peaceful resolution to the conflict in Israel/Palestine. Two other Palestinian Muslims of note are Abdul Rahman Abbad and Mohammed Majeeb Ja'bar, both founding members of Al-Liqa' Center for Religious and Heritage Studies in the Holy Land, in Jerusalem.

Yossi Beilin is known most widely for his work with the Oslo Accord, the Geneva Initiative and the Israeli/Palestinian peace process as it has moved, or not moved, in the past thirty years of his political life. Beilin was with the Israeli Labour Party from 1977 until 1984, serving as the party's spokesperson. Beginning in 1984, he served as an Israeli Cabinet Secretary, for two years, and then served another two years as Director General of the Foreign Ministry. In 1988, he was elected to the Knesset (the Israeli parliament) where he served as a member of the Labour Party until 1996. In 2003, having been basically dismissed by the Labour Party, Beilin and Yael Dayan joined the political party Meretz. He was reelected to the Knesset under Meretz. Once back in the Knesset, he and Dayan founded the Shahar Movement, which merged with Mereta to form Yachad. He now heads Yachad. Beilin's moves within a given political party and into new political parties are indicative of the way politics shift and political parties change within the State of Israel. Israeli political parties are very different to our two-party American system. There are larger and smaller parties in the Israeli system, with the majority of the parties being variations or offshoots of earlier Zionist parties. In the Knesset there are Arab members, but they are in the minority of the minority having just eight members in 2001 (Ruether 1989: 148).

While Beilin was virtually redefining the political structure of the Knesset, he was, at the same time, working on peace initiatives. He is best known for his 1992 leadership, with Palestinians Mahmoud Abbas and Ahmed Qurei, in creating the Oslo Accords (also known as the Declaration of Principles, DOP). At the time that the Oslo Accords were being organized (1992), he worked as Deputy Foreign Minister under Shimon Peres, who was then the Foreign Minister of Israel. The Oslo Accords were planned and brought about in secrecy, illegal under Israeli laws at that time. Interestingly enough, the Oslo meetings took place in a home in Oslo, Norway, far away from the usual glare of prior (and recent) peace meetings. An American friend, who is from Norway, knew the people in whose home the peace negotiators used to hold their meeting in Norway. She said they sat down at the simple kitchen table and laid out the plans for peace in Israel/Palestine – man-to-man, without the usual fanfare of cameras rolling and reporters writing. It worked, she felt, because the people were relating in an environment that was familiar – around the family table in a homely environment.

While the United States was not invited to this meeting – nor was anyone from other than Israel/Palestine and Norway – former U.S. President Jimmy Carter was kept informed of the progress of the meeting (Carter 2006: 133). It strikes me that one reason the

Oslo Agreement came into being and offered a promise of succeeding is exactly because the United States, England, Russia nor any other outside nation participated. It has been that kind of outside 'help' which has created the situation today – from the partition to the occupation. Sometimes if people are given the opportunity to sit down and talk, out of the limelight, they get a lot more done. Perhaps it is because no one is watching, which allows them to be more honest and direct in their statements, rather than trying to hone the correct sound bite before the public. This aside, from the beginning the Oslo Accords were seen more favorably by Israel than by Palestine which meant they were doomed to failure. Edward Said, a Palestinian scholar and educator, wrote: 'The deal before us smacks of the PLO leadership's exhaustion and isolation and of Israel's shrewdness. Many Palestinians are asking themselves why, after years of concessions, they should be conceding once again to Israel and the United States in return for promises and vague improvements in the occupation that won't all occur until the 'final status' talks some three to five years hence, and perhaps not even then' (Wagner 2000: 220). Said and other individuals, including members of the Palestinian political parties Hamas, the Palestinian Liberation Organization (PLO) and Fateh opposed the Oslo Accords. Many felt the most pressing issues were not addressed in the Accords, including: the status and right of return of Palestinian refugees, Jerusalem, Jewish settlements, the borders between Israel and Palestine and foreign policy with Israel/Palestine's neighboring Arab states (Wagner 2000: 220).

Beilin's work since the 1993 signing of the Oslo Accord has included leadership on the Multilateral Peace Process and continued discussions with those involved in the Israeli/Palestinian Taba Talks, which have carried on since the Clinton presidency. Perhaps most importantly he was an Israeli signee to the Geneva Accords or Initiatives in 2003. He is the founder and leader of a recent Israeli peace party, 'Beilin', and a founder and employee of the Economic Cooperation Foundation. A man most passionate about his goal to secure peace and justice for both Palestinians and Israelis, Beilin is an international figure doing an intricate political dance in the land he is trying to make whole for all its inhabitants.

Ehud Barak is a controversial figure, in that to some Jews he is seen as a peace maker and to others, he is seen as duplicitous at best, particularly in his dealings with Yasser Arafat. Even though

Palestinians, and some Jews who would critique Barak's peace dealing might not agree, Barak is included in this section because he has been involved in various aspects of the peace process, in the most part due to the political positions he has held. Because of this I believe it is important to see who the man is and what he represents.

He was born Ehud Brog on 12 February 1942, on the Kibbutz Mishmar HaSharon, during the period when the presently contested area of Israel/Palestine was still called Palestine, overseen by the British under the British Mandate. He has three brothers. Barak and his wife, Naava, have three daughters. Naava and Ehud Barak are now divorced.

In 1959, he joined the IDF, where he served for thirty-five years. When he entered the military, he changed his family name to Barak, which in Hebrew means 'lightening'. During his time in the IDF, among other things, he commanded tank divisions and was part of overt operations, including being part of the 1973 Operation Spring of Youth in Beirut, where he went into Beirut disguised as a woman, with the intention of assassinating PLO members who had purportedly been involved in the raid on the Israeli team at the 1972 Munich Olympics, in which eleven Israeli athletes died. (In the Operation Spring of Youth raid, three PLO leaders were assassinated. Their main target, Yasser Arafat was not killed.) Barak left the service as Chief of General Staff, with the highest rank offered, that of Rav Aluf. He received the Medal of Distinguished Service and four other citations. He is one of the most honored IDF soldiers in Israel.

Barak's political career began in 1995, when he served as Minister of the Interior and then Minister of Foreign Affairs. He was elected to the Knesset in 1996. He became Prime Minister in 1999, and served as such until he, and the Labour Party, were replaced by Ariel Sharon and the Likud Party in 2001 (The term of Prime Minister is usually six years. He was replaced early in his term as a result of a special election.) During his brief tenure as Prime Minister, he formed a coalition which included the Shas Party. The Meretz Party quit the coalition when an agreement about division of powers could not be agreed upon. While this internal squabble was going on, Barak saw that Israel withdrew from Southern Lebanon, he initiated peace negotiations with Syria and was a member of the failed Camp David Summit, in 2000. He, also, represented Israel at the Taba

Summit in January 2001, following his service as Prime Minister. According to Jimmy Carter, during the talks held at Taba', …it was later claimed that the Palestinians rejected a 'generous offer' put forward by Prime Minister Barak with Israel keeping only 5% of the West Bank. The fact is that no such offers were ever made. Barak later said, "It was plain to me that there was no chance of reaching a settlement at Taba. Therefore I said there would be no negotiations and there would be no delegation and there would be no official discussions and no documentation. Nor would Americans be present in the room. The only thing that took place at Taba were nonbinding contacts between senior Iraqis and senior Palestinians" ' (Carter 2006: 152).

In 2001, Barak worked in the United States with two companies, each focusing on electronic data and security. Returning to Israel in 2005, he partnered with an investment company in Pennsylvania, naming his company Ehud Barak Limited. At that time he also ran for leadership of the Labour Party, but withdrew in support of Shimon Peres. Finally, in 2007, he regained leadership of the Labour Party, to which he has belonged since he entered politics. As a review of present Prime Minister Olmert's decisions in the 2006 war against Hezbollah takes place, Barak is positioning himself to take over as Prime Minister if Olmert is removed. His real life drama continues, as do cinematic and literary versions of Barak in the Munich film and a novel, *The Devil's Alternative*.

How a man who was educated in the military, by the military in covert operations, can come into a place as tense as Israel/Palestine as a peace broker is yet to be seen. Whether the people who have been his enemy can trust him, whether his alliances with the United States will assist or deter him from peace brokering and whether his leadership role in Israeli politics will remain stable is all yet to be seen. Other leaders, who have come out of a military background, have worked for peace to ensure that there will be no more wars. If this is part of Barak's makeup, he may yet be a peace broker. For him to be considered a man working for peace is a statement of the possibility for change in itself. How much peace-seeking is a core part of the man, and how that search for peace plays out is yet to be seen. Certainly his business and military relationships with the United States could be an advantage or disadvantage. In Barak's case, only time will reveal the true depths of the man.

Another military man, who has come to be seen as a man of conscience and integrity, is Yitzhak Rabin who was born in Jerusalem on 1 March 1922, when the city was still part of Palestine. His father had emigrated to the United States from the Ukrainian Soviet Socialist Republic, changed his name from Rubizov to Rabin and in 1917 emigrated to Palestine with the Hagdud Ha'ivri (Jewish Legion) volunteers to settle the land for Israel. Rabin's mother, whose father was a rabbi, came from a family that was opposed to the Zionist Movement. She emigrated from Mohilev, Belarus, to Palestine in 1919 to work on a kibbutz, later moving to Jerusalem.

Yitzhak Rabin's early years were spent in Tel Aviv, where he graduated from Kadoori Agricultural High School with the intention of becoming an irrigation engineer. As it turned out, he did not receive an advanced degree. He married Leah Schlossberg in 1948. They had two children, Dahlia and Yuval. Dahlia Rabin-Pelossof became Deputy Minister of Defense in 2001.

Yitzhak Rabin took part in the 1948 War as a commander of the Haganah (standing army), rising to the rank of Chief Operations Officer. Upon leaving the IDF, Rabin was in full command of the IDF. When his memoirs were published, *Yitzhak Rabin, The Rabin Memoirs*, he broke the unspoken rules and spoke of what really happened during the 1948 War, from an Israeli military man's perspective. Compared to the accepted Israeli story which denied the Lod survivor's stories and halved the number of Palestinian refugees, Rabin told how David Ben-Gurion (the first Prime Minister and founding father of Israel) ordered Christian Palestinians to leave their towns of Lydda and Ramle. Rabin wrote: 'We walked outside, Ben-Gurion accompanying us. Allon repeated his question: 'What is to be done with the population?' BG waved his hand in a gesture which said: 'Drive them out'. The population of Lod (Hebrew for Lydda) did not leave willingly. There was no way of avoiding the use of force and warning shots in order to make the inhabitants march the ten to fifteen miles where they met up with the legion' (Wagner 2000: 129).

Rabin was ambassador to the United States from 1968 until he was elected to the Knesset in 1973. He was appointed Minister of Labour. He succeeded Golda Meir as Prime Minister of Israel in 1974 (Meir, the founding 'mother' of Israel, was known as the 'Iron Lady'. She emigrated to Palestine from Wisconsin in 1921.) Rabin served one term as Prime Minister (1974–1977), then resigned due to the breakup of his political coalition over F-15 jets being delivered to Israel on the Sabbath and the discovery that his wife still had a bank account in the United States when it was illegal for Israeli citizens to have foreign currency accounts. The Likud Party's Menachem Begin was elected to serve as Prime Minister in 1977. Rabin remained a member of the Knesset, serving on the Foreign Affairs and Defense Committee and as Minister of Defense.

In 1992, Rabin was elected chair of the Israeli Labour Party and became Prime Minister for his second term (1992 until his death). He is perhaps best known for his part in the Oslo Accords, which created the Palestinian Authority and granted it partial control over parts of the Gaza Strip and West Bank. PLO Chairman Yasser Arafat, at the same time, renounced violence and officially recognized Israel. Rabin officially recognized the PLO. Yitzak Rabin, Yasser Arafat and Shimon Peres were awarded the 1994 Nobel Peace Prize. Rabin was also awarded the 1994 Ronald Reagan Freedom Award. Unfortunately, Rabin's work on behalf of peace polarized the population – some saw him as a hero, others saw him as a traitor, giving away land.

On 4 November 1995, Yitzak Rabin was assassinated by Yigal Amir, while Rabin was leaving a Tel Aviv rally in support of the Oslo Accord. Amir was a right-wing Orthodox Jew who opposed the Oslo Accord. Rabin died in the hospital in Tel Aviv. The impact of Rabin on the international community was visible in the Heads of State who attended his funeral. Among them were: U.S. President Bill Clinton, Egyptian President Hosni Mubarak and Jordanian King Hussein. Despite his military beginning, Rabin has become an Israeli peace hero. The square where he was killed is named after him and the anniversary of his death is honored.

On the Palestinian Muslim side, Mahmoud Abbas (Abu Mazen) was born in Safad on 26 March 1935. During the Zionist military takeover of Palestine, in 1948, his family moved to Syria as refugees. There he was educated, first working as an elementary school teacher, later receiving a BA Degree in Law from Damascus University in Syria and a Ph.D. in History from the Oriental College in Moscow. Abbas was one of the founders of Fateh, where he presently serves as Prime Minister. He has also been a member of the Palestine National Council since 1968, and served on the PLO Executive Committee until recently. When Abu Jihad was assassinated in 1988, Abbas replaced him on the Executive

Committee as Chairman of the Occupied Territories. In 1995, after having lived out of Israel/Palestine for forty-eight years, he was finally able to return to live in Gaza and Ramallah. The following year, in 1996, he became Yasser Arafat's deputy and the PLO's Secretary General of the PLO. That same year he was head of the Central Election Commission for the Palestine Legislative Council elections, a much-awaited and debated event. In March, 2003, he was named as the first Prime Minister of the Palestinian Authority, but Yasser Arafat would not relinquish control and Mahmoud Abbas would not dismantle the infrastructure of the Palestinian Authority. The result was an impasse which affected the peace process as well as the leadership of the Palestinian people for the next few years. Following Arafat's death on 9 January 2005, Abbas was elected President of the Palestinian Authority, but was replaced in 2003 by Ahmed Korei. He presently serves as Prime Minister of Palestine through the political party Fateh.

Considered a moderate, Abbas has been devoted to finding a solution to the Israeli/Palestinian situation. As early as the 1970s he was involved in peace negotiations with Jewish and other groups. In 1977, he and Matiyahu Peled worked on and presented the two state 'principles of peace'. He coordinated the Madrid Conference in 1991 and co-headed, with Ahmed Qurei (Abu Ala), the Palestinian side of the Oslo Peace Talks in 1993. In 1995 he collaborated on a 'Framework for the Conclusion of a Final Status Agreement Between Israel and the PLO', referred to as the Abu-Mazen-Beilin Plan. In 2006 to 2007, following a political struggle in Gaza that became violent – with many deaths and injuries, some caused by the military actions of the IDF and others by the extremist members of Hamas – Abbas has been left with a fragile hold on the West Bank of Palestine, while Hamas has retained control of Gaza. The United States, as of the summer of 2007, began brokering a peace conference with Israel, the Palestinian people as represented by Fateh and Abbas, as well as other Arab neighboring countries with boundaries contiguous to the borders of Israel/Palestine. To this date, Hamas has been left out of the planning for this gathering.

Khalil Al-Wazir, a man seen as a Palestinian freedom fighter, who came out of the post-1948 years determined to reunite Palestine, may seem like an odd choice for a peacemaker. He saw himself as a liberator. He is in many ways the mirror image of many Jewish leaders who have fought for Israel's place in Israel/Palestine. Khalil

Al-Wazir had the same potential to bring together the Palestinians, as have other leaders, many of whom came from a place of violence into a stance for peace. Al-Wazir could have been a peacemaker. As it turned out he was a martyr, a counterpoint in some ways to Che Guevara, in the earlier confrontations that took place in Colombia and Argentina (Che Guevera was a revolutionary in the Central and South American wars. He will be discussed under the chapter on Liberation Theology).

Khalil Al-Wazir was born on 10 October 1935, in Ramla, Palestine. In 1948 he was forced to go from his hometown to the Al-Bureij refugee camp in Gaza. He later married his cousin, Intissar Al-Wazir. Together they had three sons: Jihad, Bassem and Nidal and two daughters: Iman and Hanan. Al-Wazir's life is offered as an example of a person who came out of a refugee existence with a desire to bring freedom to the Palestinian people. Like others living under similar situations, with similar desires to restore the rights of the Palestinian people, he made his choices. His was to utilize violence as a means to the end. Others have chosen to utilize nonviolence as a means to the same end. It is hoped we might learn from both perspectives, as we consider the ways to bring about peace in a nonviolent way to Israel/Palestine.

In Cairo, Egypt, in 1954, where he was an affiliate of the Muslim Brotherhood, Al-Wazir received his military training and was briefly imprisoned for possible involvement in violent acts against Israel. He attended the University of Alexandria in Egypt, but did not graduate. From 1959 to 1963, he worked as a teacher in Kuwait. It was here that he became involved with the people who would found the movement which became the political party Fateh. In 1963 Al-Wazir moved to Algeria where he opened an office for Fateh, recruited people for membership in Fateh and for training as 'soldiers' of Fateh (Al-Asifa, 'The Storm'). He co-founded and edited *Filastinuna* (the official newspaper of Fateh). It is in Algiers that he became familiar with military leaders from a variety of socialist countries. In 1964 he went to the People's Republic of China. He later visited North Vietnam and North Korea. In spite of these associations, he never became a Communist, himself.

In 1965, he moved back to Damascus, Syria. Here he was able to link Fateh underground groups in Israel/Palestine with the growing external and internal Palestinian national movement. At the end of the 1967 Six Day War, Al-Wazir moved into a top position with both the PLO and Fateh parties. His previous political work within the Palestinian community in exile and his reputation as a person expert on liberation propelled him to this place in politics. While still living outside of Israel/Palestine, he became the head of Palestinian commando operations inside Israel. At the same time, he took on more responsibility within the refugee community outside of Israel/Palestine.

In the 1970s, as an aide to Yasser Arafat and a leader in the 1970–71 Black September clashes in Jordan (Black September was a Palestinian group named after a 1970 massacre by King Hussein's troops of PLO forces. In the fall of 1972 the Black September group kidnapped and murdered eleven Israeli athletes.) Abu Jihad was behind many other military operations against Israel. It was during this time that he moved to join other PLO leaders in Beirut, Lebanon. He is best known for his work developing underground groups in the West Bank and Gaza. As the PLO fighters within Israel/Palestine gained numbers and support, Al-Wazir wanted to see them retain the focus of the original 'people's liberation forces'. To this end he moved to be near them in Kayfun, near Alayh in Mount Lebanon. From here he is considered to have been behind several attacks on Israel. While Arafat and the PLO became known for their corruption, losing much of their earlier discipline, Al-Wazir remained respected by the Palestinians and separate from the ongoing dissolution of the party. In spite of his differences with the direction the PLO was taking, he remained associated with Arafat and the PLO, moving with the other leaders to Tunisia in 1982. It was here, however, that Al-Wazir finally broke with the PLO. He turned his focus on organizing the people of the West Bank and Gaza, sponsoring youth committees and other groups that eventually coalesced into the previously mentioned First Intifada in December, 1987.

On 16 April 1988, Khalil Al-Wazir was assassinated in his home with his wife and children present. It is said that a commando team of Israeli soldiers went into Lebanon to assassinate Al-Wazir. This was never proved. Ehud Barak has been named, by a Maariv newspaper report, as the commander who oversaw the assassination of Al-Wazir, but the State of Israel and Barak have never commented on this report (Wikipedia: 18 July 2007). The United States protested the intrusion into Lebanon for the purpose of committing the assassination. To the Israelis, Khalil Al-Wazir is a terrorist. To the Palestinians he is a freedom fighter and a martyr.

And so he is rarely referred to by his birth name, rather he is best known by the name Abu Jihad (father of the struggle). He is also known as Al-Wazir (the top minister), for being one of the founders of Fateh. His widow, Intissar Al-Wazir is also known, now, as Kunya: Umm Jihad (mother of the struggle). She was the first female minister in the Palestinian National Authority and has continued in politics in her own right. Perhaps Abu Jihad would have died as a disgraced commando or perhaps he would have died as an honored soldier or diplomat. Having been assassinated we will never know what his true potential was. Now he is a martyr to one side and a terrorist to the other.

Unfortunately, in spite of people working for peace – or for a resolution – aggressive behavior, on both sides, continues. The behavior of the Israeli government, in my opinion, reflects the mentality of those who have been victimized becoming the victimizer – those who have been abused becoming the abuser. And perhaps, with the new generation of Hamas leaders struggling for power, are we seeing evidence of the powerless resorting to violence to regain a sense of power? These are the first and second – even third generations – of Palestinian refugees who are coming onto the political scene in Gaza and elsewhere. Patience may have run out for them. As the world becomes more focused on the Middle East, and as the 'truth' of what has happened and what is happening becomes revealed, the tragedies of the Jewish and Palestinian peoples – past and present – seem to be before us, as Americans in particular, to reexamine and to take responsibility for these many generations later.

Land seems to be a constant – a given – bandied about as if no one – no one – upon the earth cared. We have carved up the earth, built defensive structures upon the earth, destroyed orchards of ancient olives and vineyards as if in doing so we could eradicate the memory of the hands who planted and harvested the fruit. We have done all this – we continue to do all this – in the name of our God – our individually owned God, bartering God as we barter the land, its peoples and all that belongs to the land.

A person who is becoming more of a peacemaker and a disturber of the peace, as he continues to speak out his truth is our former President of the United States of America, James Earl (Jimmy) Carter, Jr. His latest book, *Palestine Peace Not Apartheid*, by its very title demands attention. By using the word 'apartheid' (strict racial segregation) he has invoked the images of South Africa, something the retired Archbishop of the Anglican Church in South Africa, Desmond Tutu, and others have also done when they have spoken about Israel/Palestine. The word 'apartheid' is relevant to Israel/ Palestine because there is a real separation between the Israeli occupiers and the Palestinians who are being occupied. A separation, not just of walls or politics, but a separation between who gets the electricity, sewage and water. A separation between who gets good education and their rightful tax dollars put to use. A separation between just and unjust living conditions and rights as a 'citizen' of either Israel or Palestine. Jimmy Carter has written and spoken the truth as he knows it – the truth as much of the media in the United States has not presented it – the truth that the majority of this nation can not see or hear. Carter's words are not prejudicial or anti-Jewish; they are words of reality. They are words that the world needs to hear if a solution to the situation in Israel/Palestine is to be secured for both sides.

Probably the most highly recognized of American citizens speaking out about Israel/Palestine, President Carter comes from Plains, Georgia – a farm town where he was born on 1 October 1924, and where he presently lives with his wife Rosalynn Smith Carter. Their four children are grown and married: John William (Jack) Carter, James Earl (Chip) Carter, III, Donnel Jeffrey (Jeff) Carter and Amy Lynn Carter. Carter's own siblings, two sisters and a brother predeceased him.

Coming as he does from a farming and nuclear physics background, as well as his experience as President of the United States, Mr Carter brings a knowledgeable, down-to-earth and scientific approach to issues. In the Middle East, particularly in Israel/Palestine, these understandings are invaluable. Carter knows from the ground up about agriculture, business and the issues of the land.

From the Navy and nuclear power planning back to farming, to-be-President Carter entered into local and national politics. After his 1962 election to the Georgia Senate, Carter moved rapidly to become the thirty-ninth President of the United States of America in 1977. He served one term in office. While some of his domestic and international policies were not highly regarded at the time of his presidency, he is recognized today for having established the Camp David Accords (the treaty of peace between Egypt and Israel);

the SALT II Treaty with the Soviet Union (nuclear); and diplomatic relations with the People's Republic of China. He was involved in worldwide human rights programs and at home established the U.S. Energy Program, the Department of Energy and the Department of Education, as well as the environmental Alaska Lands Act.

Before becoming President of the United States, Jimmy Carter had developed personal relationships with Yitzhak Rabin, Moshe Dayan, Golda Meir, Abba Eban and other Israeli political and military leaders. In part, these relationships developed from a visit Yitzhak Rabin made to Georgia, when Carter was Governor of the state. Following Rabin's Georgia trip, the Carters (Jimmy and Rosalynn) went to Israel in 1973 as Rabin's guest. While in Israel/ Palestine, the Carters visited Christian sites, a Kibbutzim (collective farm or settlement), a settlement on the Golan Heights and a military training camp in Bethel. The Carters had virtually no interactions with the Arab Palestinians. These experiences, combined with later understandings that came from interactions with both Palestinian and Israeli leaders, informed Carter's presidency.

While president, Jimmy Carter's ability to interact with the key politicians in the Middle East led toward the 1978 Camp David Accords and the 1979 Egyptian/Israeli peace treaty. Carter worked primarily with President Sadat, of Egypt, Menachem Begin, then Prime Minister of Israel, King Hussein of Jordan, and President Assad of Syria (dealings which had to be done indirectly as the PLO was classified as a 'terrorist organization' by the United States, precluding a direct one-on-one visit between the presidents of these two nations) and Yasser Arafat, Head of the PLO. After leaving the presidency of the United States, Carter has continued to remain involved in the politics and policies of the Middle East.

Since 1982, Carter has been the University Distinguished Professor at Emory University in Atlanta, Georgia. In 1986, he established the Carter Center that focuses on a wide range of subjects, including: national and international issues of public policy, resolution of conflict, promotion of democracy, protection of human rights and issues related to the prevention of disease and agriculture in the developing world. Besides Emory University's Carter Center, the Jimmy Carter Library and Museum is located at Plains, Georgia. It is a national historic site. He and Rosalynn are known for their volunteer work with Habitat for Humanity. He also teaches Sunday School and is a deacon in the Maranatha Baptist Church in Plains,

Georgia. The Carter's have chosen a humble and authentic way to live out their faith, keeping grounded in the Plains, Georgia life style, while working on international and domestic issues of great importance. Mr Carter won the Nobel Peace Prize In October 2002.

Jimmy Carter has had over twenty books published, *The Blood of Abraham*, in 1993, and his latest, published in 2007, *Palestine: Peace Not Apartheid* focused on Israel/Palestine. In *Peace Not Apartheid*, Carter has hit a nerve in the American public. By using the word 'apartheid', there is an immediate comparison drawn between the Palestinians' situation under Israeli occupation and the indigenous Africans' racial segregation in South Africa. Did Carter mean there should be peace, not apartheid or did he mean that there is apartheid, already, and peace is the only alternative? He said, in an interview at the Carter Presidential Library on December 8, 2006, that he meant for his book to be deliberately provocative because 'there is an impenetrable wall between American citizens and what is going on in Palestine'. Some reviews of his book have indicated that the reviewers never got beyond the title. Alan Dershowitz, a former supporter of Carter, gave a harsh critique of the book. While the book went on the New York Times Best Seller List, the book was not reviewed by the *New York Times*. I find the book to be an insightful reflective journal of Carter's (and others) political interaction with the Israelis and the Palestinians. He uses facts and personal experience to put before the reader the reality of the Israeli/Palestinian situation as he knows it. Speaking as an ex-president and a Nobel Peace Prize recipient one would hope that people might be receptive to what he has to say.

The Wall, The Fence, The Barrier

Perhaps the most egregious of recent actions, on the part of Israel, has been the erection of The Wall, referred to by Israelis as 'The Fence'. This wall, sometimes as high as three stories and as wide as two football fields are long, is a heavy presence in a heavy time. Built on the pretense of trying to secure Israel's borders, while making for a terrorist-free nation state, the Wall is cutting into Palestinian territory, dividing homes from their adjacent farm lands, people from one another, segregating and segmenting a peoples while, at the same time, expanding the Israeli claim to the land. The Wall is a reminder of the Berlin Wall, which fell in November 1989.

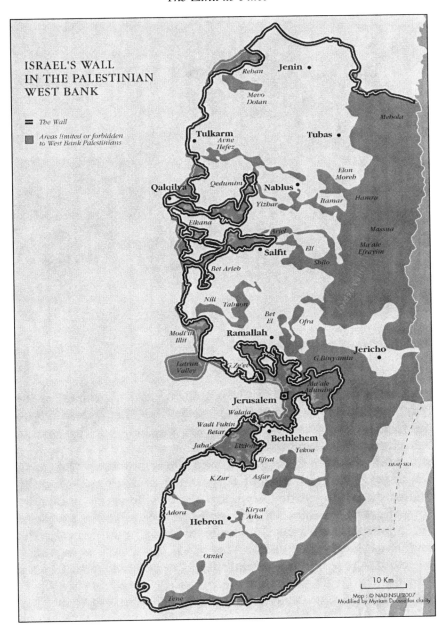

Israel's Wall in the Palestinian West Bank, © NAD-NSU 2007, modified by Myriam Dousse for clarity, permission kindly granted by Anna Baltzer.

Wall Long Shot, Peter J. Nagle CFP, M.A.R

And, now, as the question of the building and placement of the Wall goes before the International court at the Hague, few believe the judicial decisions, when they are reached – if they are in Palestine's favor – will be carried out.

A wall, as Robert Frost has said, does not make for good neighbors. This wall, patrolled by armed soldiers and specially trained guard dogs from Argentina, overshadows the possibility of peace. At Christmas 2003, I was heartbroken for the people of Bethlehem and those who wished to enter Bethlehem for the traditional services. Just before Christmas, the Wall was extended to exclude those wishing to enter the City of Jesus' birth. For the first time in 2,000 years, according to the Anglican Bishop of Jerusalem in his Christmas letter, there were no services. How bleak it felt, to sing, 'Oh, Little Town of Bethlehem', knowing the place of our beginnings – the place that brought our 'Christmas' into its sacred, festive place in our lives – the oldest Christian community in the world – was without its own annual, holy remembering of the birth of Christ.

Now, Bethlehem is encircled by a wall that restricts and inhibits the movements of both residents of Bethlehem and those wishing to enter Bethlehem. In 2006, I took a cheroot (local bus) from Jerusalem to Bethlehem. Driving into Bethlehem, one used to crest the gentle hills that ring the city and looked down on the pastoral hillside scene unchanged for eons. Now, there is no hill top view into the city, rather there is a grim wall, that blocks the view – that blocks the entrance and exit for many. Upon arriving at one of three entrances through the wall into the area that surrounds the city, we who held American or European passports were allowed to walk – with an armed escort – through the maze of wire-fenced, metal turnstiled pathways that lead into an open area, virtually walled into the wall. Armed soldiers were on top of the wall, looking down upon us and out to the hillsides we could not see. Once through this open area, we were released through the wall into a desolate area, far from Bethlehem proper, where taxi drivers waited in hopes that someone would hire them for a ride into the city. While we, Americans and Europeans, were going through the security system of the wall, the Palestinians who had been with us on the bus were taken in another direction, into a windowless appearing building where they faced further security measures.

Later, when we were in the center of Bethlehem, we found Manger Square, usually bustling with people and activity, completely devoid of life, save for two Roman Catholic nuns who were walking across the square (they live in Bethlehem). Very few tourists come to Bethlehem any more, either out of fear or because of the restrictions and difficulties imposed upon them entering and leaving Bethlehem. The residents of Bethlehem are, subsequently, suffering from a lack of income – either because they can not leave Bethlehem for previous places of employment or because the tourists, and others, who used to provide sources of income can no longer come. A young woman I met through mutual friends lives a life that exemplifies existence in this walled city. She has a Master's Degree in Hotel Management. Previously, she worked in a large hotel in Jordan, preparing to take on the management of a hotel, which turned out to be in Bethlehem. She came back to the city where she was born – a city where her family has been for countless generations – to be in charge of the new Intercontinental Hotel in Bethlehem. The hotel was formerly a palace. Two modern wings were added to the palace, including beautiful pools and the latest amenities one might expect to find in any high end hotel. The ambiance of the place is lovely. She is keeping the hotel clean and protecting it at great expense to the Intercontinental Hotel as the place remains virtually empty (when we were there only six people were staying at the hotel, which could house hundreds). Only a year or two before, the IDF entered the newly restored and expanded hotel, severely damaging the place. It took a year to repair what had just been restored or newly constructed.

As the hotel manager, she should go to Jerusalem, and other areas, as part of her job. Because she is under thirty-five years of age she is unable to leave Bethlehem to go to Jerusalem. This is a new age restriction imposed by the Israeli government on Palestinians. Along with age, and other factors, Palestinians in Bethlehem (and other areas of Israel/Palestine) now are required to carry a Visa-like card to leave or enter the city. These cards must be entered into a machine upon leaving or returning to a given city or town. The machine is programmed to determine whether a given person can leave or not. If one is allowed to leave, the time one is allowed to be out of the city or area is proscribed, varying for the person and the reason for exiting. There is a curfew imposed at midnight, or earlier, in Bethlehem and other towns and cities.

One man, a well-established, longtime Bethlehem resident and business owner, said to get to Jerusalem and back, using the same check point, is most difficult (people must exit and reenter at the same place). According to him, and others, the fines and consequences for not meeting the deadline are severe. Young educated men (as well as women) are leaving Bethlehem, as they can not find work within the walled city, nor can they exit for work outside the walls. Our young hotel manager wants to remain – as do the many – in her hometown near her family. She is a Christian Palestinian, born in Bethlehem, with no immediate hope for her professional future, with no hope for a personal future which would under normal conditions include the possibility of marriage and children. The restrictions are constricting the life of the city that brought Christian life to the world.

This kind of walling off of populations is only going to bring about more resentment, fear and a deeper loss of hope, which in turn will bring more 'martyrs' into Israel on bombing and other suicide missions. When one has no hope left, a despair settles in – a resolution takes hold – and the feeling of fearful hopelessness expands. Did Berlin teach us nothing? Does our own nation's ongoing argument over building trenches and walls between Mexico and the southern parts of the United States teach us nothing? Reconciliation does not come with barriers being erected. Reconciliation comes when barriers are breached and the strong allow themselves to be open to the other – to be permeated by the other.

For those who feel, as the Zionist Christians and Zionist Jews do, and as the followers of the Halakha (Jewish codified oral law from the first centuries BCE) feel, that, '...for the boundaries of the Land of Israel, there are no arguments; they are clear axioms' (Harkabi 1986: 183), there seems no alternative to violence. Likewise, for the members of the extremist Palestinian militias who do not recognize Israel's right to exist, there seems no alternative to violence. Jews, Christians and Muslims offer both the solution to the problems and are the problem. As mentioned before, extremist groups, whatever their name or their allegiance, are counter-productive to a peace that unifies and embraces all with a claim to the place of Israel/Palestine.

The Law Ancient, The Reality Today

In the midst of this ongoing, ever-erupting shift of ownership and possession, it appears that aggressive legal actions have preempted human rights and the theology of 'God among us' has been shelved. In the world's desire to right one wrong, another was committed. As John Bright says in referring to the law of the Hebrew Bible, '...the law, as law, is ancient, irrelevant, and without authority. But what of the theology of the law?... It seeks to tell us that the land is God's and that we live on this earth as aliens and sojourners, holding all that we have as if it were on loan from God' (Bright 1967: 153). We are aliens – sojourners – guests of God on God's own home planet, yet we behave as though the land is ours – for this generation – for this moment in time – forever.

The Native Americans who believe that we should make decisions based on what is best for the seventh generation to come, are more in tune with Genesis and Exodus and our holy scripture than we who so rudely grasp at the ground, abuse it and one another in our attempts to gain what we see as our needs – our wants – our rights. Sometimes God is seen as giving us a touch of ironic injustice, as when,

> 'Yahweh (leaves) the Canaanites in the land to punish Israel for its illicit contacts with the inhabitants and their gods, and specifically to test Israel's faithfulness, to train Israel in the arts of war, or to preserve the environment against predatory wild beasts' (Gottwald 1979: 141).

When I read this I was reminded of Maryhill on the Columbia Gorge, in Washington State. At the side of this small jewel of a museum is a lovely picnic area, overlooking the Gorge and the environs of the museum. It is a dry, high desert area, not unlike parts of Israel/Palestine. Imagine my surprise when we took our lunch out to the area, only to find the tables and benches guarded and patrolled by peacocks. Peacocks are not native to Eastern Oregon or Eastern Washington, but rattlesnakes are! The peacocks were brought in to roam the grounds of the museum to protect the visitors (and staff) from invading snakes. Peacocks are one of God's few creatures that will attack, kill and devour a rattlesnake. And so we consumed our lunch, with the benefit of the beauty of the peacocks and the knowledge that we were safe from intruders. How like the use of the Canaanites by the Israelites is this use of the peacocks by the museum!

For peacocks, the 'sentry' duty is natural. For human beings sent out as sentry decoys is not natural or right. To use one people to teach another people a lesson, or to use them like peacocks left to strut about the boundaries and parameters of an open land as protection against invasion by dangerous intruders of nature – that is a completely different thing than having peacocks do what peacocks do as part of their nature. It sounds diabolic and not of God. Again, I wonder, is this really the voice of God as heard in Judges, Deuteronomy and Exodus, or is it the voice of man explaining his behavior and rationalizing his relationship with God and his sibling rivalries?

PART 2

LIBERATION THEOLOGY

Exodus

Then Moses stretched out his hand over the sea. The Lord drove the sea back by a strong east wind all night, and turned the sea into dry land; and the waters were divided. The Israelites went into the sea on dry ground, the waters forming a wall for them on their right and on their left. The Egyptians pursued, and went into the sea after them, all of Pharaoh's horses, chariots, and chariot drivers... Then the Lord said to Moses, 'Stretch out your hand over the sea, so that the water may come back upon the Egyptians, upon their chariots and chariot drivers. So Moses stretched out his hand over the sea, and at dawn the sea returned to its normal depth... Thus the Lord saved Israel that day from the Egyptians; and Israel saw the Egyptians dead on the seashore. Israel saw the great work that the Lord did against the Egyptians. So the people feared the Lord and believed in the Lord and in his servant Moses (Exod. 14:21-23, 26-27, 30-31).

Men and women, seemingly at odds, living within the prophetic voice of God, come together in the Exodus story as it is revealed and lived out in the twentieth and twenty-first centuries' Liberation Theology of South America, Central America, South Africa, the Philippines and, now, Palestine. When I worked in the Immigration and Naturalization Service's (INS) Detention Center, in Boston, Massachusetts, with the Refugee Immigration Ministry (RIM) – a ministry I founded and led from 1986–1989 – no one had been released until he (and they were all men in the facility) was given political asylum or other legal status. Cases had been known to drag on, with appeals, for as long as five years, with the detainees remaining in this one-day-room, one-sleeping-room environment. It was only because of a question asked, on 'People Are Talking', a local television program in Boston, Massachusetts, and an answer given, that I was granted access to the INS Detention Center. The program was focused, that day, on the Sanctuary Movement in the United States – a movement that was giving sanctuary, or refuge, to 'illegal aliens' who were fleeing the wars in Central America.

The Assistant Deputy Director of INS had responded, angrily, to a statement that one of the Sanctuary representatives had made. The Assistant Deputy Director said, 'My men are God-fearing men...'. I responded by asking, 'If your people are God-fearing, does that then mean that we can have (religious) services at the Detention Center on a regular basis?' Before 75,000 viewers, the answer was 'yes'; whereas before when an individual or group had made such a request, the answer had always been 'no'.

In the 1980s the Detention Center was a place where accusations between the INS and religious leaders had accelerated and feelings of negativity had festered – a place where even the lawyers were suing to gain access to their clients or those held without legal representation. In this climate of mistrust, fear and hostility, I found myself as the priest/chaplain to fifty-plus detained men. After some weeks, one of these men, John Amankwaah, came to me with a list and said, 'Constance, you must go to the District Director of Immigration and ask that we be released'. I told him that no one had previously been released from the facility until the immigration court had ruled on a decision in their case. John persisted. I met with John and the others (eighteen in total) and they, also, argued their cause. Then John said, 'Constance, you will be like Moses opening the Red Sea for his people. You will open the doors of this place and we will be free!' Not having a Moses complex – nor John's sense of the prophetically possible – I did, nonetheless, agree to take the list to the District Director of the INS, Mr Charles Cobb. Mr Cobb, as he said, to show me the kind of people I was dealing with, agreed to look at the list. We were to meet, a week later, to discuss the men's cases. He seemed assured that, once I knew the character of the men, I would reconsider my request.

We met again. It turned out the men were all in detention because they had escaped their native lands for reasons of a well-founded fear of persecution for their race, religion, ethnicity or membership in a particular organization or political group. These are the established protocols for determining if someone qualifies for political asylum. They were not thieves, murderers or criminals of any kind. I pleaded for their release and offered to take the men out of detention on my own recognizance, meaning I would be personally responsible for them – for their housing, food, health and general welfare. The District Director was not impressed. I pleaded that if they were released, they would no longer be a burden on our society, rather they would be working, tax-paying productive people while they awaited the verdict of the courts. I promised none would flee the country or the legal process. (Only one left the United States and went to Canada after his appeal process ended). The director said he would look at the list, again, but assured me that I was foolish to put this idea forward.

And then, while in New York for a meeting, I got a call from the director that John Amankwaah was being released! I said, 'Hold him until I can get back to Boston!' That night began an exodus of detainees from the Boston – and later the New England, Eastern Seaboard and other INS facilities. From John's witnessing to the powerful potential of God among us, came a change in immigration policy and law. From John's belief came new life, new hope and new beginnings for men and women and children formerly held in custody. The Exodus came alive in the musty, cigarette smoky, dull colored, overly lit, barred environment of captivity. The door opened – and opened again – and remained open until recent political decisions have once more closed the door – stemmed the flow – of freedom for those deserving of an opportunity to live anew in this land of liberty. John Amankwaah – a man of faith – heard God's voice, read God's word, prayed God among his fellow detainees and, yes, the door opened, just as he said it would. But who was the Moses figure in this Exodus story? It was John – the one who believed and acted out of faith – the one who challenged me to challenge the powers that be – the one who said, 'It will happen – it will be' – and it was!

Exodus is one of several such stories of liberation used frequently in liberation theology circles. Exodus is a vivid, vital story about a people enslaved – a people oppressed – a people caught in a quagmire, to some historical extent of their own making, if one recalls how the Israelis got to Egypt originally and how they lived before they left. The undoing of the situation, the breaking of the Pharaoh's hold over the Israelites – complete with a plague of frogs and gnats and flies, dying fish and a ruined river, a pestilence upon all the livestock of the Egyptians and the Egyptians themselves, hailstones from heaven, locusts, darkness and finally the death of all first-born Egyptian animals and children – has all the captivating power and drama of any great story. No wonder people oppressed – wherever they were – caught the spirit – related to the potential for hope and change and liberation! It is truly a story of God working among us, through a speech deficient man (Moses) – through a faith deficient people (the Hebrews) – through all the obstacles of a nation and of nature. God prevailed and the Hebrews went on to the 'Promised Land', the land held forth in this story of the Hebrew people as they exited Egypt.

Of course, what is not said, is how the Egyptians felt about losing their wealth and their working class, and what is not said is how the Canaanites (the Palestinians) felt about being intruded upon – in fact moved-in-on and displaced. Often, I think, what is not said is what is important: the other side – the yin of the yang – the back side of the front side – the view of those benefiting from God's grace and the view of those damaged by the grace so freely given to the other. We see it in today's Israel/Palestine, which one might assume is no less dramatic, painful or different than the combining of the two populations post-exodus from Egypt.

This is not to take away from the belief in the 'power of God', as experienced in Exodus by those being freed, but it is to say there are two peoples – two perspectives – two experiences and two realities – and what does the 'power of God' mean to those Canaanites upon whom the Hebrew people descended? Without acknowledging this, there can be little hope for mutual understanding or mutual agreement now or in the future. Michael Prior states, in *The Bible and Colonialism*, that, 'Readers of the biblical narrative are easily impressed and consoled by that story's capacity to lift the spirits of the oppressed. However, one's perspective on the Exodus story takes on a different complexion when read with the eyes of the "Canaanites", that is, of any of several different cultures, which have been victims of a colonialism fired by religious imperialism' (Prior 1999: 39).

Peacemakers Versus Disturbers Of The Peace

The power of scripture – be it used by a Jew, a Christian or a Muslim (or any other religion for that matter) – is a power with a life of its own. There exists the word of God as a peacemaker and there exists the word of God as a vengeance taker. There is revealed in scripture, much about God, and sometimes more about the one selecting the word and using the word of God. For what we choose as a passage and how we use that particular passage in a given context can shape the meaning of the word and of God to the one hearing – the one receiving the word.

Following talks at the White House and the signing of the Palestinian-Israeli Declaration of Principles peace agreement, on 13 September 1993, President Clinton presented to the world Israeli Prime Minister Yitzhak Rabin and Palestinian Chairman and PLO President Yasser Arafat. Rabin and Arafat joined hands in what has become known as 'the handshake', with President Clinton pushing each of them to turn to the other. At that time, President Clinton said that both leaders had been, 'shaped by the values of the Torah, the Koran and the Bible' (Prior 1999: 39). That is the blessing and that, apparently, is the curse. For in spite of the handshake that sparked hope for the world, the peoples connected through time have not been able to make a connection that is satisfactory or even reasonably acceptable to all concerned at this time in history.

The blessings of God, the promises of God and the actions of humans seem to be a living contradiction to the giftedness of life. Between religions exist contradictions of understanding, differences of definition and vast gaps in the realities each group accepts as the reality of their own, personal and scriptural experience. And not only between religions, but within religions, exists a polarity of understanding that fires challenges of orthodoxy and action. Where do we go from such a stand off, where extremists – be they Jews or Muslims or Christians – are firmly placed in opposition to one another?

My original thesis has been that the minority Christian population – the moderate (that is not extremist, Zionist Christian population) – joined with the rest of Christiandom's peace-based faith communities can be the force that joins the extremes together. This is what happened in El Salvador and in Guatemala – where much is still, unfortunately unresolved – and in South Africa. I believe the main stream Christian community is a strong and viable hope for Israel/Palestine at this time. Given the rising tide of anti-American and anti-Christian feelings in the Islamic world (following our actions in Afghanistan and Iraq and our ongoing military and economic support of Israel), I see this hope becoming more of a sliver than a wedge. Those Christians who truly follow the Prince of Peace – those Christians who believe deeply in the liberating power of Jesus – those Christians who see Jesus the Christ as embodied in the suffering of the world, still can be – can provide – the slim sliver's wedge of peace needed in Israel/Palestine.

While I recognize that South and Central America were basically Christian and predominately Roman Catholic countries, ensuring that Liberation Theology had an immediate base to operate from, and while I also see that today's Israel/Palestine is predominately Jewish and Muslim, I believe the Palestinian and international Christians have the potential to do in Israel/Palestine what the base communities did in Central and South America. Certainly the situation in Israel/Palestine is not simple, but perhaps – just perhaps – South and Central America were the previews of what can bind and bond and bring healing to the land of the origins of our common faiths: Jewish, Christian and Muslim.

I find it no more impossible to envision an all-encompassing theology of liberation within the Abrahamic community than within the Roman Catholic and greater Christian community. After all, these great religions have at their core the same statements of liberation – of peace – of compassion – of justice. The fragment of Jesus' people remaining in Israel/Palestine can be the beginning of a new union of faith within the larger, international Christian community itself, and within the sisterhood and brotherhood of Abrahamic relational religions, remodeled or broadened to encompass the diverse theologies of the three Abrahamic faiths. This kind of union could bring an opportunity and an offering of independent yet equal bonding that would allow each to operate out of its own faith stance in step with one another, yet separate from one another in a cooperative and compatible rather than a combative way.

Later, I will address Palestinian Liberation Theology as it exists today. For now, I suggest what began in the 1960s can continue in a new way into this new century and into this place of shared holiness. One thing is certain, among many things that are not certain, and that is that something needs to shift dramatically for a real peace process to take place. The present peace process is a rather bleak and pathetic remnant of what was, with little hope for what might still be. The procedure is in place for bringing an energetic change of a positive nature to Israel/Palestine: it is called Liberation Theology. It has proved the potential of its effectiveness in Latin America, as well as South Africa and other parts of the world. May it not expand upon its theology and effectiveness in the land of Christ – the birthplace of all hope?

Liberation Theology and Vatican II

What is Liberation Theology? To understand the evolution of Liberation Theology, one really needs to know the context in which Liberation Theology arose. As we all know, nothing transpires in a vacuum. Certainly the second Vatican Council's (Vatican II), held between 1962-1965, while it was not the beginning of Liberation Theology, came about from a reality where the 'poor' were not given preference, or deference, or even recognized as human beings of equal worth with those of means – the oligarchy and the rich. Vatican II took place as the great imbalance of power and wealth in the Southern Hemisphere was beginning to be felt and acknowledged. There were cracks and shifts in society, resulting in revolutions in Mexico (1911); Bolivia and Guatemala (1952); Cuba (1959) and in Santo Domingo, where the people resisted a United States' invasion (1965).

Liberation Theology grew and developed in this context of terror and repression. People had nothing tangible to cling to, and so they turned to a God of compassion and strength to help them live through the darkness and desperation of their time. They also supported new leadership in opposition to the dictators who had oppressed them for so long. Chile elected Salvador Allende, a Marxist, as President. He was supported by the people, including Priests for Socialism, a group within the Catholic church. Allende was overthrown in a coup, in 1973, that was sponsored by the United States through the Central Intelligence Agency (CIA). Nicaraguans overthrew Anastasio Samoza, another U.S. sponsored dictator, and the Sandinistas came into power. El Salvador's civil war was carried out between the right wing U.S. sponsored ARENA party and the revolutionary Farabundo Marti Nacional Liberation Front (FMLN). The people were seeking a better way of life, free of the suppression and restrictions of the past. In Cuba and Nicaragua, for example, the health care, literacy levels and land reform programs have become models for other countries. In fact, in 2007, Cuba has a higher percentage of literacy in their country than does the United States, and an outstanding health care program that serves all the people for little or no charge. And yet the government of the United

States still sees Cuba as a threat to our national security and imposes an embargo on the country and restrictions on travel to and from Cuba.

During the early years of uprisings, in an attempt to unify themselves, the Roman Catholic National Council of Brazilian Bishops (350 in number) was established in 1952, followed by the establishment of the Council of Latin American Bishops (CELAM) in Rio de Janeiro in 1955. They met, for a Tenth Assembly Meeting, in Mar del Plata, Argentina, in 1966. CELAM met for a second time as a General Council, in Medellin, Colombia in 1968, where the phrase 'preferential option for the poor' was placed in the council's document, primarily due to Liberation Theologians like Gustavo Guttierez. Unfortunately, most Latin American bishops were not present at this conference. Once the reactionary bishops realized what had happened, they moved to block its development by the time the Council met for the third time at Pueblo, in 1979, and had reversed it by the 1980 Council meeting in Santo Domingo. The Vatican was behind the conservative swing back to pre-Vatican II theology. Pope Paul VI, who became pope following Pope John XXIII, systematically replaced progressive bishops with right wing theologians. In addition, the Vatican closed progressive seminaries and centers of pastoral education that featured Liberation Theology. I remember one of the leading lights in theology – in the minds of young seminarians and priests in Rome – who was without warning sent off to a hill town where he no longer had contact with other liberal thinkers and was for all extents and purposes 'silenced'. It was part of the church's policy of removing or silencing progressive thinking people within the church.

Elected in 1978, Pope John Paul II, continued this replacement of progressive priests by conservative ones, continuing to close down liberation centers of pastoral education. One example of this is Bishop Helder Camera, who, upon retiring in North Eastern Brazil, was replaced with a right wing bishop. His school and faculty were replaced by a traditional seminary. By 1989 the base for Liberation Theology within the Roman Catholic Church was virtually nonexistent. Some of those who had been involved in Liberation Theology, including Pablo Richard and Franz Hinlelammert, joined lay or ecumenical organizations or Protestant-funded programs like Costa Rica's Departamento Ecumenico de Investigaciones (DEI) and Nicaragua's Centro Valdivieso.

In 1976, the Ecumenical Association of Third World Theologians (EATWOT) met, for the first time, in Dar es Salaam,Tanzania. During these early years, Dom Helder Camera, of Brazil, and Dom Manuel Larrain, of Chile, became leaders – 'prophetic minorities'. They created 'Le Christ et l'Eglise servante et pauvre' (Christ and a Poor Servant Church) and 'L'Eglise et l'aide aux paus en voi de developpement: conditions d'une action efficace' (The Church and Aid to Developing Countries: Conditions for Effective Action). All of these organizations and movements, according to Leonardo Boff, 'helped create the spirit of Vatican II' (Leonardo Boff 1984: 7-8) as they helped create a space for the 'Spirit of Vatican II' to breathe new life into the church. These were the forerunners – many independent of one another – of what was to be a major movement within the church universal.

It seems I all too frequently am heard to say, 'The church should be proactive – leading the secular world, not reactive – following or doing catch-up to the rest of society'. The second Vatican Council is a point in case. As Leonardo Boff, O.F.M., wrote in, *When Theology Listens to the Poor* : 'The second Vatican Council can be regarded as the terminus of a long, toilsome process of *aggiornamento* (modernizing) from Pope John XXIII. The Church has finally succeeded in adapting to the modern culture in what was the upshot of the bourgeois revolution – an upheaval in economic, scientific, technological, and political expressions' (Leonardo Boff 1984: 1). The people were heard, the reality of the grassroots movement received an official stamp of approval and before The Church of Rome knew what it had done, Liberation Theology had become a force within not only the Roman Catholic Church, but in Protestant churches as well. What had been happening was taken up by others in what became a growing groundswell for liberation, freedom and justice. For what is human liberation but the freeing of a person or a peoples, and what is theology but the systematic study of religion or belief systems? United on this scenario, they stand for a union with God in the spirit and the liberating will of Christ.

In 1959, Pope John XXIII called for Vatican Council II. (Vatican Council I had been held between 1869–1870. It was then that the concept of and the term for 'papal infallibility' was established.) Vatican II commenced in 1962 and ended in December of 1965. According to Myra Poole, SND (a member of the Sisters of Notre Dame), for the first time, there were women auditors – twenty-three in number – who were formally invited to observe. On many levels, it was a whole different forming and reforming of what had been known and heard and taught and cherished in the church. This is not to imply that other important critical thinking and theology was not going on within the Roman Catholic Church prior to Vatican II.

Liberation Theology took Jesus out of heaven and put Jesus in the midst of the people – with the poor, the underprivileged – with those kinds of people with whom Jesus associated and worked and lived in his time on earth. No longer was Jesus 'up there'. No longer were heaven and hell places apart from our earthly lives. The cosmology of Christ was brought back to embrace the people in the here and now – not in the hereafter. This was and remains a major theological shift. The conservative and more evangelical Christian concept of accepting the now, knowing one's rewards will be greater in heaven, came face to face with the concept of heaven on earth, now, and Jesus amongst us. The liberating call to use one's gifts and faith to change one's life rather than accepting the unacceptable, shocked and stunned those versed in the more traditional conservative theology of Christianity. Evangelical preachers went to the garbage dumps of major cities in Latin America – where people lived off the excesses of others' lives – telling the people to rejoice for their reward would be great in heaven. Liberation theologians went to the same places and gathered together similar people telling the people they had minds and God-given talents that would allow them to change their lives and their world. These ministers – lay and ordained – led the people into Base Christian Communities, where the people learned of a God of power and might and reform and change – the God of the radical life-changing thought-provoking love of Christ.

Vatican II brought theological reflections, theological actions, the theology of the past and present together in, according to Berryman, '...a radical shift (in which) the church began to see in 'human progress' evidence of God's working in human history' (Berryman 1987b: 17). As so often happens, even though the church of the Southern Hemisphere had brought many of the issues and questions into the council, it was the Europeans and North Americans who set the agenda for the council. But, after the council ended, it was the South and Central Americans who took the church's changes and adopted them to their church in the Southern Hemisphere.

According to Leonardo Boff, 'The presence of the bishops of Latin America at the Second Vatican Council had no theological impact. One even heard of a 'church of silence'...their impact was in the pastoral area. The Latin American bishops voiced the restlessness of the poor. They made the universal Church aware of the issue of social justice' (Leonardo Boff 1984: 7). It was some of these very same bishops and theology advisors who took the words of the council home and birthed the options and words of Vatican II into a life of their own, breathing them in and embodying them out into the world in which they lived.

Vatican II, as it happened, was beginning its last year in session when I moved to Rome. One of the first people I met in a Roman Italian language class introduced me to his cousin Bishop Lawrence Michael Graziano – a man born in New York, who, according to his family, served as the first Anglo bishop in El Salvador. Bishop Lawrence, as he was called, had been offered the office of bishop two times. Two times he had refused the offer. According to his family, on the third time he was told that his obedience would be called into question if he refused. He accepted and became one of the bishops involved in the movement for change – within the church, within the country and within the larger area of Central America. We enjoyed many meals and conversations, during the remaining time of Vatican II.

Of course, at that time what did I know about Vatican II? I was a young woman from the Northwestern part of the United States, an Episcopalian, more out of the church than in the church at that moment. The whole Vatican scene was amazing and, at times, overwhelming. The grandeur, the richness of art and architecture – of history – of presence, let alone the wealth and land holdings, in Rome, the politics and networks of societal and religious intrigues were both appalling and appealing. The Bishop and his stories added just one more prism to a stone already complex with facets of beauty and mystery, scandal and corruption. When Bishop Lawrence told us about losing the stone in his bishop's ring, we all laughed! People would kneel to kiss his ring and, instead of kissing the ring and receiving his blessing, they would attempt to bite out the beautiful, large stone. (He had lost the stone under these circumstances twice, when I met him in 1964–1965.) Many of his stories were designed to entertain, some were educational, others were simply the kinds of things one talks about with friends and acquaintances over a congenial Italian meal. When he told us about priests running guns to the peasants – the 'guerrillas' – that did catch my attention, but it was so very, very far from my own experience at that time, in the church or in the world, that it was more shocking than eye-opening. When I went to seminary, I thought, 'Ah, hah!' and understood. When I learned, recently, that he had indeed been a bishop in El Salvador – a place where, in the eighties, I spent time working on the same liberation issues within the church – I had another surprising revelation of a more personal nature.

And so Vatican II, at the heart – away from the glitz and glamour of such Vatican gatherings – made a dramatic shift in the way the Roman Catholic Church had been and presently was in the world. While Luther and the other reformers of the Protestant Church in the sixteenth century, gave the Bible to the people in the vernacular of the times (the language of the people), the Roman Catholic Church, up until this time, had continued to entrench itself in its ongoing use of Latin (the language of the past), and set itself in a defensive stance, protecting its religious practices – its very religious system and theology (Berryman 1987b: 16). With Vatican II, no longer were services to be done in Latin; rather the language of the people was to be used. (In response in Italy, Romans for example, walked out of churches in large numbers, not appreciating the service in its new, modern understandable form. For many, part of the mystique and the mystery went with the Latin, at least during the initial years of the implementation of the edicts of Vatican II). Not only were services to be conducted in the language of the people, but the Bible was to be made available to the people. As astonishing as this may seem, to modern Roman Catholics and Protestants, with the exception of a movement in the nineteenth century and another in the first half of the twentieth century, before Vatican II the sole purveyors and interpreters of holy scripture for Roman Catholics were those ordained in the Holy Mother Church of Rome. Suddenly scripture was of the people and God's word began to be lived out in ways that quickly became unsettling to those in places of authority within and without the church. No longer was it acceptable to accept abuse, servitude, inhumane treatment, subhuman standards of living, all for the benefit of a few. Now, God's word was revealing itself in a new way – a way of peace and justice and dignity in the now, not in the after life – in the present moment, not in some future undefined time. Exodus was read, discussed, believed and lived out on the streets of South and Central America and on the streets of Mexico. The cry of freedom was in the air. The 'Hallelujahs' sung in the churches and meeting places resided in the hearts of the people, where hope began to live anew. Some, however longed for the old ways. In 2007, Pope Benedict XVI, counter to the decisions of Vatican II, authorized a return to a wider use of the old Latin Mass. Whether this and other decisions will affect the decrees of Vatican II and the mandate for the poor has yet to be seen.

Economic Development and Developing Revolutions

As this revolution within the church – first Roman Catholic and then the larger Catholic and Protestant Churches – was taking place, politicians and governments were moving forward with their own plans for Latin America. At this time, our President, John F. Kennedy, brought the American sponsored Alliance for Progress into being. The Alliance for Progress was established in light of the 1959 Cuban Revolution, with the intent of preventing further revolutions. It took place during the Cold War with Russia. It existed from 1961-69. This alliance was created to promote democratic reform and assist with development within the individual countries in South and Central America. The center left Social Democratic and Christian Democratic parties were chosen, by the United States, to be Latin America's partners with North America. The Alliance was seen by us, in North America, as a way of helping our neighbors to the south – of bringing them to a higher socioeconomic level. This alliance was considered, by Leonardo Boff, to bring in an, 'euphoria of developmentalism' which actually further brought 'exploitation and marginalization' to the laborers and members of the working class. As Penny Lernoux wrote in, *Cry of the People*, '…the stated goals were to promote development and contain communism, and few then realized the ambiguities contained in that statement. Only later was it learned that development, as practiced, benefited the rich at the expense of the poor, and that containment of communism was often simplistically equated with protecting an unjust and unchristian status quo' (Lernoux 1982: 284).

From 1965, when Vatican II ended, until the end of the 1980s, South and Central America (particularly Brazil, with its military coup in 1964, Argentina, Chile, Uruguay, Paraguay, El Salvador and Honduras) were dominated by national security (fascist military) states. All were by and large put into place and supported by the United States, who had supported the Cuban dictatorship that was overthrown by Fidel Castro. The U.S. saw these continuing Latin American revolutions as a communist or socialist threat. As early as the 1960s, the United States was giving counter-insurgency aid to the right wing elites and the military. I personally met some of the United States' 'contractors' and 'advisors' who were in actuality military personnel traveling undercover or independently contracted 'mercenaries'. In one case, I flew into Honduras on a new airline, 'Challenge', that turned out later to have been a cover for the CIA, full of out-of-uniform American military, obvious in their buzz cuts and Hawaiian shirts. It turned out I was on the airline's second flight. On the first, I was told, they had given free bottles of liquor to all passengers. On my flight, there were free alcoholic drinks. The airline offered cheap flights but it was only in business for a few years, then it disappeared just as quickly as it had appeared.

These national security-dominated states governed through terror, with their death squads and brutal methods, many of the leaders and military having been trained by the U.S. sponsored School of the Americas. Democracy was nonexistent as we understand 'democracy' to be in the 'democracies' we supposedly supported. According to Rosemary Radford Reuther, in a lecture she gave titled, 'Liberation Theology is Not Dead: Who has wanted to Kill it? these national security states '...can be described as a colonial fascism, dependent on foreign aid from neocolonial centers of power, that (acted) as a conduit for economic exploitation of the country on behalf of the interests of elites and those of foreign powers...The ideology of these national security states (focused) on the prevention of "communist subversion", often seeing themselves as defending "Christian civilization" '.

Developers – one could say colonizers – were moving forward at the same time as liberation theologians were establishing their new way of being in Christ. A clash was inevitable, as one group worked to develop the country – furthering the advantage for those already wealthy – and another group worked to bring parity and strength to those of the poorer class. As the disparity between the classes grew – as the division between the rich and the poor grew – so, too, did the unions grow as well as the human rights, farm workers, peasants and student organizations and solidarity groups made up of university professors and students and some Christian activists, most of whom were also found, in those early days, on university campuses. As a result of this imbalance of power, guerrilla movements were beginning in most countries in Latin America. 'Latin American economists were saying', according to Ruether, 'that Latin America was not so much 'underdeveloped' as misdeveloped by five hundred years of exploitation by colonialism and neocolonialism. This had created a legacy of small elites who owned all the best land, and all the large factories and mines, often controlled by foreign corporations, while the masses of urban and rural Latin Americans toiled in deep misery. What (was) needed (was) not more 'development' of that same exploitative type, but liberation, nationalizing Latin American resources, taking them from foreign control and creating an integral development to meet the needs of the Latin American masses, a development from the bottom up, not from the top down'.

Europe and the United States were seen, by Latin America, as the 'center of peripheral capitalism' – The United States and Europe being the power brokers, in the center, with the Central and South American countries being external, or outside, the center, held tight by the Unites States' economic grip (Leonardo Boff 1984: 9). We were the ones who placed our corporations on their land, industrialized and urbanized their cultures and their countries, used their raw resources and their cheap labor for our own ends and for our own financial benefits. The very few, who were of the elite class, benefited from this rape of their land. Amy Chua, the author of *World on Fire*, has said that capitalism has often mistakenly been equated with democracy by our Western leaders. In those days, promoting the church's understanding of equality – of justice – of shared opportunities and shared rights to own land – those speaking from a Christo-centric place were labeled 'Marxists' and 'Communists'. Those who stood for the ideals of their faith and the democratic rights they were guaranteed in their own North American and European nations, were denounced.

The Alliance for Progress not only continued this colonization process, but it provided political and military 'advisors', as well, who quickly were seen as 'oppressors', put in place to contain and to sustain a system corrupt at the center of its being. Instead of bringing a democracy of equal opportunity, a racial, cultural and ethnic bias that already existed was cemented in place – just as it is in place in Israel/Palestine, today, where European and North American Jews receive preferential treatment from the developers of today, primarily the United States. This speaks to what I see as a comfort level people feel in relating to the known and familiar, rather than the unknown and unfamiliar. This also speaks, I feel, to a prejudicial bias that permeated our white-based culture, then, in the early days of Liberation Theology, and today, in our international dealings with other nations and peoples.

It was in response to this governmental involvement by the U.S., in Latin American affairs, that U.S. peace groups and U.S. church groups organized and joined with our counterparts in Latin America. It was from our own sense of responsibility as citizens of the United States, combined with a sense of moral obligation and moral outrage, that many of us became involved in the situation in Central and South America. It was, also, from a desire to give voice to the voiceless, that many of us went to Central and South America to see for ourselves, to hear for ourselves what was really going on in those countries and to come back to speak for those not being seen or heard. It is, today, the same situation in Israel/Palestine.

It was in this conflicted arena of differing understandings and interpretations of ethics – be they business or religious – that Pope Paul VI said of capitalism that it is a system, 'which considers profit as the key motive for economic progress, competition as the supreme law of economics, and private ownership of the means of production as an absolute right that has no limits and carries no corresponding social obligation' (Sigmund 1990: 26) Unfortunately this statement, and some of the pope's other frequently cited quotes, seemed to be in opposition to one another and ultimately presented an ambiguous, rather than an unified statement of support for what was becoming a peace and justice movement based on Vatican II's proclamations. According to Sigmund, 'Liberation Theology began as a revolt against 'developmentalism', the (falsely) optimistic view associated with the Alliance for Progress that economic development would solve, or at least considerably ameliorate, Latin America's social, economic, and political problems' (Sigmund 1990: 179).

When one realizes that 1-5% of a given nation's population in South and Central America controlled the individual nations and when one realizes that this 1-5% was made up almost entirely by ethnic groups of European origin, primarily from Spanish descent, then one can begin to see that capitalism does not necessarily equate with democracy or that development does not necessarily equate with an improved socioeconomic status for all. Illustrative of this discrepancy in power and ethnicity, Radford said in her lecture on Liberation Theology, that 'Bolivia is 30% Quecha, 25% Aymara, 30% mestizo (a person of mixed parentage) and only 15% white. Guatemala is 55% mestizo and 43% indigenous. Peru is 37% mestizo, 45% indigenous and only 15% white, even Mexico is 60% mestizo and 30% indigenous, and 9% white'. That would translate into our own country, population-wise today, with the Spanish speaking population becoming the dominant ruling class, a mirror reflection of what happened in Central and South America, without the terror and corruption.

My cousin – the person most like a brother to me – constantly tried to show me how wrong 'these people' were and how dangerous it was for me to be involved with 'them'. He was, as it turned out, a 'Spook' (an undercover agent) for the Central Intelligence Agency (CIA). He was an incredibly bright man who believed in this, our nation, and in the legitimacy of what we, the people of the U.S. – through our government – were doing. He believed in the dogma of the Alliance and in our policies and practices that grew out of and continued from the Alliance and from the Cold War that preceded it. He believed in the concepts that overlaid the Alliance, particularly the underlying fears of Communism that the United States held in respect to other nations and their governments. He felt those in opposition were 'misguided', 'misled' and needed to be stopped. It was from him that I first learned that we – the United States of America – had, indeed, brought about the killing in El Salvador of the Jesuit priests and their housekeeper/cook and her daughter, which will be discussed in the section on 'Martyrs of Liberation Theology' (These killings were revealed, later, to the public, but were kept as a government secret for many years.) He told me things to try and dissuade me from carrying out my own work in opposition to our government's involvement and policies in Central America. He tried to bring me to my senses, as he used to put it, so I could see 'the other' for what he believed they were. He told me that I was a liability to him. I responded that he might very well be a liability to me. I am afraid I proved to be more of a liability to him, as he talked and I listened, and as he later died.

Why, I ask, do individuals – do religions – do nations turn to violence to preserve what is an imbalance of power, rather than work toward a collaborative, cooperative alliance? This holding onto the land – the wealth – the riches of a place is exactly what is happening in Israel/Palestine. And, it is what is happening, as I write, in Iraq. Over and over and over again, a small group is seen to struggle to hold onto a large portion of the people's land and their resources. Hundreds of thousands died in South and Central America, some fighting for equality and justice, others fighting to hold onto their power over the majority. Many power brokers simply reacted – joined in the struggle – to maintain the status quo, never realizing the moral and ethical issues before them – simply feeling threatened, and in a defensive stance, fighting out in desperate ways. I am reminded of a woman, who sat next to me on a flight to El Salvador. She spoke about the 'inconvenience' of having to live in Miami, having left her home in San Salvador in the care of her husband (who had a business in El Salvador) and their household staff. She was returning to El Salvador only because the stress of the 'situation' had made her husband ill. She saw no relationship between the poor, the church, her status as a wealthy landowner and the lack of opportunity and justice that lay as wide as a canyon between the two groups, with the church in the middle. For her the war was deeply personal and could easily be brought to a peaceful end, once the irritating insurrectionists were eradicated.

Her story was not only one family's story, but a story reflective of one small group's advantage and the perspective it held against the remaining majority of the population in El Salvador. She and others of her class – most of them – went to church, they worshiped, they believed, but their theology was not one of liberation – their church's theology was not of liberation. The division in the Roman Catholic – and later many Protestant Churches – widened as some chose to align themselves with the status quo and others chose to side with the Liberation Theology Movement. In the capital of El Salvador, San Salvador, exists a cathedral, unfinished to this day. Archbishop Oscar Romeo refused to allow the cathedral to be completed until the poor were fed and clothed and housed and had jobs of equal opportunity. At the same time, when I visited San Salvador between 1985–90, there was a finished 'cathedral' of a more opulent style, to which the oligarchy went to worship. The worshipers in both edifices considered themselves Christians – Catholics – and people of faith.

Founders of Liberation Theology

While there are many promoters of Liberation Theology, or many who were involved in the movement of liberation, some of the 'fathers' of Liberation Theology are generally recognized as being the Roman Catholic academicians Gustavo Gutierrez, Jon Sobrino, Leonardo Boff and his brother Clodovis Boff. There are others of importance, some not published in English, such as Ignacio Ellacuria. Jon Sobrino wrote of the need for 'spirit' in liberation. As he said, '…surely liberation practice provides us with a necessary, just, and good channel for our energies. But that channel must flow with 'spirit'. What else will remedy the limitations of those engaged in the various liberation practices? After all, they are human beings' (Sobrino 1989: ix). Sobrino quotes Leonardo Boff as calling for 'contemplation in liberation'. Finally Boff credits Gustavo Gutierrez' call to *Drink from Our Own Wells* (1983), as inspiring him, and others, to fill themselves with the life-giving, liberating power of the spirit (Sobrino 1989: ix). These men's voices brought the concepts of Liberation Theology to the world view for consideration. These men's voices – and others – brought Liberation Theology to the world view whether the world wanted to look and see or not.

Gustavo Gutierrez, a priest born into poverty himself in 1928, in Lima, Peru, studied in Rome and France and, later, taught theology at the University of Lima where he chose to return to the slums of Lima, where he still lives and works among the poor. His book, *Toward a Theology of Liberation*, was first published in Spanish in 1968, later in English, in 1971, under the title, *A Theology of Liberation*. This book was seen as the first major Liberation Theology publication – the book that awoke the rest of the world to the newly emerging theology that addressed the plight of the poor in Latin America. As one who lived and worked as one with the poor, Gutierrez' own life gave special weight to his words of theology – words that came out of the reality of his own experience.

Jon Sobrino, a Basque, was born in 1938 in Barcelona, Spain. He was ordained as a priest by the Jesuits and sent to El Salvador where he has remained these past thirty years. He serves as a professor of philosophy and theology at the Central American University, Universidad Jose Simeon Canas, in San Salvador. He is also the director for the Center for Theological Reflections.

Christology at the Crossroads (first published in 1978) established him as a theologian of liberation.

Quoted earlier, Leonardo Boff, a Brazilian priest and Franciscan Friar, was born in 1938, in Concordia, Brazil. He studied in Brazil, London and Germany. He taught systematic theology in the city of Petropolis, Brazil, and has written profusely. He and his brother, Clodovis Boff, are well-known in liberation theology circles. They complement each other with their wide-ranging theological perspectives. Leonardo Boff interprets Christ's message as a revolution in thought and action that involved the liberation of the 'oppressed consciousness' of his time and the creation of (a theology that addressed the needs of) the social outcasts (prostitutes, tax collectors, and former guerrillas) and crossed class barriers...Jesus produced a social and cultural revolution without violence that became the basis of Western civilization (Sigmund 1990: 81). Christ represents a *liberation praxis* 'of love above the law (that) transcends class differences' (Sigmund 1990: 81).

Leonardo Boff's first major book focusing on Liberation Theology was published in 1972, *Jesus Christ Liberator*. In this book he wrote, 'The Christology of the future should emphasize the anthropological over the ecclesiastical, the utopian over the factual, the critical over the dogmatic, the social over the personal, and orthopraxis over orthodoxy' (Leonardo Boff 1986: 43-47). *The Theology of Captivity*, which he wrote in 1980, took examples from the Hebrew Scripture and applied them to Latin Americans. As noted earlier, the Exodus of the Jews from Egypt became one of the major stories – one of the key scriptural texts – for the impoverished of Latin America who were looking for their own liberation from an environment that virtually enslaved them to the wealthy and the landowners. In *The Theology of Captivity*, Leonardo Boff wrote, 'We live in Egypt. The poor are suffering in Babylon. In their veins runs the blood of martyrs. But we are in a different Babylon and Egypt. The sun of justice has already appeared on the horizon. In Him is anticipated the liberation of all those in captivity. Against all despair, there is still hope – because of Jesus Christ and his resurrection' (Leonardo Boff 1986: 55-56).

Leonardo Boff's work also ventured into church structures (*Ecclesiogenesis*, published in 1977), covering Base Communities, including 'extraordinary ministers', those lay leaders whom he felt should be allowed to celebrate the Holy Eucharist when an ordained priest was unavailable. He even touched upon the subject of the ordination of women, stating that he found no theological rationale that would support the continued refusal to ordain women to the priesthood. He was bold enough to suggest that women ordained would contribute to the spiritual and the liturgical life of the church. In 1979 he published *The Maternal Face of God*, which placed him firmly on the side of the newly emerging feminine theological movement in Latin America. Unfortunately, for these statements, views and other reflections, Leonardo Boff was silenced. He was first investigated, by the Vatican, for his views and his 'orthodoxy' – or lack of orthodoxy – in 1976 and 1980. In 1984, he published *Church: Charism and Power*. On 15 May 1984, the Vatican censured him. On 2 May 1985, the Vatican asked the Franciscan superiors to impose upon Boff an 'obedient silence for a convenient time. He was not to preach, give interviews, or continue as the editor of the *Revista Ecclesiastica Brasileira* and his writings were to be subject to prior censorship' (Sigmund 1990: 160). This silencing was lifted on 29 March 1986. In 2000, he decided to give up his priesthood and his ongoing battles with the Vatican. Leonardo Boff remains a theologian for change and an active member of the Brazilian Christian Community, continuing his work with the Base Christian Communities, and as a professor of ethics at the University of Rio de Jeneiro.

Clodovis Boff was also born in Concordia, Brazil. He is a Servite priest (in the Order of the Servants of Mary), teaching theology for six months a year at the Catholic University of Sao Paulo, Brazil and spending the other half a year working in the Amazon basin with Base Christian Communities. He has written *Theology and Praxis* (1978) and co-authored *Introducing Liberation Theology* with his brother. His 1987 book, *Feet-On-The-Ground-Theology, a Brazilian Journey*, is a handbook – a journal – a theological reflection for others use and adaptation. As Clodovis Boff wrote, '...liberation theology aims at being a 'critical reflection on the praxis of faith' ...this theology is based on a journey a people is making, and seeks to serve that people. But it sheds light only on the next steps, not on the whole course of the journey' (Berryman 1987a: xii).

Liberation Theology would not be totally 'liberating' if it were only limited to the male priests who were the original leaders and theologians. There were many others – lay men and women or men and women, not ordained, but members of religious orders –

who taught and defined Liberation Theology and lived out the theology in their lives. One such person is Peruvian Diego Irarrazaval, who brought the 'indigenous voice' to Liberation Theology, which from the mid-1990s to today is discussed in theological circles as 'teologia India'. He theologized what the indigenous people were doing, bringing Mary, the mother of Jesus, into the people's understandings of 'Pachamama' or Mother Earth. Among the early women, who were confined to 'feminine' topics of 'Mary' (not the Mother Earth Mary) and 'women and the theology of liberation', were Ana Maria Tepedino, Nargarida Brandao, Maria Clara Bingemer and Ivone Gebara.

Ivone Gebara, a Brazilian Sister of our Lady (Canoneses of St. Augustine), who was born in 1944, is an example of the early women liberation theologians. She is regarded, today, as a leading Latin American theologian, whose focus is on Liberation Theology and Ecofeminism. A professor at the Theological Institute of Recife, Brazil, she is the author of *Longing for Running Water: Ecofeminism and Liberation*. Her work in the slums of Brazil has informed her theology. She sees what she calls 'urban ecofeminism' as being born out of the environment of poverty in which she has worked.

In 1995, Gebara was silenced by the Vatican for two years following an interview she gave to the magazine, VEJA (Old Woman). In the interview, she said that abortion was not a sin for poor women. She said that the 'preferential option for the poor demanded by Liberation Theology called for more tolerance of women's choices for abortion than that of the official Roman Catholic Church', according to Lois Ann Lorentzen at the University of San Francisco, California. The Conference of Bishops of Brazil, in 1994, cleared her of charges; however, the Vatican's Congregation of the Doctrine and Faith silenced her. As part of the silencing, she could not give lectures, teach or write for two years. In addition, she was forced to move to France for 'theological reeducation'. When she returned to Brazil, she resumed her work, among other things, she founded the 'Shared Garden' theological program in 1997, which has had programs in Santiago, Chile, Washington, DC and Recife, Brazil. In addition to teaching, speaking and writing, she advocates for safe drinking water, better nutrition, clean streets, operating sewers and health care for the poor with whom she also continues to work.

As Liberation Theology has evolved, it has also expanded to include feminist thought, African-American, Afro-Caribbean, ecological, gay and lesbian theology. Unfortunately, the poverty in Central and South America that brought about Liberation Theology has not abated; in fact it has worsened. Liberation Theology comes from and is for those who are attempting to throw off the burden of their oppression. It is, also, for those of us who are party to the oppression, even if we are unaware of our role. As in Israel/ Palestine, for one group to be free and liberated, both groups must be aware of their implicit or explicit participation in the injustice of their situation. Freedom comes when both sides are equally liberated and there is justice for all. This may, in fact, be happening in South and Central America. 'In recent years', according to Reuther, 'this acceptance of the Washington Consensus in economic matters in Latin America, suppression of dissent and the quest for alternatives, has begun to shift…Hugo Chavez (Venezuela's newly elected president) has sought to position himself as the leader of a Latin America that bonds together against domination by the United States'. She further noted the following presidents have been elected in recent years: in Bolivia, a socialist Indian president; in Chile a socialist, Michelle Bachelet, its first woman president; in Brazil a Worker Party union organizer, Luiz Inacio Lula de Silva and Nicaragua re-elected Sandinista Daniel Ortega. If they can, indeed, address the needs of their countries and their people – bringing an end to the poverty and oppression that has been part of their story – then there will be a restoration of hope in both the southern and northern Americas. As these countries grapple with their own nations, may our nation – the United States – allow these people to define themselves and independently work out their own solutions to problems we have, to a large part, helped create in the past.

Leaders and Martyrs of the Revolution

Now, let's back up to look again at the origins of Liberation Theology in the mid- to late-1960s. In Colombia, Fr. Camilo Torres, an educated upper-class Colombian from the city of Bogota, became the first of many prototype martyrs for Liberation Theology. He began as an academician, having been a fellow seminarian with Gustavo Gutierrez, moving from a place of privilege and acceptance to a place of organizing the people – peasants, laborers, professionals, men and women alike – in a movement he called the United Front. He was a charismatic figure – a passionate man – who chose to live out the words of Jesus Christ in his words and in his own life. As he moved from being an educator and a sacramental priest to becoming a guerrilla for Christ, Fr. Torres said that revolution is, '...the way to bring about a government that feeds the hungry, clothes the naked, teaches the ignorant, puts into practice the works of charity, and love for neighbor, not just every now and then, and not just for a few, but for the majority of our neighbors'. For him, the church that should do these things had failed him and the people he served.

In 1965, seven months before Vatican II came to a close, the United Front became a public reality. At that time, Fr. Torres was speaking widely in Colombia to divergent groups, be they Christian or Communist, military or student, unionist or peasant, men or women. Because of his political work and the contacts he had made with the Army of National Liberation (ELN) – a growing guerrilla group in Colombia – Fr. Torres was forced to renounce his priestly vows. Much like others, forced into silence, or forced out of the priesthood by the church, he continued working at what he felt was his 'priestly calling'. He joined ELN and was killed in combat on 15 February 1966. He remains among a small number of priests, throughout South and Central America, who aligned themselves in solidarity and in battle with the guerrillas. According to Berryman, what captured the imagination of many about Fr. Torres, 'was Torres willingness to follow his convictions to their ultimate consequences' (Berryman 1987b: 19).

Another such man, Ernesto Che Guevara, was born in Argentina on 14 June 1928 and was executed in Bolivia on 9 October 1967. (Che was a nickname, somewhat like 'buddy', in English). Between his birth and his death, he became a doctor, specializing in dermatology, was married to Aleida March de la Torre, had five children and lived in and/or was involved in revolutions in Chile, Peru, Colombia, Venezuela, Bolivia, Guatemala, Mexico, Cuba and Zaire the Congo, most notably in Cuba where he sided with Castro. An author of two revolutionary handbooks, he also coined the ideal of the 'new man'. He was not considered to be a liberation theologian, but rather a liberator theoretician – a revolutionary pushing for the ideal of the 'new man'. It is interesting to note that he used the same identification with Jesus, as the prototype 'new man', as did Leonardo Boff, later. (It should also be noted that in that era, 'man' linguistically included 'woman'. Later, some in South and Central America came to speak of 'woman' separately.)

While for Leonardo Boff the 'new man' image had more of a sense of being new in Christ and liberated, for Guevara it held a secular sense of liberation and liberator. Guevara felt – as did liberation theologians – that liberation does not come from heaven, but from within and from without, through one's actions. He was driven, it would seem from the following poem, by love, not hate – by disappointment in the system that led to his revolutionary actions around the world. This poem, considered to be his favorite, was written by Leon Felipe and found in the papers of Guevara following his execution. Perhaps this gives a sense of his love – his passion – and his hope for his people:

Christ I love you

not because you descended from a star

but because you revealed to me

that man has blood

tears

anguish

keys

tools

to open the doors closed to light

Yes! You taught us that man is God…

a poor God crucified like you

and the one who is at your left on Golgotha

the bad thief

is God too! (Gutierrez 1973: 211)

Che Guevara remained a force for change long after his death – his image found on t-shirts, his words on banners, as at the April 1982, International Conference of Christians for Socialism, where his words were displayed, 'When Christians dare to give full-fledged revolutionary witness, then the Latin American revolution will be invincible…' (Berryman 1987b: 28). He became a byword – an electric switch for change in the United States, particularly with farm workers and union organizers, one of the strong voices for change during the years of struggle for equal rights. The entire Liberation Theology Movement is punctuated by lives lived out and lives lost in the actions that came out of the faith of those who believed deeply, physically and spiritually in the message of Christ – and those who believed in the oneness of humanity and the rights of the whole fabric of humanity.

Unfortunately, people of faith – people of great hope and belief – are sometimes pushed by that very faith to respond in violent rather than nonviolent ways to the hopelessness and despair they feel for the situation and the stubbornness they observe within the systems, both political and religious. It is a fine line, I believe, between those who are able to maintain a stance of continuous nonviolent behavior under any and all conditions and those who, out of their frustrating and disheartening experiences, fight back and retaliate in a violent way. Certainly, even all of those with Jesus in the Garden of Gethsemane were not able to maintain a vigilance of uncompromising nonviolence – some fleeing and one striking off the ear of a slave. As Daniel Berrigan wrote in, *No Bars to Manhood*,

> "...Of course, let us have the peace", we cry, "but at the same time let us have normalcy, let us lose nothing, let our lives stand intact, let us know neither prison nor ill repute nor disruption of ties...". There is no peace because there are no peacemakers. There are no makers of peace because the making of peace is at least as costly as the making of war – at least as exigent, at least as disruptive, at least as liable to bring disgrace and prison and death in its wake (Daniel Berrigan 1970: 174).

This happens, it seems to me, when the religious system no longer supports the religious person. The person is either expelled, for reasons of orthodoxy – for having views outside the box of understanding of the given denomination – or the person chooses to exit, voluntarily, seemingly pulled away from the church on his or her own path, in another direction. Whatever the reason, a person living and active outside of a community of faith no longer has that faith community's support and common conscience to critique them as well as to protect them. Those who are forced or those who choose to go it alone are, I feel, more susceptible to becoming like Torres and Guevara. Oscar Romero (murdered Archbishop of El Salvador) and the Jesuits and the Maryknoll Sisters (also murdered in El Salvador, they will be discussed in detail later) and the many,

many, many others – martyrs and those living the dream of faith still – stayed within a community of faith, operated out of a community of faith, spoke from a community of faith and received their physical and spiritual strength within their respective communities of faith.

Being on one's own versus being part of a group is key, I believe to being able to maintain a nonviolent versus a violent stance. Given the same circumstances, the same risks, the same scenarios, those who manage to stay in communion seem better able to stay centered in Christ. Christ was not a warrior king. Christ was the Prince of Peace, the King of Love and he lived and died as an example of this way of life.

I know, in my own self, that it would be easy enough to respond to the injustice, violence, inequity and all the biases and hatreds in our world by joining a resistance group and going out in a blazing flame of reaction and response. But, the path of pacifism, the path of nonviolence, is for me the path I have chosen. In the end, as I have said since my experiences in El Salvador, it is how we live that matters. We will all die, no matter how protective we may be of our lives – our possessions – our positions in life. We will all die. How we live and how much life we can give back to the world is what really matters. The liberation theologians in El Salvador – and in South and Central America in general – lived in the face of death, of torture, of horrors beyond horrors and yet the vast majority knew that living in the face of death – laughing in the face of death – simply being in the face of death was more important than killing to avoid death. They knew we will all die. In community, the fears were acknowledged, the fears were lifted up to God, the love of Christ was shared.

Out of the deepest fear – out of the fearfulness that comes at staring into the muzzle of an M16 – or into the equally steel-hard eyes of a soldier – out of a fear that goes beyond the fears of 'normalcy' I have witnessed, myself, and I have experienced, myself, the joy of letting go of the fear and living in the lightness of the moment. That does not dissipate fear, forever, nor does it give life, forever, but it does keep one on balance for the evers of our human time. It does not take post traumatic stress or nightmares or reality out of life, but it does provide an alternative that is life at its essence. Jesus, at Gethsemane, was not happy. He was human. But Jesus was able to be at peace, in the end, so we could live in peace in our time. 'Whoever would save his or her life will lose it, but whoever loses his or her life for my sake will find it', said Jesus (Mt. 16:24-25) Those keeping the non-combative faith may die from violence, but they will have chosen life.

There still is no real, solid life-giving peace of equality in South and Central America, even though many have lived and died for liberation and even though others still remain as active, vocal, vital proponents for a peaceful, liberating, Christ-centered change. Certainly one could expect the ideals of Christ would lead one to a non-combative stance – a non-retaliatory response – a 'turn the other cheek' response – a peaceful-peace-centered-response. As Berryman has said, 'No liberation theologian has provided a theological rationale for killing. To the extent death is theologized, it is in reflections on martyrdom, the willingness to give one's life for others, not to take others' lives' (Berryman 1987b: 193). The ideal is to be centered in Christ, unmoving in the face of violence. Yet, some are unable to maintain that stance as the passions of their convictions and as their outrage over what they have witnessed and experienced builds.

The guerrilla movement, to a great extent, grew out of the new understandings that were coming from the Base Christian Communities. Certainly the military saw the church as siding with the opposition, the rebels, the guerrillas. Being found in some parts of Central America with a Bible could be seen as a sign that one sided with the guerrilla forces. I know this from personal experience when a person in our van, on a trip in El Salvador, brought a Bible to identify us as friendly to the rebels – if we should be stopped on the road by them. As it turned out it was the Salvadorian military that stopped us and saw the Bible. Their response was to see us as rebel supporters. We were fortunate to escape with our lives. It was dangerous to profess one's faith openly and publicly. And as the violence grew and the persecution increased, the lines were sometimes very shaky between those who professed a peaceful liberation and those who would liberate by force. In a way, Fr. Torres was a man who, one might say, was expelled by the church into the world of violence and guerrilla warfare. And although in the minority as a member of the guerrilla fighting force, he was not alone in his struggle for liberation.

Torres and Guevara were the 1960s Central and South American rebels with a cause – the ones who struck out on their own. The liberation theologians who followed worked from a faith stance rooted deeply within their faith community. It was this group identity, as I indicated earlier, that added substance and strength to the Christians struggling for change. The times were no less dangerous; in fact, the Death Squads had become a visible reality and no group was exempt from their scrutiny, nor their actions. In El Salvador, where I personally had the most experience, human rights' workers, unionists, church workers (ordained and lay), farm laborers – anyone who dared to organize and to protest, was subject to the Death Squad's surveillance, apprehension, torture and death. In 1980 alone, 3,000 people were killed a month, according to human rights records at the time. Their bodies were left in streets and streams and on garbage dumps. The human rights' organizations kept seemingly unending stacks of books with photos of the bloodied, beaten, tortured bodies, the names of the individuals (if known) and the date of their deaths.

In 1985, when I was in El Salvador, I saw these books and I photographed some of them. I met with Salvadoran church and activist groups and high level governmental leaders, both Salvadorian and American. I saw the Jeep Cherokees, with their darkened window glass, that the United States provided to El Salvador as part of our military aid program to the country. These Death Squad vehicles followed us everywhere we went. In our meetings, I took photos of those gathered to show back in churches and at other meetings in the United States. Ten years later, as I was preparing to show some of the slides to a group, I was shocked to see how many people I had met had, subsequently, been murdered. Unnamed in history books, unsainted in the church, these men and women and even children believed and lived and died in their faith.

Martyrs of Liberation Theology

Besides the thousands – hundreds of thousands – of everyday people killed, there were those more notable in the world press, who will be discussed later.

- 24 March 1980, Archbishop Oscar Romero was gunned down at his altar as he was saying mass.
- 12 December 1980, Maryknoll sisters Ita Ford, Maura Clark,Ursuline Sister, Dorothy Kasel, and lay minister, Jean Donovan, were apprehended and killed.

- 16 November 1989, six Jesuit priests, their housekeeper/cook and her daughter were murdered.

Oscar Romero has always struck me as such a human person, rather like Peter, as both individually struggled with the reality of being Christ's representative to the people of their pastorate in the time of their leadership. Romero really did not want to be involved in the Liberation Theology Movement, originally only wanting to remain in his conservative, scholarly priestly place, safe in the background, apart from the ongoing war that was affecting both the secular and the Christian world of El Salvador. Born on 15 August 1917, in the Ciudad Barrios of San Miguel (a district near the Honduran border, in the region of Cacahuatique), Romero had been elected bishop as a compromise choice – a safe person whom the conservative bishops trusted. At that time, Romero openly criticized those doing Liberation Theology.

As a new bishop, he was not supportive of a priest who was under his care: Rutilio Grande. Grande had become one with the peasants of his congregation, helping them as they organized into farm cooperatives. As a result of his work with the people – living out the ideals and ideas of Liberation Theology – Rutilio Grande was killed by the Salvadorian military, along with an elderly man and a seven-year old child from his parish, as he was driving in his car to bring communion to a sick person. The night of the assassinations, as Archbishop Romero viewed the three bodies, his theology and his ministry changed forever. Like many of us, faced by a moral and ethical challenge, he had to choose between defending the words of Christ in his words and in his actions or to continue to deny them. In the midst of the killings and the persecutions and the injustices that he could no longer avoid seeing, he chose to side with Christ and the people whom he was consecrated to serve. As a result of the killing of Rutilio Grande, Romero became an outspoken and supportive voice for Liberation Theology and for the impoverished people of his nation. As a result, the bishops who had formerly supported his election, now felt abandoned by him. All but one bishop in El Salvador signed a secret document that was sent to the Vatican, denouncing him for having become politicized. The elites of El Salvador turned against him, as well. This denunciation came, in part, due to public statements and actions made by Romero. His refusal to attend any government functions until the repressive violence against the Salvadorian people ended, did nothing to soften Romero's new image or to alleviate the conservative church's and the elites concerns about him.

At one point Romero said, 'If they kill me, I will be resurrected in the Salvadorian people'. These words have been the words of resurrection and hope to a nation yet to revive from the war of the 1980s. Unfortunately for El Salvador, for the church and for the world, he was killed. His life was sacrificed at the very altar of Christ's sacrifice.

As Archbishop Oscar Romero was celebrating a funeral mass for a friend's mother, on 24 March 1980, a man entered the sanctuary and shot and killed him. Alvaro Saravia, a Salvadoran living in Modesto, California, was found guilty of providing the gun, transportation to and from the church and the payment to the assassin. The actual assassin's name has not yet been revealed. The day before, on Sunday, 23 March 1980, Romero had resumed his customary preaching over radio stations YSAX and Radionoticias del Continente. The stations had just gone back on the air, having been off the air due to earlier damage by the Salvadorian right wing (Brockman 1982: 209). The violence was escalating, the Death Squad killings were rampant and fear among the people was palpable, as no one knew for certain who the enemy was, for the enemy could be anyone: a family member, friend, neighbor or other unnamed informant. In his sermon, Romero said:

> I would like to make an appeal in a special way to the men of the army, and in particular to the ranks of the *Guardia* people. You kill your own campesino brothers and sisters…No soldier is obliged to obey an order against the law of God… It is time to recover your consciences and to obey your consciences rather than the orders of sin. The church, defender of the rights of God, of the law of God, of human dignity, the dignity of the person, cannot remain silent before such abomination. We want the government to take seriously that reforms are worth nothing when they come about stained with so much blood. In the name of God, and in the name of this suffering people… I beg you, I ask you, I order you in the name of God: stop the repression' (Brockman 1982: 217).

The response of the military was to kill Oscar Romero. As we shall see, elsewhere in this writing, this same killing of blood brothers and sisters is going on in Israel/Palestine, and the same pleas to stop are being made at peril of the pleader's life.

Nine months after Romero's death, on 2 December 1980, four American church women were killed as they were leaving the airport at San Salvador. The women were Maryknoll Sisters, Ita Ford and Maura Clark, both of whom worked in Chalatenango and were returning to El Salvador from a meeting in Nicaragua; Ursuline Sister, Dorothy Kazel, and lay missioner, Jean Donovan, both of whom worked in La Libertad (a small coastal town in El Salvador), and were at the airport to pick up the other two women. They were in El Salvador, under the auspices of the Archdiocese of San Salvador, who supported their work with refugees and displaced persons fleeing the violence of the war within the confines of El Salvador. As with the Jesuit murders, it was found that the head of the National Guard, two officers investigating the case and Salvadorian military and American officials all conspired to cover up the facts of the case. The United Nation-sponsored Commission on the Truth for El Salvador, found that the abductions and murders were executed and carried out by the military under the authority of orders from people higher up in the military and government.

It was further found that the murders had been planned. In 1984, five members of the Salvadorian military were found guilty and sentenced to thirty years in prison. Three were released in 1998. Accused senior Salvadorian government officials and Salvadorian generals escaped to Florida, where they were given legal status by the United States, according to the Religious Task Force on Central America and Mexico. In all, over 75,000 civilians were killed and over 8,000 were missing at the end of the war in El Salvador.

On 16 November 1989, nine years after Archbishop Oscar Romero's assassination, the military entered the grounds of the Jesuit University of Central America in San Salvador and assassinated six priests, their housekeeper/cook and her daughter. Since then, these eight have been added to the long list of martyrs of El Salvador. The priests were: Ignacio Ellacuria, university president and rector; Ignacio Martin-Baro, liberation theologian and author of opinion polls in El Salvador, which counterbalanced claims being made by the government of El Salvador; Segundo Montes and Martin-Baro, colleagues at Georgetown's Center for Immigration Policy and Refugee Assistance; and the following pastors Joaquin Lopez y Lopez; Amando Lopez; and Juan Ramon Moreno. The housekeeper/cook, Julia Elba Ramos, and her fifteen year-old daughter, Celina Mariset Ramos, were killed as they slept in beds in the Jesuit house where they had stayed for reasons of safety.

The Jesuits were supportive of the church's Liberation Theology movement and were seen as being intellectually supportive of the FMLN political uprising. The Jesuit faculty members were known to be outspoken against human rights abuses. It is a sad irony that their deaths were, in fact, human rights' abuses of the most violent and outrageous nature.

As a result of these killings, and the ensuing public outcry in the United States, U.S. policy toward El Salvador was reevaluated. Congressmen Tip O'Neil and Joseph Moakley, both from Massachusetts, were courageously persistent in seeing that an investigation of these killings took place. It took several years, but eventually it was found that, indeed, the United States military, through our 'advisors', had been involved in planning and carrying out the killing of these eight people. Three years after these killings, in February 1992, a cease fire was declared. The hundreds of thousands of Salvadoran deaths did not bring about the cease fire; rather it took the deaths of Oscar Romero, the Jesuits and the Maryknoll Sisters to garner enough international support and recognition within the United States for the killings and repressive tactics of the Salvadorian government to cease.

In 1990, I led a delegation from the Episcopal Diocese of Massachusetts to El Salvador for the celebration of the life of Oscar Romero, held on the tenth anniversary of his death, 24 March 1990. There was a jubilation within the streets of San Salvador and within the spaces of the cathedral. People came in waving branches broken off from trees and posters with Oscar Romero's picture and banners citing his words. As my delegation entered the cathedral (in an informal way, just mingling with everyone else), a man broke away from across the cathedral and rushed over, carrying his little child with him. When he got to us, he asked me (in my clergy collar) to bless his child. What a blessing – what an absolute blessing for me to be asked to do such a thing in the cathedral of Oscar Romero, in the cathedral of the Roman Catholic Church, in the place where women are not ordained! It was just one of many shatterings of the expected in this land where liberation was and is still bubbling up molten-like, as lava waiting underground to erupt in a more all encompassing life-changing way.

While the jubilation continued within the area of the cathedral, and in the various churches and meeting places for those involved in Liberation Theology, on the roads leading into and out of the city there were military blockades, more heavily reinforced with soldiers and munitions than in my earlier visits. Where before we had been able to talk our way through the check points, we were not able to do so on this trip. We had many boxes of clothing, medicine and other humanitarian items for the city of Suchitoto. We left them with an Episcopal priest to distribute to those in need in his area of San Salvador. Back in the capital, all was seemingly normal. I say 'seemingly', if one did not read the newspapers and did not listen to the television in Spanish. People speaking English, in the hotels and on the streets, heard only what others wanted them to hear and did not see or hear the 'truth' of the situation. The war was not over. The strife had not ceased. The spirit of Archbishop Oscar Romero was infused within the people, but the work was not yet completed. The people were not yet freed of their impoverishment. The imbalance of power still existed.

Base Christian Communities (Communidades de Base)

Ecclesiastical Base Communities or Base Christian Communities, as they are also called, began as early as 1955, according to Boff (Leonardo Boff 1984: 9). Paolo Freire's religious education of the poor and oppressed joined with the Base Education Movement in the 1960s to address the core question of the meaning of Christianity and the role of individual Christians in a world so overwhelmingly populated by the poor and the oppressed. According to Leonardo Boff, it became clear that, 'The only way to be a Christian was to be at the service of liberation', otherwise, in the words of Boff, '…poverty meant forced impoverishment at the hands of economic and social mechanisms of exploitation' (Leonardo Boff 1984: 10).

But there was also a pragmatic concern that priests were in short supply and the people wanted to worship and to study the Bible. Having not enough clergy – not enough religious trained sisters or brothers – the church by the very nature of the situation was forced to look upon the laity as viable resources for leadership. The early proponents of base communities saw these communities as working within the context of the established church, or as L. Boff said, in 'permanent coexistence' with the church. L. Boff wrote, as well, in

Ecclesiogenesis, the hierarchy of the church, the pope, bishops and priests should, '…exercise their function within the communities and not *over* them, integrating duties instead of accumulating them, respecting the various charisms (gifts), and leading them to the oneness of one and the same body' (Sigmund 1990: 83).

There was no intention, as mentioned previously, to remove the base community from within the context of the church; in fact, the original concept was to broaden the leadership within the church. Of course, that solution to a paucity of leadership created a problem with the existing leadership within the institutional church. So what are – and what were – *Communidades de Base*, as they are called in El Salvador and other Central American countries and Mexico?

Basically, a Base Community is comprised of a group of laity of varying ages, who come together to study the Bible. Sounds familiar, to those of us who have sat in Bible classes. But this Bible study is revolutionary in its very being. As was mentioned, earlier, the people who were coming to the classes did not read, for the most part; they were uneducated, impoverished and they had never held the scripture in their hands before. They came and they sat together. Usually, they were given photocopies of a particular piece of scripture (because there was no money for Bibles and because one piece of paper is easier to carry, to study, to make one's own).

Often the beginning biblical story focused on Exodus or another such liberating story. The participants were taught to read, they were asked to relate, to exegete – explain and understand the scripture from their own experience. They were invited to be a part of the scripture and to let it be part of their life as a community. They were urged to see their world through a different set of lenses. The very process of the Bible study and the very direction the Bible study took, was in itself revolutionary. The people taught, themselves, they theologized, as one member among others, they related the scripture to their lives, themselves. The priest sat in the background, as a resource, or was not even present, as the base community became established. The word was as it had been in the time of Jesus – with the people – breathing new life into the people – awakening them to new possibilities and new arenas of being.

In the beginning days – weeks – months of such a Base Community, the priest or sister would gradually cede his or her power and authority to leaders within the group. Many of these lay leaders became Catechists (instructors in the faith and preparers for baptism). As they grew in their confidence, their responsibilities expanded and the priest or sister gradually withdrew from the place of leadership, to being one person among those gathered, or else leaving to start another group. Clodovis Boff has written about the Base Communities in his book, *Ecclesial Base Communities and the Practices of Liberation* (1980).

I experienced Communidades de Base in the early stages in Cuernavaca, Mexico, in 1981, and then later in Honduras and El Salvador. In 1985, I went to Honduras under the auspices of the United Nations' High Commission on Refugees (UNHCR) to visit the refugee camps – camps full of people who had fled the wars in El Salvador and Guatemala. Before I left, as an aside, I got a letter from then Massachusett's Governor, Michael Dukakis and my Episcopal Bishop, David Johnson, asking that I be allowed into the camps. I had them put impressive gold seals and ribbons on the papers. As it turned out, these letters – along with my official papers from UNHCR and the Catholic Relief Service (members of whom traveled with me in Honduras) – helped get me through what was incredible red tape and stonewalling tactics. The government of Honduras did not want outsiders in the camps of the refugees, or for that matter, within the country of Honduras. This was the time when the Death Squads in Honduras were beginning. It was a time of elections and a time of incredible tensions – of disappearances and death.

Needless to say, anything I witnessed or experienced was nothing compared to what the refugees had been through. The two largest camps, at that time, were Mesa Grande and Colomoncagua. I also visited other sites and met with the people working with the refugees, as well as a variety of representatives from the churches in Honduras. In these refugee camps, I witnessed the Base Communities in all their power and faith-filled conviction. Living on tortillas, rice and beans (and very little of that) – living away from families, from homes, from the land of their beginnings and the land of their ancestors – living as spartan and cruel a life as one can, in a place hot as Hades during the day and cold as a freezer at night – these people were living their faith, in faith and in joy and in hope. In one class, in Colomoncagua, the leader was just thirteen years-old. She was a beautiful young girl, trained by the priest to read and to be a catechist. The people in her group were given sheets of paper with the scripture lesson on it – folded, refolded –

treasured. A part of the Exodus story was on the paper they were using at that time. They sang. They read. They talked. They spoke out for justice, for freedom for peace. They planned for the time when they would be free – taken out of captivity – led back to their land in El Salvador. They did all this in the most harsh of circumstances.

I learned from them. I grew with them as I sat with them (as an observer, not as a leader, not as a resource, but as one there to learn). The young woman, Maria, and I had many conversations. We agreed to write to one another after I left. She was a delightful girl turning into a young woman, with dreams and aspirations just like any girl of her age, perhaps made more mature by her circumstances, but still young and full of promise – a truly delightful young girl/woman.

I also planned to keep in touch with some of the internationals present – those there to try and keep the people safe from the unpredictable raids by the Honduran military – to see that the 'truth' of their experience was able to get out to the world. Two weeks after I left, the Honduran military, including several blond-haired, blue eyed English speaking soldiers, entered the Camp of Colomoncagua, raping and killing several, including Maria. The internationals sent me the news and a picture of Maria that she had intended to send to me. I shall never forget her beautifully bold profile, still so innocent and so full of hope. I shall never forget, either, what we as a nation have done to the innocence of those not yet come into the fullness or the potential of their lives, as I shall never forget, either, what our government has done to our own innocence and trust in the United States of America.

The irony, in the horror of this event, is that I was initially supposed to be with a group from San Francisco. They felt it was too dangerous to go when I went, putting off their trip for two weeks. They were in the camp when the military entered. They survived, by crouching, hidden away from the bullets and the violence, observing what happened. They became witnesses to the violence they had hoped to avoid, and as such became a voice for the truth of their experience.

Some forty years later, the Base Christian Communities have continued to grow and expand in places in the world where there is a desperation and a need for hope. In South Africa and other parts of Africa and Palestine, there are Bible study groups designed to liberate the people by letting the people liberate themselves. As for Base Christian Communities in Latin America, some have faded away as the nations have undergone change following the wars of the 1980s. However, in 2007, there were over 100,000 Base Communities in Brazil, alone. It is obvious to me that death can not stop the movement of the Spirit, as the word of God is integrated into the lives of the people and lived out in the world in which they and we all live.

Liberation Theology in North America

When I entered Harvard Divinity School in 1982, I had my own experiences of Liberation Theology and Base Communities, but no academic foundation undergirding my new understandings. I had no idea who Henri Nouwen was. My room was across the hall from Divinity Hall's chapel and so my dorm mates elected me to be the one in charge of our chapel's services. The first morning we had a service, I found the priest in the chapel arranging the chairs in a circle in a base community style of worship. And so we sat in a circle, with the priest among us, as one with us. During the homily, our celebrant looked up and away, frequently, as if communicating with another being. He also gestured, frequently, with hands that seemed larger than life size (when in reality they fit his size and frame). As I soon found out, this was Henri Nouwen, a man I came to know, a man I learned from, a man who blessed me with his friendship, his books and at my installation as rector at St. Stephen's Parish in Portland, Oregon, with a very special chasuble and stole from Guatemala.

Henri Jozef Machiel Nouwen was one of many who brought Liberation Theology and the construct of Base Communities to the United States, where we formed communities of faith. Nouwen, a Roman Catholic priest, was the eldest son of his family, born in The Netherlands on 24 January 1932. He died on 21 September 1996. A fellow at the Menninger Clinic in Kansas, he taught at the University of Notre Dame, Yale Divinity School and Harvard Divinity School. His last residence was at the L'Arche Community of Daybreak in Toronto, Canada, where he was pastor and lived with the adult community of mentally and physically handicapped adults. One of Nouwen's earliest and most appreciated books, *The Wounded Healer*, exemplified his own life's struggle with brokenness. It was this kind of honesty and openness that resonated with his readers and with those of us who were privileged to know him. Nouwen used to say that *The Return of the Prodigal Son* was the book he wrote to address his own father/son issues but it was *Love in a Fearful Land, A Guatemalan Story* – and others from his missionary work in Bolivia and Peru – that made the issues and the people of Central and South America real. As Harvey Cox, Professor at HDS wrote concerning *Love in a Fearful Land*, 'Henri Nouwen with his characteristic feel for the concrete and the personal, helps bring us back to the reality with this engaging story of two men who remind us that the 'Central American issue' is about real people'.

In those days in the seminary, it seemed to many of us that the impoverished of the Southern Hemisphere were bringing to us in the United States the riches and the richness of their faith – bringing new life into the impoverished spirituality of our northern Christian Church. The people of South and Central America came as refugees – as political asylum seekers – sometimes bringing only their faith with them. They came with a sense of gratefulness and gracefulness that defied our own perspectives and our own North American lives of over abundance. They came with, as Nouwen put it in his book *Gracias!* a sense of thankfulness. The people of Bolivia and Peru, with whom he interacted between October 1981 to March 1982, taught Nouwen '…that everything that is, is freely given by the God of love. All is grace. Light and water, shelter and food, work and free time, children, parents and grandparents, birth and death – it is all given to us. Why?' Nouwen asked, 'So that we can say gracias, thanks: thanks to God, thanks to each other, thanks to all and everyone' (Nouwen: 1983:187). This time in South America was a time of discernment for Nouwen. Should he remain in South or Central America? His question arose, in part, out of an awareness of the disparity within and between the secular and religious lives in North, South and Central America. Later, on 27 August 1984, he went to Guatemala to join his North American priest friend, John Vesey, as he took a new post in Santiago Atitlan. Peter Weiskel, a friend and photographer, accompanied Nouwen. They remained for ten days. Three years earlier, on 28 July 1981, the priest in Santiago Atitlan, Stanley Francis Rother, had been murdered at the rectory of the church. The room of his death was subsequently used as a chapel – bullet holes and blood stains remaining on the wall and in the tabernacle (Nouwen 1985: 20).

Entering into the drama of a nation at war, a nation traumatized by the same nightmarish reality as El Salvador was experiencing, brought Nouwen to realize that, 'In the end, prayer summarizes the most needed response to the reality (he) encountered' (Nouwen 1985:10). Vesey, as priests before and after him, was radically changed by the environment and his sense of being in Christ with the people of Christ. As Nouwen wrote, 'John never (pointed) an accusing finger at anyone. He (invited) people to conversion, to a reshaping of a heart and mind in the service of Jesus. In one of his homilies (John) said: 'Nobody is killed by a gun without first being killed by the tongue. We need a new heart, because only from a new heart can peace be born' (Nouwen 1985: 108). John Vesey was still serving in Guatemala when Nouwen wrote *Love in a Fearful Land*, in 1985. As Nouwen pondered, I have pondered: am I called to serve in Central America or, now, Israel/Palestine, or am I called to serve wherever I am out of the spirit and knowledge of Christ's love as witnessed in Central America?

Another stellar person I met at Harvard Divinity School was Harvey Cox, Hollis Professor of Divinity. He, as I, had just been in Cuernavaca, Mexico, working with the growing Base Community there. He had been a visiting professor at the Mexican Baptist Seminary (Seminario Bautista de Mexico) as well. The author of many books, including *Secular City* and *The Silencing of Leonardo Boff: Liberation Theology and The Future of World Christianity*, Cox's class on Liberation Theology was seminal in my growing understanding of the situation in South and Central America. It was in this class that I first heard of the 'Discipleship of the Poor', a term Leonardo Boff coined, to explain the reality of the new church being born from the poor. What I had seen and experienced myself, Cox, in his lectures, grounded in the context of the broader picture of Liberation Theology and Communidades de Base. He also brought some of the leading figures in Liberation Theology to Harvard, Gutierrez and Sobrino among them, each of whom brought much to the reality of what was being read about and spoken about but not truly known in North America.

While Nouwen focused on the spiritual and the prayerful aspects of the liberation process, Cox's focus was more on the process and the theology. Together, they made for an exciting learning atmosphere at seminary. At that time Professor Cox's church, Old Cambridge Baptist Church (OCBC), was a sanctuary church, as was the city of Cambridge, later on. Sanctuary churches gave refuge to political asylum seekers, and in this case, to one woman in particular. Cox's lectures and his actions as a Christian combined to bring a strong witness of presence to the seminary's community and to the community at large. The two, Nouwen, the Roman Catholic, and Cox, the Baptist, were strong models for my coming ministry in the Episcopal Church.

Others brought Liberation Theology to North America, as well. William S. Coffin, Presbyterian minister and Yale University Chaplain, who called for the 'National Conference on New Politics'; Charles Bayer, author of *A Guide to Liberation Theology for Middle Class Congregations* and minister of First Christian Church, St. Joseph, Michigan; Charles H. Briggs Professor of Systematic Theology, and James H. Cone, Charles Augustus Briggs Distinguished Professor of Systematic Theology at Union Theological Seminary in New York City. Dr. Cone wrote several books including, *A Black Theology of Liberation,* and *Speaking the Truth: Ecumenism, Liberation and Black Theology* . Finally, as might not be surprising, the American-based Maryknoll priests and nuns and the Jesuits who were so active in Central America brought base communities into their own American church's sphere. In addition, the Berrigan brothers: Daniel, a Jesuit priest and Philip, a former priest, a married member of the Jonah House Community; Penny Lernoux, journalist and author of *Cry of the People*, with many others, added to our nation's understanding of the southern half of our shared continent's people and their process toward liberation.

And, as with other transferred ideologies, practices, educational programs and theologies, the South/Central American version of Liberation Theology was both adopted and adapted to fit the needs of the people and the multiple cultures of this nation: impoverished African-Americans, females, young, old and even middle-class. While our poverty level is on a lesser scale, some people and some parts of the United States of America remain at an impoverished level in society. While our democracy is not subject to the corruption of some of the South and Central American countries, we are not free of corruption. In fact, in recent years, we have become more entrenched in politics of isolationism and 'terrorist'-focused policies that deny basic human rights to others and to our own citizens, while bringing into question the power of the few over the rights of the many. There is work to be done to shore up, not tear down, the goodness of our nation and the spiritual life of our religious bodies – whatever they may be in this polycultural, polyreligious time.

Liberation Theology: Jewish and Islamic

As we have noted earlier, the Torah, the five books of Moses (the Pentateuch) tells the Jewish story of a people enslaved, struggling to be free, obtaining freedom through the grace and guidance of God and then resisting or abandoning the rules of God as prescribed in the Jewish history with God. For the Jews, freedom is dependent on recognizing the equal rights of all peoples, be they Jewish or not. Freedom is also dependent on the rich sharing so that none are poor, or even more importantly, sharing so none are dependent, but rather have the opportunity to be independent. Freedom, as well, is dependent on sharing not only on an individual, but a communal level. And freedom is dependent on following the laws and commandments of God. The sense of a Jewish Liberation Theology goes back to the beginning and works its way into the stands of modern day Reform and Conservative Judaism, as opposed to Orthodox Judaism, which is more 'conservative' by Liberation Theology and social justice standards. The New Jewish Agenda is seen as being part of this liberating leaning in American Judaism. *A Jewish Theology of Liberation* by Marc Ellis is an example of this focus in Jewish theology.

For Christians, it is not spelled out as clearly, or as detailed and authoritatively, but nonetheless, an underlying dependency on our freedom – or our spiritual well-being – clearly relies on our following the first and great commandment to love God and our neighbors as ourselves. Implicit in this are the Hebraic admonitions that preceded our own Christian guidelines, the directives that have been reinterpreted for us through the teachings and the preachings and the life of Christ.

For the Muslims, it is much the same. In fact, it is my understanding and my experience that peoples from the Middle East – be they Jewish or Muslim or Christian – have a much stronger sense of family ties and communal ties than do we Westerners. This regard for and respect for the family brings with it an obligation and a duty that is apparently instilled at an early age and lived out through one's lifetime. In North America, while it is 'good' to give back to the community, to volunteer, to contribute, it is not necessarily an obligation nor a cultural norm as in the Middle East, especially in the American urban and less personal, more family-fragmented areas of our nation. While we Christians grow up with a certain familiarity with the lessons of the First and Second Testaments, most of us are not aware of similar Islamic scriptural dictates. In actuality, the Jewish, Christian and Islamic scriptures call for liberation, justice and peace. We, Christians, who have coined the term, 'Liberation Theology', have no copyright on either the term or the concept. All three Abrahamic religions call for the same law-abiding, peace-providing, justice-bringing behavior. Claiming ignorance simply allows a problem to exist; making informed decisions is liberating. Now if we, as members of our given religion, do or do not choose to become informed and to follow the edicts of our faith, that should not be a reflection on our faith, but rather on us as practitioners of our faith.

Desmond Tutu, (left) retired Anglican Archbishop of South Africa, Naim Ateek, Founder and Head of Sabeel and Constance Hammond, author, at the Sabeel Conference in Boston, 2002. Reproduced by kind permission of Sabeel.

Liberation Theology: Palestinian Christian

Palestine Liberation Theology, or as The Rev. Dr Naim Ateek calls it, 'Palestinian Christian Theology' or 'Palestinian Theology of Liberation', has come out of the times of challenge that began in 1948 – times that even more deeply impacted the Palestinian Christian community following the Six Day War in 1967. Dr Ateek wrote, 'Any theology of liberation must of necessity address the issue of justice. It is, after all, the major issue for Palestinians regardless of their religious affiliation' (Ateek 1989: 75) Like the people of South and Central America, the Palestinian Christians were faced with life and death issues, not only on a personal level, but on a community and church level. The thriving Christian community that existed prior to the 1948 Partition Plan, in the 1960s – and even more so, the Palestinian Christian community today – has become a mere remnant of itself. How to resurrect the people of the resurrection, was (and to some extent still is) the overall abiding question.

Dr. Ateek has addressed this qustion by looking at the sources of the problem in his chapter, 'The Emergence of a Palestinian Christian Theology', in *Faith and the Intifada, Palestinian Christian Voices.* Ateek feels the problem lies in the following four areas:

1. *The rise of Jewish religious fundamentalism,* following 1967, when Gush Emunim (block of the faithful), Zionist settlers on the West Bank; Chabad Lubbavitch, Hasidic Jews; and other fundamentalist Jewish groups all came into being or prominence. Because the Six Day War had been won in such a brief time, some religious Jews felt that this was a sign that the land was being given back to the Israeli Jews by God. The land, therefore, acquired an overlay of significant religious meaning. The former primarily secular Jewish State, suddenly became more religious, and as such, more determined to keep the land (Ateek 1992:2).

2. *The rise of Western Christian fundamentalism* also came into being following the 1967 war, when the quick ending of the war and the return of the Israeli Jews to East Jerusalem was seen as a forerunner to the rebuilding of the temple and the Second Coming of Christ. It is these same fundamentalist Christians who have supported the fundamentalist Israeli Jews, seeing in them the means to their end, which will be the glory of their Christian rapture. According to Ateek, in 1992 there were over

sixty million Christian fundamentalists in the United States, and the group has grown since then (Ateek 1992: 2). According to Rosemary Radford Ruether, 'For Falwell, an unshakable bond ties Jews and Christians together in the promises of God…Whoever blesses the Jew (and the Jewish state) will be blessed by God. Whoever curses the Jew (and the Jewish state) will be cursed by God (Gen. 112:1-3). Thus Americans and Christians assure their own prosperity by protecting the Jews and supporting the State of Israel. This then, is Falwell's vision of the world – a vision and a commitment that one has every reason to believe is totally sincere…The Christian messianic Zionism of Falwell…has great affinity with the militant political messianism that has arisen in Israel in the Gush Emunim settler movement' (Ruether 1989: 179). And so Ruether ties together two of Ateek's points, the fundamentalism of the religious Jews and the fundamentalism of the non-indigenous Christians and the fervor of the settlers and those who support them.

3. *The Jewish development of Holocaust Theology*, which, according to Ateek, came about as the religious Israeli Jews saw an 'interconnection between the Holocaust and (their own) Jewish empowerment' (Ateek 1992: 3). According to Marc Ellis, a widely read and respected Jewish theologian, 'The Holocaust represents tragedy and worthlessness, while Israel represents empowerment and redemption'. Ellis further 'believes that with empowerment, the ethical side of Judaism has suffered. Holocaust theologians have refined the notion of practicing Jew from one who engages in ritual and observance of the Law to one who cherishes memory, survival, and empowerment… (Ellis) adds to that definition "a critical and efficacious pursuit of justice and peace" ' (Ateek 1989: 69).

4. *The Christian Zionist Theology came into being* and aligned itself with the Jewish Zionist Theology, its politics and its aspirations. It was, according to Ateek, at this time that Israel – as a nation – began to focus upon a divine plan that would support the Jews to the exclusion of the Christians in Israel/Palestine (Ateek 1992: 3). According to the recently retired Anglican Bishop of Jerusalem, Riah Hanna Abu El-Assal, Zionism, while it was originally conceived in a secular framework, has become increasingly '…seen as a fulfillment of prophecy, a renewal of the covenant between God and his Chosen People, giving them

an exclusive right not only to dwell in the land, but to take it by force as did Joshua and the kings of Israel, killing or expelling those already living here or making them "hewers of wood and drawers of water" ' (Abu-El-Assal 1999: 56). One can see why this is a problem for the Christians – those who are not Zionists, themselves – and for the Muslims. One can also see how the fundamental movements in the Christian and Jewish faiths are so dangerous to finding any peaceful resolution of the present conflict in Israel/Palestine.

Out of the extensive background and history of the first Christians came a need for the present day inheritors of the faith, the Palestinian Christians, to find their own strength in their own faith in this, their own time. Heart-sickened and alienated by the use of God in the rhetoric of the opposing factions, battered by the battles that continue within their towns and villages, and dazed by the ongoing stress living in such an occupied zone brings, Dr Ateek sees four ways of addressing the faith issues of his people:

1. *In a pastoral/grassroots way*, looking for God in the moment of their lives – looking at the God of the Palestinian Christians' occupation and their oppression, to see if God is still with them in this time of seeming abandonment (Ateek 1992: 4).

2. *By looking at the indigenous factor.* As it had been in South and Central America, foreign-born clergy have dominated the church in Palestine. Ateek feels that Palestinian Christians – lay and ordained leaders – are needed to 'define the meaning of the land', to be in charge of their own lives and their own churches (Ateek 1992: 4).

3. *By addressing the biblical question.* For many of us in the Episcopal Church in the United States, adding the First Testament readings back into the service in the 1979 *Book of Common Prayer* was a way of reconnecting with our Jewish heritage – Jesus' Jewish heritage. For the Christians in Israel/Palestine the references to the First Testament are offensive, having as they do an overlay of meaning for Israel as conqueror and the Palestinians as the ones conquered. The Christians wanted, according to Ateek, to, '…find in the Bible the God of justice, the God who is concerned with the oppressed', concerned with them, the Palestinian Christians, not only the Israeli Jews (Ateek 1992: 4).

4. *By addressing the theological factor.* Where is Jesus in relation to the Palestinian people, in an historical, biblical and incarnational

sense? As Ateek says of his people, 'How do we relate the coming of Christ to the Jewish people and to the Christian Church?' (Ateek 1992: 4).

Out of these problems and issues, both historic and present, Dr Ateek has formulated his concept of Palestinian Liberation Theology. As he has written, 'We are desperately in need of finding a theology of liberation for ourselves that will also be a theology of peace and reconciliation for the peoples of this land, for Israel and Palestine as two people of this land' (Ateek 1992: 5). Looming before the Christian community, living within the Christian community, are the ongoing questions involving God and holy scripture – peace and justice – redemption and forgiveness – violence and nonviolence.

Another person who is helping expand this concept of Liberation Theology in Palestine is Nadia Abboushi. Born in a primarily Muslim city, she now lives in the Christian city of Ramallah. Her degrees are from Beirut University College and State University in Potsdam, New York. In her article, 'The Intifada and the Palestinian Churches', Abboushi writes, 'The Christians of Palestine are an integral and vital force in the national struggle for liberation. Their influence has been felt and demonstrated overtly, as in the valiant case of Beit Sahour's nonviolent acts of civil disobedience, and covertly, as individual members of underground local committees lay the new infrastructure for the independent Palestinian State in the various fields of education, agriculture, medicine, industry, and public relations' (Ateek 1992: 58). She feels, however, that the churches in Palestine have been – as churches tend to be elsewhere – bogged down by their desire to keep the status quo, especially in regard to interdenominational and holy site issues. In addition, Abboushi feels the churches are trying to keep their ties to the past, as is illustrated in the individual denominations' hierarchical and ritualistic ways, while they, also, maintain their paternalistic attachments to European and American churches. Finally, she feels that the Palestinian church's reluctance to offend the authorities by becoming politically active, is weakening the positive impact that the churches could have (Ateek 1992: 58).

Abboushi states in her article that, 'The challenge facing these churches in the age of the Intifada is the formulation of a holistic vision of peace based on justice in the Holy Land… A comprehensive framework of a Palestinian theology of liberation will put the churches back in the mainstream of events, get them involved in the ongoing struggle against oppression, and empower them toward achieving salvation' (Ateek 1992: 59). Abboushi is part of a growing circle of people, both lay and ordained – Christian and Muslim – who are attempting to address the needs of the Palestinian people through their faith-based stances. She, and the others, offer a hope that the political system that has been so fractious and divisive in the recent past seems unable to offer. As with the earlier people of the Liberation Theology Movement, it is this combination of faith and hope for a future that may, eventually, move the political system and the governments that are involved to take actions that will bring about a just resolution to the present occupation of Palestine by Israel.

To this end, to help people feel they are not alone and isolated, a Christian organization working for peace and justice, Sabeel (the Arabic name means 'the way' or 'a spring of life giving water'), has joined with other grassroots peace groups to work toward building a sense of commonality and community within the confines of Israel/Palestine – Christian, Jewish and Muslim persons are involved. Founded by Episcopal Anglican priest Naim Ateek, with members of the thirteen indigenous churches of Palestine, Sabeel is an example – the most widely recognized example – of a Palestinian Christian organization that is devoted to nonviolent resistance. Sabeel strives to foster peace and understanding by working with American Christians and others of goodwill around the world. Sabeel, also, is involved with the indigenous Christian churches, working to bridge differences between them as they seek to find the common Christ among them – becoming one in Christ rather than ones in separate denominational units of division. To bring this about, Sabeel's mission, according to The Rev. Dr Richard Toll, Chair of Friends of Sabeel-North America, includes helping the Palestinian Christians to free themselves of their past prejudices against one another; working together to speak with one voice, rather than the many conflicting voices of the recent past.

Ateek's hope for peace and justice for Israel/Palestine comes out of his understanding of Liberation Theology. He has reformulated Liberation Theology, placing it within the context of his own place and his own people, and in the process has created a Palestinian Theology of Liberation that is relevant to the now of the context of Liberation Theology – Palestinian Liberation Theology. Sabeel has established two primary goals: one, to offer Palestinian Christian youth and adults Bible study that will give a scriptural relevancy to their lives and 'sustain their faith and hope'; and two, to work with international visitors and delegations so they may learn more about the Christian community in Israel/Palestine and the possibilities that exist for a peace settlement in the region (www.sabeel.org).

As with Liberation Theology in Central and South America, Ateek is working to help his brother and sister Christians in Palestine to see that they have hope in the presence of Christ-with-them as they struggle for a new place in their old land. Unlike the Liberation Theologians of Central and South America who focused on Exilic literature, Ateek focuses on three biblical readings, each with a different theme: 1 Kgs 21, 1 Kgs 22 and Pss. 42 and 43. In 1 Kgs 21, Ateek emphasizes 'God's justice for the poor...God's intervention to defend the poor, the weak and the defenseless and liberation to the oppressed' (Ateek 1989: 86-87). In 1 Kgs 22, he reminds people that 'Often the powerful want to hear only what pleases them...(and) those who view events with an eye for justice are disliked and often hated' (Ateek 1989: 90). In Pss. 42 and 43 Ateek sees the biblical theme as being one of liberation and hope, as heard 'in the cry of the oppressed' (Ateek 1989: 91). It is these themes of liberation, hope and faith which he feels directly relate to the Palestinians in their situation in Israel/Palestine, today.

While Sabeel can work in these ways to bring about community and hope, the desire to find and install people to serve in the indigenous priesthood lies really in the hands of the bishop (or other Christian heads of denominations) and the Israeli government, which controls the coming and going of all Palestinian people. To exit Israel/Palestine could mean there would be no guarantee of a lawful reentry. In these present days when land is being confiscated because the land owners are not able to cultivate it (even when living next to the land, but separated from it by the Wall), to leave for seminary offers many potential side implications and issues. Even bringing in, from neighboring countries, persons ordained has proved to be problematic. Those who serve the Christian churches now, in Israel/Palestine, are at best isolated in their options.

Others not ordained are moving forward in their own way to create an atmosphere of nonviolence and hope. Mubarak Awad, a lay Christian from Bethlehem, has brought into being a nonviolent resistance program that trains Palestinian villages in nonviolent living. Mohammed Gandhi's grandson has participated in this program, as have others from various parts of the world. The idea is for an entire village – each and every member – to refuse to live in a violent, retaliatory way. The result: Awad was deported and now lives in Washington, DC, where he heads Non-Violence International. In his absence, the village program is continuing through the leadership of family members who remain in Israel/Palestine. It appears that in a violent world, violence sometimes seems more the norm and less threatening than nonviolence.

Remaining committed to a nonviolent stance in an ever escalating violent situation within Israel/Palestine, Ateek, and those who work with him in Sabeel, are desperately seeking the God of the transforming and regenerative spirit, just as those before him, in South and Central America, sought their God for solace and strength and change. But this time, in this place, there are three religions calling upon God in their own righteous and religious ways. As long as each speaks God to the other, as if he or she owns God, the work of those like Naim Ateek will continue to be laborious, difficult and dangerous. But, the alternative is to give up hope and the prospects for peace, and that is even more dangerous, more life and soul-threatening.

Palestinian Resistance Groups

As with the Liberation Theology Movement in South and Central America, all resistance groups are not pacifistic or non-violent. The Islamic resistance group most widely recognized is Haqamat al-Muqawamah al-Islamiyyah (Hamas), begun in the 1930s as an outgrowth of the Society of the Muslim Brothers in Egypt (the first modern Arab Islamist movement). Hamas and the Society have remained linked, yet separate. In the 1980s, the Israeli government supported Hamas in order to divide the Palestinian Movement and hence weaken the PLO. Late in the 1980s, in the first years of the first Intifada, Hamas, according to Karen Armstrong,

> ...fought both the Israeli occupation and the Palestine nationalistic movement. They were fighting the secularists for the Muslim soul of Palestine... It was a violent movement that, yet again was born of oppression. HAMAS terrorism escalated after the killing of seventeen Palestinian worshipers on the Haram al-Sharif on October 8, 1990. Impelled by a fear of annihilation, HAMAS also attacked Palestinians whom they judged to be collaborators with Israel... HAMAS saw the

> Arab-Israeli conflict in religious terms...(they) believed the Palestinian tragedy had come about because the people had neglected their religion; Palestinians would only shake off Israeli rule when they returned to Islam. HAMAS believed that the success of Israel was due to Jewish faith, and that Israel was dedicated to the destruction of Islam. They claimed, therefore, to be fighting a war of self-defense (Armstrong 2001: 352).

Recent events have shown this sense of defensiveness still lingers, growing out of the long-held fear of being annihilated and the sense that the faith of their people is being lost. If the leaders and members of Hamas could allow others to coexist, whatever their faith or political stance, and if Hamas could realize that faith is something that can not be implemented by force, the great benefits Hamas is capable of bringing to the Palestinian people would be recognized and accepted by the wider global community.

In spite of the often violent and militant base of Hamas, which we, in the West, have seen on our television sets and read about in newspapers and magazines, it should be noted that both Hamas and the Society have done much to upgrade the living conditions and the moral and the societal standards of the Arab population, specifically the Muslim Palestinian people. Unfortunately, Hamas' more recent hard extremist Islamic line runs counter to actions being done to bring about a unifying Palestinian presence, where Muslim, Christian and Jew can live in peace and harmony. Any benefit to one group, at the expense of the others, is not beneficial in the end to Israelis, Palestinians or to the peoples residing in the larger Middle Eastern region, or for that matter in the world at large.

The Al-Jihad Al-Islami (Islamic Jihad Organization), formed in the early 1980s, is separate from but often identified with Hamas. More and more, this group is identified as a violent, militant group. While I do not condone violence, and I do support the concept and the practice of conscientious objection and nonviolent resistance, I feel it only right to point out that what to one side is a resistance fighter, to the other side is a terrorist and conversely, what to one side is a terrorist to the other side is a resistance fighter. In the Second World War, the French Resistance was supported enthusiastically by the United States in a variety of tangible and supportive ways. To the Germans, the resistance fighters were people to be found and to be executed. They were traitors and enemies in the mind of the occupying Germans, just as they were patriots and heroes in the mind of the occupied French. As always, I believe, it is important to see the reasoning behind the resistance – passive or aggressive – and to see, equally, the reality of the other: the occupier and oppressor.

The Peacemakers in Israel/Palestine

A sampling of those persons who are most widely accepted as being Palestinian Christian peacemakers in Israel/Palestine, are Mitri Raheb, Jean Zaru, Hanan Mikhail-Ashrawi, Naim Ateek and Elias Chacour.

The Rev. Dr Mitri Raheb, a Lutheran pastor, is a Palestinian Arab born in Bethlehem in 1962. He presently serves as the General Director of the International Center of Bethlehem (ICB, or in Arabic *Dar Annadwa Adduwalia*), which was founded in 1995, and as the founder of Dar al-Kalima School and Academy, which was founded in 1998. He has served as Pastor of the Evangelical Lutheran Christmas Church in Bethlehem since 1988. Raheb received his undergraduate degree from Hermannsburg Mission Seminary, Germany, in 1984. His major was Protestant Theology. He completed his master and doctoral degrees, from Philipps University Marburg, Germany, with the same major. He and his wife, Najwa, have two daughters.

Dr Raheb's International Center was the place to which people were bringing food and water and medicine during the military invasion of Bethlehem in April, 2002. As I read his book, *Bethlehem Besieged, Stories of Hope in Times of Trouble*, I was reminded of that time in 2002, for I was in Jerusalem trying, with others, to bring needed items to besieged Bethlehem. Along with members of the Christian Peacemaking Team, I went in a car to deliver supplies to the people in Bethlehem. This was at a time when the Israeli forces had said there would be a lifting of the curfew for people to go out of their homes and for others to enter the city for humanitarian reasons. However, all normal entrances into Bethlehem were impassable – we tried several – due to road blocks and military checkpoints. (At that time a wall did not ring the city of Bethlehem). We ended up going to an area where other humanitarian groups were gathering, off the main road, on a hill looking down on the city. Our cars – lightweight Volkswagens and similar small cars not intended for off-road driving – were marked with black tape as

'Media' or 'News' or 'TV'. Seemingly the news media could get through more safely than the Red Crescent (the Arab equivalent of the Red Cross). As we were organizing, members of our various groups were in constant telephone contact with persons in Bethlehem. While the telephone lines, electricity, water and sewage had been damaged or shut off, the cell phones still managed to keep up a moment-by-moment account of what was happening. Just as we were ready to drive in, we received word from Dr Raheb that it was too dangerous for him and the others to leave their homes and go to the center. A cease fire had indeed been declared by the IDF, but as people were going out of their homes, they were fired upon by the IDF. Dr Raheb was apologetic that they would not be able to welcome us! In the midst of utter chaos, his own home and church complex severely damaged, he remained a hospitable person, unchanged by all the changes going on around him. (Later, groups were able to go in with the supplies we had brought).

The Church of the Nativity, which was also under siege for two days, suffered great damage as well. And this after the Episcopal Church in the United States, along with other Christian denominations worldwide, had raised hundreds of thousands of dollars to refurbish the Church of the Nativity for Jerusalem 2000, the second millennium Christian celebration! Following the 2002 damage that was done to the ICB, Raheb was able to have it repaired and rebuilt. The center now has a cultural and conference center which contains a three hundred and fifty seat theater, media center, restaurant and bar, guesthouse and meeting rooms. In spite of the ongoing occupation of Bethlehem, the ICB has remained a center for cultural and social activities for the people of Bethlehem. Not only that, Bethlehemites picked through the rubble, following the 2002 invasion, and took all the glass fragments they could find to the ICB art workshops where they made angels for Christmas of 2002, ordered by the Christian Council of Norway. We Americans have a saying about making lemonade from lemons. Raheb's people made angels out of shards of glass!

Raheb writes, in *Bethlehem Besieged*, that what he remembers about the Six Day War, when he was almost five years old, is the sound of the Israeli airplanes flying overhead, the bomb that dropped into the home next door to his family's home, and his mother taking him by the hand to the place she thought would be safest, the Church

of the Nativity. His father remained at home, listening to the radio.
After several days he and his mother were able to leave the church
and go home. Fortunately his father was alive, but the occupation
of Bethlehem had begun, with Israeli soldiers on the streets.

When Raheb was thirteen his father died. Raheb managed to
continue his studies while working in his father's bookstore,
graduating from high school – without a graduation ceremony. A
fellow student had been imprisoned for taking part in a
demonstration. Since the boy, Samir, could not graduate, the class
decided to forgo their own graduation. While Raheb says he did
not participate in actions during the Intifadas, the Intifadas have
had an effect on him and his family. He and his wife were unable to
have the normal wedding celebration (just the ceremony) due to
Israeli restrictions. And the ongoing stress, the violence, the pastoral
and personal concerns associated with the occupation continue to
be a part of his family's life.

Dr Raheb is known as a Palestinian theologian who has developed
a contextual Christian Theology specifically designed to be used
within the Arab Palestinian context. Like Naim Ateek, Raheb is
involved with interfaith dialogue as he works to bring peace and
justice to his city and his fellow Palestinians. An author of several
books, his first book in 1995, *I Am a Palestinian Christian*, offers a
number of lectures and sermons collected over several years which
give an insight into his contextual Christian Theology. As Rosemary
Radford Ruether wrote in the Foreword of *I Am a Palestinian
Christian*, 'Mitri Raheb ends his book with a line from Martin Luther
King, Jr: 'I have a dream'. Raheb's dream is that of two peoples and
three religions all sharing the one land of Palestine in justice and
peace. He calls Western Christians to be helpers, rather than
hinderers, in realizing that dream' (Raheb 1995: x). In 2003, he was
awarded the Lutheran Institute's Wittenberg Award for his service
to the Lutheran Church. The Holy Land Christian Ecumenical
Foundation gave him their award for his work with Christians in
Palestine. His work goes on, for as he says in *Bethlehem Besieged*, 'At
times when we feel as if the world must be coming to an end
tomorrow, our call is not to wait, not to cry, not to surrender.
Rather, our only hopeful vision is to go out today into our garden,
into our society, and plant olive trees. If we don't plant any trees
today, there will be nothing tomorrow. But if we plant a tree today
there will be shade for the children to play in, there will be oil to

heal the wounds, and there will be olive branches to wave when peace arrives' (Raheb 2004: 157).

Jean Zaru, Clerk of the Friends Meeting House (Quaker) in Ramallah and a founding member of Sabeel, was born in Ramallah in 1940. While she is among the fortunate who did not go into exile, she witnessed the reality of those who were uprooted by the Zionist takeover of her land. Her family home became a refuge to fifty people for six weeks, and home to a family for two years. She understands the reality, as well, of people needing to emigrate out of Israel/Palestine (her two sons have left Palestine). Zaru assisted in establishing the Friends International Center in Ramallah, which, according to their literature, 'works to lift up and nurture a Quaker presence in Ramallah; find ways to enrich and support the local community; and hold up and further peace and justice issues in the community'.

Zaru has written two booklets, *A Christian Palestinian Life: Faith and Struggle; and Overcoming Direct and Structural Violence : Truth and Peace-Keeping in the Palestinian Experience*. She has served on the Central Committee of the World Council of Churches (WCC) and on the WCC's Working Group in Interfaith Dialogue. Jean Zaru has also been a member of the International Council of the World Conference for Religion and Peace, she was President of the Board of Directors of the Jerusalem Young Women's Christian Association (YWCA) and served and was an officer on the national and world boards of the YWCA. She is committed to women's rights and to assisting women, whom she sees as having the majority of the burden for holding families together under the Israeli occupation. As a volunteer, she presently works with the Middle East Council of Churches on Islam and human rights.

Perhaps the most important, underlying aspect of Jean Zaru is her commitment to nonviolent resistance that is based on her Quaker values. The Swedish Fellowship of Reconciliation gave her their 2005 award for nonviolence. In an interview with Marianne Arbogast on 22 August 2007, Jean Zaru said, 'I am a pacifist myself – I am a Quaker. I don't believe that violence will lead us anywhere, neither morally nor strategically. And there are also some people in Israel who feel that way…we have crossed boundaries and networked with these Israeli groups, as small as they are, to work on these issues…But now the nonviolent movement (including Europeans, Americans and Jews from Israel) is becoming also a threat to

Israel...(which means) the nonviolent movement has been effective...'. While Zaru is able to leave the country for conferences and for personal reasons, she is unable to move her car two miles north or south or east or west of her home in Ramallah, which means although she is on the board of Sabeel, whose offices are located in Jerusalem, she can not attend meetings. And if she should need to go out of Ramallah for medical treatment, she is unable. And yet, she remains a lay minister with a strong voice for a peaceful solution to the occupation that has been a part of her life for most of her life. Her sister-in-law is Dr Hanan Mikhail-Ashrawi.

Hanan Mikhail-Ashrawi was born in the city of Nablus on 8 October 1947, in a Palestine that was as yet to face the 1948 partition plan and the reality of the State of Israel. She grew up in the traditionally Christian city of Ramallah, her father's hometown, which is now part of the West Bank. Following the establishment of the State of Israel, but before the 1967 War, Ramallah was under Jordanian control. Ashrawi attended The Friends Girls' School (a Quaker school), where students, both Muslim and Christian, interacted without any discrepancies or problems. When she was ten years old, her father was imprisoned for his political beliefs. Perhaps this early recognition of what it means to stand up for one's beliefs and go to prison for those beliefs, coupled with a strong identification of herself as Christian helped forge Hanan Mikhail-Ashrawi into the person she is today. In addition, her early interaction with Muslims and people from different backgrounds has seemingly freed her from biases and prejudices that come when the 'other' remains unknown.

Ashrawi went to the American University of Beirut, where, after the 1967 war, she found herself unable to return to Palestine because of Israeli restrictions on Palestinians' right to return to Israel/Palestine. This was the sixties, a time to rebel and idealistically proclaim one's views. Ashrawi was no different than Americans protesting the war in Vietnam when she joined a resistance cell in Beirut. 'Sacrifice and the *feda'yeen* (the freedom fighters – 'those who sacrifice') were the operative words as the new generation of Palestinians embraced the struggle for the liberation of Palestine' (Ashrawi 1995: 25-26). As a freedom fighter, she worked in refugee camps, doing menial labor to help those made refugees by the war in her country. She also began writing material about the revolution, taking reporters through the refugee camps and setting up other women's organizations. Her political feminist role began, in 1967, as she started or joined groups and served as a delegate to various conferences and gatherings (usually as the only woman delegate). Still unable to return to Palestine, after her graduation with a Master's Degree from the American University of Beirut, she went on to the University of Virginia at Charlottesville, as a graduate student, working on her Ph.D. in Literature. Here, Ashrawi continued organizing and joining groups as diverse as the American Friends of Free Palestine to the Appalachian Mine Workers and the Black Student Alliance. Her home was home to many organizations. Her life was already one that reached out to others. Her mind was ready to relate and support and learn from or teach others.

Once back in Israel/Palestine, in the early 1970s, Ashrawi continued to organize, teach and learn, as the Palestinian Minister of Higher Education and Research, a member of the Palestinian National Authority and as the official Palestinian Spokesperson at conferences and peace negotiations (including the failed Madrid Peace negotiations between 1991 and 1993). She served, also, as Chair and Dean of the Faculty of Arts at Bir Zeit University in the West Bank. Establishing the University Legal Aid Committee for Palestinian students (which became the Human Rights Action Project), feminist study groups and other groups and organizations, it appears that she is incapable of simply letting things go, rather she has a history of responding to a given situation by organizing and assisting.

Ashrawi decided to not serve on the National Authority, upon Arafat's return to Israel/Palestine after his exile out of the country. She chose, instead, to be a member of the Board of Commissioners of the Palestinian Independent Commission for Citizens' Rights. Her work with Nelson Mandela and the African National Congress members helped her decide to make this switch from politics to, 'serve the people and the cause with *amanah* (free will)' (Ashrawi 1995: 297). It is easy to see why, following the Palestinian 1996 election, Arafat told U.S. President Jimmy Carter that Hanan's elected position on the Legislative Council was equal to ten other women combined – he could have said 'men', as well (Carter 2006: 146). She has shown she has the intelligence, the humility, the vision and the political and religious center to be more than one expects of any given individual.

Hanan Mikhail-Ashrawi belies the stereotype of the Arab or
Palestinian woman. She moves easily internationally as well as within
her own culture – a culture that far predates our own in the United
States. As she writes, in 'The Intifada: Political Analysis', 'Most
people, when they understand that we come from families that go
back centuries, are amazed. They're not aware of the truth of the
Palestinian people or of the age of this nation. We are also the product
of two thousand years of continuous Christian presence in Palestine.
This fact has to be kept in mind: Palestinians are an ancient and
proud nation. We are not an accident of history' (Ateek 1992: 9).
Hanan Ashrawi is no accident of history, either. She shines forth as
a gift to the Palestinian and world's history, illustrative of her own
words, spoken to a gathering in Portland, Oregon: 'Ignorance is
our worst enemy. I would like to count on you to speak out...to
shine light into the dark places' (Abu-Jaber 1901). Asrawi is a person
who brings light into the places of darkness in her world and ours.

Ashrawi's life has shifted, as she has become a respected voice
for and within the Palestinian, Israeli and international communities.
She is a woman of integrity, who speaks her truth for her people
and to the world. As a person of faith who is a politician, she
represents the best of the 'new woman' of this present day Liberation
Theology Movement and she serves as a model to Palestinian Muslim
women who are yet to emerge internationally as leaders in their
own right. In the spirit of Guevara and Leonardo Boff, who defined
the 'new man' in their time, she has taken on a new role, redefining
herself as she has lived through her different life experiences.

The Rev. Dr Naim Ateek and The Rt Rev. Riah Hanna Abu El-
Assal and The Rt Rev. Suheil Dawani, all Anglican Episcopalians,
have been shaped and molded as well, by their life experience.
Ateek has broken from the expected role of priest in the diocese to
become the father of a new ministry and program that reaches out
from the Palestinian Christians to the rest of Christendom and to
the other religions of the world. Abu El-Asal, becoming bishop on
15 August 1998, in one of the holiest of Christian places as well as
the most conflicted of places in Christendom. Dawani, consecrated
bishop on 15 April 2007, facing a diocesan congregation that is
segregated and isolated as a result of the occupation. Before their
new leadership roles, these men had lived as refugees or displaced
persons in their homeland under the present Israeli occupation. They
see themselves as Palestinians, Arabs, Christians and Israeli citizens,

coming as each does from a lineage that goes back to the first Christians in the first century. Abu El-Assal, rector for twenty-eight years at Christ Church in Nazareth (the hometown of Jesus), calls the land not the Holy Land, but, '…the land of the Holy One' (Abu-El-Assal 1999: x). Of course the land is not holy, now, nor is it the land of only the Holy One, Jesus the Christ, but renaming and rethinking the familiar words is a beginning – a way out of the old ways that seem to no longer work.

The Rev. Dr Canon Naim Stifan Ateek, an Episcopal priest, is both a native born Palestinian and an Israeli citizen as well. Born on 2 February 1937, in Beisan, Palestine (now Bet Shean, Israel), Ashrawi and Ateek both were born into the historical times of change that have brought Palestine under the occupation of Israel. In the case of Naim, he lived through the Zionist (Haganah) troops' occupation of his hometown, when he was eleven, and was subject to the subsequent overturning of what had previously been a life full of the stability and beauty of family and friends, church, home and garden. Prior to the invasion, his family's home was one alive with family activities: 'family' consisting of nine siblings, an elderly relative, an aunt and an uncle and their respective families and missionaries from England, all living in adjacent homes that his father had built. The home Naim lived in was also the center for Christian activities, including the Orthodox Church's Sunday School. (Later, Naim's father became an Anglican and built the first Episcopal/Anglican church in Beisan.)

Ateek's family illustrates what happened in 1948 to thousands upon thousands of families. When the troops entered the town of Beisan, many residents fled, as they had heard of the massacre in Deir Yasin. As people left town, many gave valuable items, including their house keys, to Naim's father for safe keeping. The senior Mr Ateek vowed he would not leave Beisan.

This is what the people of Beisan – and other villages feared. On Friday morning, 9 April 1948, slightly over a month before the troops entered Beisan, Zionist commandos, headed by Menachem Begin, attacked Deir Yassin, a Palestinian village of about 750 residents. At the time the British still had a mandate over Palestine. By noon over one hundred people – half of them women and children – had been systematically murdered. After several days it was found that 350 had been murdered, ten homes had been dynamited and the cemetery had been bulldozed. Shortly after the killings in Deir Yasin,

Jacques de Reynier, the Head of the International Red Cross Emergency Delegation, forced his way through the military into the village. His eyewitness account verified what some of the fifty who escaped said. The bodies had been thrown into a well, to conceal the act, but the word had spread. By September, Orthodox Jewish immigrants from Poland, Ruania and Slovaia had been settled in what had been Deir Yasin.

On 12 May 1948, two days before Israel was declared a state, the Ateek's family town of Beisan was occupied by the Zionists. On 26 May 1948, the remaining Palestinian men of the the town were gathered in the military headquarters and told, 'If you do not leave, we will have to kill you'. They had two hours to gather what they could carry. Driven to the center of town, the Muslims and Christians were separated. Muslims were sent to Transjordan (Jordan). Christians were sent to Nazareth, a Palestinian city, now flooded with displaced persons – refugees within what had recently – only days before – been their own country. Ten years later, Israeli Palestinians were able, for the first time, to leave their area of residence and travel to other parts of occupied Palestine. Ateek's family found their town of Beisan, and their previously owned homes, occupied by Israeli Jews, their Orthodox Church falling apart and the Episcopal/Anglican church left as a storehouse. Following this visit, Naim's family returned to Nazareth, where his father suffered a stroke. He died two years later.

At the time of his father's death, Naim Ateek was in the United States attending university. His father's last gift to him were these written words: 'To my son Naim: read Psalm 37:5… "Commit your way to the Lord/trust in him, and he will act"' (Ateek 1989: 7-12). I have heard these family stories from Naim Ateek, as we have driven on the roads of Oregon and Washington, but they are available for others to read with more detail in his book *Justice and Only Justice*.

Ateek has acted upon his faith. He is married and has three children. Ateek has degrees from Hardin-Simmons University, Abilene, Texas; Church Divinity School of the Pacific, Berkeley, California; with a Doctorate of Ministry Degree from San Francisco Theological Seminary, San Anselmo, California. Ateek was ordained a deacon in Nazareth on 16 October 1966 and a priest in Haifa, on 21 May 1967. He has served as a parish pastor, Chapter Canon and Pastor of the Palestinian Congregation of St. George's Cathedral and as an interim priest primarily in Israel/Palestine, but in the United States as well. Presently, he is founder and director of Sabeel Ecumenical Theology Center in Jerusalem, where he has served since founding Sabeel in 1992. Since 1977, he has also served as a member of the Consultation on the Church and the Jewish People of the World Council of Churches (WCC). Somehow, with all this to do, he has given hundreds of lectures, overseen Sabeel's quarterly publication, *Cornerstone*, and has written five books, with others in the works.

Ateek said, in a talk at St. Thomas Episcopal Church in Medina, Washington, on 22 April 2001: 'To know Christ is to have the courage to take a stand for justice, but we must work in nonviolent ways as we champion the rights of the poor and oppressed. We must not forget that we can overcome evil with good. The final word is love, not hate' (Pneuman 2001: 5). As the father of Liberation Theology in Palestine, Naim has been faced with the necessity to live out his own words in every day occurrences – at check points, at the airport (where as a Palestinian-born man, only his Israeli citizenship gets him in and out of the country) in the streets, with his family – separated by the occupation or by Israel's restrictions. In big and small ways, as Ateek evolves the theology of Palestinian liberation, he is becoming the liberating spirit of change for his people. Out of an occupation that forcibly physically restricted him and his family, has grown a man unrestricted in his faith – his wisdom and his grace.

Archbishop Elias Chacour was born in the Palestinian town of Biram in 1940. When he was eight years old, his father gathered Elias and his six siblings to tell them that the Zionist soldiers would be coming to their town in a few days. The father told them about Hitler and how these Jewish people needed to come to Palestine as they had lost their homes in Germany and elsewhere. The father said, 'A few (Zionists) will stay in each home, and some will stay right here with us for a few days – maybe a week. Then they will move on. They have machine guns, but they don't kill. You have no reason to be afraid. We must be especially kind and make them feel at home' (Chacour 1984: 28). And so the family welcomed the Zionist soldiers, giving them their rooms, as the family slept on the roof and fed and cared for the soldiers' needs.

After some weeks, the men of Biram, as with Ateek's family, were called to the town square. The commander told the men, 'Our intelligence sources say that Biram is in serious danger...fortunately, my men can protect you. But it would risk your safety to stay in your homes. You're going to have to move out into the hills for a few days. Lock everything. Leave the keys with us. I promise nothing will be disturbed' (Chacour 1984: 50). As with the Ateek family, they were told to move quickly, taking nothing, in this case, as they would be returning. After two weeks, having heard nothing, the elders returned. Their homes were destroyed, doors smashed, items removed and, worst of all, armed soldiers were there who told the elders that the land was now Israeli land. They were forced by gunpoint to leave Biram.

After having spent two weeks in an olive grove, with the weather worsening, they went to the nearest hill town of Gish which was no longer occupied by the Zionist forces. This village, too, was empty of all but a few elderly people. Even though Gish was as badly devastated as Biram, it was better than living outdoors. The villagers from Biram accepted the hospitality of those remnants of the village of Gish. Almost immediately they found a common grave of some of the missing villagers. And very soon the military came and eventually took all of the men, whom they labeled 'terrorists', they dumped them on the road a great distance away, shooting over the men's heads to disperse them. The men of Chacour's family found their way back, eventually taking jobs in their own garden in Biram, tending their cherished trees for the Israeli occupiers. The rest of Chacour's childhood reads in dramatic fashion, as he was apprehended, falsely accused, beaten and released. At the same time, the elders were petitioning for their land. Instead of returning the land, the Israeli's bombed the town, and other towns nearby, destroying anything that remained. Chacour, rather than leaving the land of his birth – with his family who went into exile – remained and studied at the Bishop's House in Haifa.

These early years when Chacour experienced so much violence and betrayal, as well as the loss of so much that was tangible, did not turn him into a bitter man, rather he has become one of the most compassionate and caring of men in Israel/Palestine. He has had moments of anger and loneliness and unhappiness, but these feelings ultimately were transformed into an ability to relate and empathize with all – be they Israeli Jews, Muslims or Christians. His two books, *We Belong to the Land* and *Blood Brothers* are personable and powerful presentations of the facts of the occupation and the way one man – one family – survived with their faith intact.

As with Hanan and Naim, Archbishop Chacour is a person with international credentials. He was educated in Paris and has a degree from Hebrew University in Jerusalem, where he studied Hebrew, the Torah, the Talmud, Aramaic and Syriac. He was the first Arab to graduate from Hebrew University. While Ashrawi and Ateek are both fluent in several languages, Chacour speaks eleven languages. Chacour presently heads the new Metropolitan of the Melkite Catholic Diocese of Akka, Haifa, Nazareth and Galilee. (The Melkite Order is an Eastern Byzantine Church in communion with the Roman Catholic Church.) Elias' first assignment as a priest in 1965 was to a forsaken, fractured Palestinian community in Ibillin. Out of a most resistant congregation and town he created a modern miracle. But before the 'miracle', he had to lock them all in church during a Sunday service, refusing to open the door until they agreed to forgive one another and exchange the peace, something I would love to have done with a few congregations I know! Out of the depressed environment of Ibillin he built a library, a kindergarten and an elementary school. Each time the Israeli government caused difficulties with the paper work necessary for such construction. Not only did the church come back to life, but the town flourished and the ecumenical and interfaith connections were reestablished. Chacour proved there is no one left out in the house or the heart of Christ.

Out of these initial endeavors came Mar Elias Educational Institutions, which now consist of seven schools, including a technical college and a teacher's resource center. Today, more than four thousand young people (elementary through young adults) come to Ibillin from seventy towns and villages throughout the area. The institution is unique in that there are both Israeli Jewish and Palestinian teachers as well as Christian and Muslim students. In addition, Chacour has invited Israeli Jews to be students at the institution. It is not surprising that Elias Chacour has been nominated for the Nobel Peace Prize three times and was selected, in 2001, with Israeli Prime Minister Shimon Peres, as Man of the Year. As with Ateek, Chacour accepted Israeli citizenship after the founding of the State of Israel. And as with Ateek, having this status assists Chacour in his frequent trips abroad.

In an interview, following his consecration as archbishop, he was asked about his new role. Part of his response was, '...I can never compromise on any Christian value or any human value, and I consider justice and righteousness to be necessary for peace and security. Everybody would love to have me compromising for his side. But I'm used to being a troublesome boy. I do not compromise on the gospels' values or on human values. Even if that makes many angry, so what?' (Lewis 2006: 18). As a man who has lived through so many personal and national changes and observed or experienced so much brutality, Chacour appears to have been purified of fear and resentment and the other emotions that can limit and hold a person back. He holds no animosity toward the Israeli Jews or the Muslims. As he noted, the Christians and the Muslims have lived together for thirteen centuries. He is a reconciler, something the Melkite diocese is evidently in need of, the priests having been more or less on their own for these past thirty years without the unifying leadership that is expected from an archbishop. He calls the Christians of the Holy Land, the 'living stones'. Now he has the responsibility for bringing together some disparate parts of the Melkite clergy as he continues to work with people of all Christian denominations and faiths. Having done what he has already done in Ibillin, one only can assume whatever is needed will take place. It is people like Ateek, Zaru, Ashrawi, Raheb and Chacour – working together while they address their own venues of responsibility – that give hope to the place of Israel/Palestine and the people of the land so lacking peace.

Liberation Theology is evolving and redefining itself through the actions of many, be they recognized outside of their communities or not. What is missing in this country is recognition of the many still growing and expanding groups working for peace in Israel/Palestine. The world seems to focus on the negatives – on those who disrupt the peace, not those who are working for peace. As in the war years in Central America, individuals and groups are rising up within the area of Israel/Palestine, while international groups are coming in to assist, to accompany, to be in solidarity with their sisters and brothers in crisis, coming out of Israel/Palestine as witnesses and spokespersons for the situation as they observed it and experienced it, speaking to those in their own countries and communities.

Israeli Jewish Peace Groups

Within the Jewish Israeli population is a growing movement for a peaceful end to the occupation, an end to the building of the barrier Wall and a removal of the settlements presently on Palestinian land. The Committee for Solidarity with Birzeit University (CSBZU) originally stood against the Lebanese war, later becoming the Committee Against the War in Lebanon (CAWL). Peace Now (Shalom Achshav), independent from CAWL, was spurred into action following a CAWL demonstration held in Tel Aviv against the occupation. They now have 'tens of thousands of Israelis to demonstrate against governmental policies in the occupied territories' (Lockman 1989: 243). Peace Now interacts with Palestinians, and demonstrates with them – a move outward from their original purely Israeli Jewish stance.

As the Intifada continued, Peace Now maintained a twenty-four hour a day vigil opposite Ariel Sharon's house until Sharon's stroke necessitated his removal as Prime Minister. Peace Now's placards and signs reminded passerbys (and it is on a heavily traveled street in the Jewish sector of Jerusalem) of the ongoing deaths of both Israeli Jews and Palestinians. According to the author of *Intifada: The Palestinian Uprising Against the Israeli Occupation*, '…Peace Now and the more radical Jewish committees shared in common negation of the occupation and a recognition of its inherent instability' (Lockman 1989: 232).

The movement called Women in Black began in January, 1988, in Jerusalem, following the First Palestinian Intifada. Israeli women who saw the injustices of the occupation sided with their Muslim and Christian Palestinian sisters and brothers by standing in black in a protest of grief and sorrow. Beginning as a Jewish protest, it expanded as Palestinians joined, and now others of like minds have joined as well. It soon became a nationwide demonstration, joined by international solidarity vigils outside of Israel/Palestine. These are held every Friday at 1p.m. In many cities and towns in Israel/ Palestine and in other major and smaller cities throughout the world and the United States – even in Olympia, Washington, the small hometown of my parents and Rachel Corrie. Women gather dressed in black to stand in a silent protest. Each person holds a small palm-shaped sign which has these words: 'End the Occupation'. In Paris Square, Jerusalem, according to Reuven Kaminer, the '…youth groups of Kahane and the Tehiya party have formed counter demonstrations...but there are also many double honks of support' (Lockman 1989: 241) during the hour's vigil with people making peace signs with their hands.

While this is a women's movement that protests violence, some men, also, stand in solidarity with the women. Black clothing remains the common identification, a sign of the 'tragedy of the victims of violence'. Besides the weekly Friday vigils, Women in Black, also gather to protest other injustices (www.womeninblack.org). At this time they have won many peace prizes from Jewish organizations and from international groups, such as San Giovanni d'Asso's coveted peace prize in Italy and the United Nation's UNIFEM Millennium Peace Prize.

End the Occupation (Dai Lakibush), has within its membership veterans from previous Israeli wars who are now waging war for peace, and people who are new to the activist scene. This particular peace group has demonstrated more than any other group, '... venting its outrage over the rising tide of cruelty and repression', according to Reuven Kaminer (Lockman 1986: 235). What I consider most innovative are their educational tours to towns and refugee camps within the occupied zone, where Israeli Jews see what was previously unseen, gaining a new understanding of the occupation itself and their own responsibility for it as individuals within the occupying State of Israel. Under Israeli law it is illegal for Israelis to go to the occupied territories without a permit. They risk fines or imprisonment for crossing the check points without the proper documentation, which makes this a particularly creative and courageous program for all concerned.

The Vietnam Vets Against the War in Central America, from the 1980s in the United States, remind me of Israel's There is a Limit (Yesh Gvul) and the Courage to Refuse, two of the most hopeful of the Jewish peace groups, coming as they do from within the IDF reserves itself. Yesh Gvul began in 1982 with 2,500 reserve Israeli soldiers of the IDF who refused to serve in Lebanon. Their present position paper, taken from their web page, states: 'We, soldiers of the IDF, men and women, hereby declare that we will take no part in the continued oppression of the Palestinian people in the occupied territories, and we will not participate in policing actions or in guarding the settlements'. By 1988, 500 reservists had signed the petition as a 'declaration of refusal' (Lockman 1986: 236). The 'refuseniks' of the group, The Courage to Refuse, are now up to 1,330 soldiers, according to their web site. There is also a growing group of pilots who are refusing to bomb and strafe the refugee camps of the Palestinians.

Bat Shalom, which grew out of a 1989 meeting between several groups, including the Jerusalem Center for Women, is a Jewish Israeli and Palestinian Israeli feminist women's peace group. Bat Shalom focuses on the '…needs, rights, values and histories of both the Israeli and the Palestinian peoples', according to their official statement.

The list goes on and on, but within Israel it is important to point out these additional Israeli Jewish peace groups: Machsom Watch (which observes the major checkpoints, watching for harassment of Palestinians); New Profile (feminist with male members, established to 'civilize the militaristic Israeli Society'); Shani (Israeli Women Against the Occupation); TANDI (Movement of Democratic Women in Israel, the oldest Jewish/Arab women's organization, founded in 1949); WILPF (Women International League for Peace and Freedom which goes back to the 1920s); Women Engendering The Peace (political and educational project founded by the Dutch government in 2001); Noga (nonprofit organization founded in 1980, it created the first Israeli feminist magazine, organizes conferences, symposiums, workshops working for greater representation of women on all levels of life in Israel, including the peace process); Bat Shalom (founded 1989 by Israeli and Palestinian women in Brussels, in 1994, they created the Jerusalem Link, Bat Shalom (Israeli women) and The Jewish Center for Women (Palestinian women). They share the same principles and work to be a model of coexistence); Gush Shalom (The Peace Bloc, an extra-parliamentary organization independent of any political party, was founded by journalist Uri Avnery in 1993. Gush Shalom objects to the illegal Israeli occupation and many specifics associated with the occupation. They won the Right Livelihood Award in 2001); The Israeli Committee Against House Demolitions (founded by Jeff Halper, it became a nonprofit organization in 2004. The group is a nonviolent, direct action group established to oppose and resist Israeli demolition of Palestinian homes in the Occupied Territories. Each summer internationals from Europe, the United States and elsewhere, set up a camp and rebuild destroyed Palestinian homes); The Coalition of Women for a Just Peace (often referred to as CWFJP or Just Peace. An international forum for justice and peace with institutions – such as Palestine Restitution Trust. There are branches of Just Peace around the world.)

Palestinian Christian and Muslim Peace Groups

The Al-Liqa Center for Religious and Heritage Studies in the Holy Land was established in 1983, in Jerusalem, by a Palestinian group of Christians and Muslims. Since then, Al-Liqa has provided a center for both these religious and historical studies and for Palestinian theological reflection. Since 1989, Al-Liqa has broadened its scope to include Jews as well as Christians and Muslims, hoping through dialogues and conferences to bring about a greater understanding between the three religions. Naim Ateek was a member of Al-Liqa, before he founded his own group, Sabeel. Both groups continue to collaborate on their mutual goals of justice, peace and better understanding between the peoples of this land so broken and scarred.

And within Palestine, as well as Israel, are the women's groups – amazingly strong and resonant, particularly so given the male-dominated society in which both Palestinian Muslim and Christian women live. The Palestinian Women's Movement began in 1920, as a result of the colonial policies of the British and French and as part of the growing sense of a new Palestinian national identity – a national identity born out of the occupation and the domination of the colonialists. Contrary to the traditional roles of women, these early Palestinian feminist women protested, organized and spoke out publicly. After the 1967 war, and the further occupation of Palestinian soil by the Israeli government, the women's movement increased in strength and number. Interestingly, according to Rita Giacaman and Penny Johnson, '...the major framework for women's organization and activity were the over one hundred traditional charitable societies located in the towns.

Among the most successful of these were In'ash al-Usra (Family Rehabilitation Society or the preservation or renewal of the family), which grew from two rooms in 1965 to a large modern building with over 100 employees, an orphanage and a wide variety of programs; and the Arab Women's Union in Nablus, which runs a hospital' (Lockman 1989: 158). Besides this, much like what happened in South and Central America in the latter part of the 1970s, the women (and men) organized themselves into trade and student unions and in youth and health movements.

Samiha Khalil founded the Society of Ina'ash El-Usra. For this she is also called Um Khalil (Mother of Khalil, as she is the Mother of the Society). She was born in the Palestinian village of Anabta in 1923, she died in 1999. During her childhood she attended the Friends Girls' School in Ramallah. Her father was Mayor of Anabta. She married Salameh Khalil at seventeen. In the 1948 Israeli/Arab War, she and her family were forced to go to Gaza as refugees. Eventually she went to Lebanon, and when it was possible, returned to Ramallah. She became the only woman on the National Guidance Committee – a committee that sets policy for the Palestinian resistance to Israel's occupation of the West Bank and Gaza. She ran against Yasser Arafat in the first Palestinian elections, and while she did not win, her candidacy spoke to the position she held – and still holds – in the community.

The organization she founded, Ina'ash El-Usra, offers emergency assistance (food, clothing and medicine), as well as the following programs: political prisoners assistance (financial aid, winter clothes, lobbies for their release); scholarships (80 Palestinian students receive money to attend local schools); free dental and medical clinics (for beneficiaries and employees); kindergarten (founded in 1967, it services up to 130 children); day care (founded in 1977, it is for children of working mothers – the children range in age from one month to three years; young girls (founded in 1984, room and board and medical needs are met and education is provided for 58 girls); child program sponsorship (working with local and international individuals and groups, 540 children have benefited to date. $600 is given, per child, to families who are in need). Money to support many of these programs comes from outside of Palestine, donated by Palestinians in exile and by other concerned persons and organizations.

From the educated women who had been activists on university campuses came the stimulus to join together in supporting one another: the Women's Work Committee and the Working Women's Committee (1978) formed first and were followed by the Palestinian Women's Committee (1982) and the Women's Committee for Social Work (1984). These committees operated much like any union organization, sending in 'seasoned women leaders' (Lockman 1989: 159) to assist in the grassroots organizing in a given area. At the same time, sit-ins at the International Red Cross offices, and other places gave a focus to the detentions of Palestinians and the conditions under which they were detained. One remembers the Mothers of the Disappeared, in South and Central America, protesting outside of the prisons as they waited for word of their missing relatives. Their first rally was held in Buenos Aires on 28 April 1977. They have continued their presence until recently. How extremely sad that the same need is being met by a similar group of women, although this time in a different culture and at a different location.

Probably the best known of the intellectual and articulate Palestinian women is Hanan Mikhail-Ashrawi, mentioned earlier, whose 1995 book, *This Side of Peace*, speaks to the women's movement and her movement out of the traditional role of being a woman into the confrontational role of being a woman advocate for truth and justice. Her writing about the 1990 Women's March and Human Chain speaks as much about the fear engendered among the occupiers and the oppressors as it does about the strength and determination that was felt by the women challenging the status quo. In this case the march was to be a peace march, going through Jerusalem. Against songs and chants, the IDF responded with tear gas and bullets. The Human Chain was to encircle Jerusalem in a ring of peace; instead, the ring was broken by IDF blasts of colored water (Ashrawi 1995: 64). Among many organizations and groups she has brought into being, Ashrawi is the founder of Miftah, The Palestinian Initiative for the Promotion of Global Dialogue and Democracy.

Within Palestine, in addition, are other organizations, including these peace groups: Palestinians for Peace Now (Salam al-Ann, formerly Yalla Salam, opposes violence, including suicide bombers, extremists, and fanatics. It believes peace must come about through talks between Palestinians and Israelis directly); Adalah (The Legal Center for Arab Minority Rights in Israel); and finally, The Coalition of Women for Peace, a leading voice for peace in Israel/Palestine. Founded in November 2000, members are both independent women and members of nine women's peace organizations. Jewish and Palestinian Israeli women citizens may belong. Their goal, to end the occupation and to bring a resolution to the present impasses. Some of these organizations have become international, moving as it were from Israel/Palestine out to the wider world.

International Peace Groups

Coming from outside Israel/Palestine are most notably the International Solidarity Movement (ISM), The Christian Peacemaking Team (CPT), The Christian Witness for Peace in Israel/Palestine, and The World Council of Churches (WCC). Other groups are: Women Peacemakers of the World, a project of Global Coalition for Peace, which sponsors Mother-to-Mother for Peace and Non Violence (a program that links mothers of different cultures, who support one another in bringing up their children in a nonviolent environment); Women Shaping Society (for non-child bearing age women); Young Women in Action (for young women from thirteen years of age and up). These are only a representative portion of a wide-ranging variety of secular and religious international peace groups involved in Israel/Palestine at this time.

The International Solidarity Movement is a secular peace group that comes out of Palestine itself, and is led by Palestinians. ISM is comprised of volunteers from all parts of the world, who are trained in Gandhian nonviolent techniques. They do many things, from assisting with the olive harvests, protecting homes about to be bulldozed, to standing in silent protest against the occupation and what they call the 'Apartheid Wall'.

The Christian Peacemaking Team is, according to their brochure, a group dedicated to giving support to '…faith-based nonviolent alternatives in situations where lethal conflict is an immediate reality or is supported by public policy'. CPT began in 1984 when delegate Ron Sider spoke before the Mennonite World Conference in Strasbourg, France, challenging attendees to address the need for a nonviolent solution to the Palestinian/Israeli situation. This happened at the same time as such groups were establishing themselves in Central America, notably the Accompaniment Program (*Accompaniamento*). These are volunteers who spend twenty-four hours a day with a person who is likely to be a target for assassination, and the Peace Delegations from the various denominations. By 1992, delegations from CPT were found in Haiti, Iraq and the West Bank of Israel/Palestine.

The Hebron peacemaking project came out of discussions between two former Peacemaker Corps members and the Mayor of Hebron. Having been in Hebron in 1998, myself, with the members of CPT who live there as a presence for peace, I am an admirer of their vigilance and their willingness to live in such a risk-taking environment. As observers, wearing eye-catching red vests and caps, it is not unusual to see one of them step between Israeli and Palestinian individuals to de-escalate an escalating situation. They are visible and they are watchful and they embody the best of Christian witnessing, in my estimation. These volunteers sign on for twelve months, spending part of their time in Hebron and Israel/Palestine, and part of their time talking to groups back in the United States.

The World Council of Churches (WCC) has its roots in the early twentieth century as an ecumenical organization. Officially established and recognized in 1948, it has grown out of a commitment to unite the Christian churches in a united world organization. Subsequently, WCC has worked equally hard with displaced Palestinians and has drawn world attention to the need to recognize the rights of the states of Israel and Palestine to exist. WCC works closely with Sabeel and the churches in Jerusalem, where its office is housed. The WCC has supported the UN's call to make Jerusalem a jointly shared city and has focused on ending the occupation of Palestine. Their Ecumenical Accompaniment Programme continues to have a presence in Israel/Palestine.

Another group that bridges the international and local peacemaking groups, that really isn't a peacemaking group, per se, but is helping to bring understanding and a different way of seeing and hearing and being with the 'other', is 'Sounding Jerusalem'. This group was founded by Austrian Erich Oskar Huetter, the Artistic Director for 'Sounding Jerusalem', and Israeli musician and conductor, Daniel Barenboim. (Daniel Barenboim also directs the Peacemaking Youth Orchestra Project in Ramallah.) This two-week chamber music festival had its inaugural season in the Old City of Jerusalem in 2004. The purpose of 'Sounding Jerusalem' was to bring Austria's leading master musicians and other international guest musicians to Jerusalem to work with talented young Palestinian and Israeli music students. The students in 'Sounding' had auditioned and been selected prior to the actual event. During this two week festival, various master musicians from Austria and Europe gave nightly concerts, tutoring the students by day. The students attended the nightly concerts and in the last two concerts performed. In the next to last concert, 'Rising Stars', instructors and students performed a 'best-of-program' selection and in the last concert,

'Bright Resonances', the Stuttgart Chamber Orchestra, Austrian soloists and local students performed selections from Wolfgang A. Mozart, Joseph Haydn and Felix Mendelssohn Bartholdy.

The purpose was to bring people together in a way that would overcome previously held stereotypes, biases and prejudices – music being the common denominator and language of those involved. The students ranged in age from five years to sixteen. As Erich Oskar Huetter wrote in the festival's brochure:

> We can learn a lot from the human tradition of making music together. Especially chamber music requires a high degree of sensitive interaction between the people involved. It asks for more than just being able to read the music. To reach mutual understanding in the group, all members of the ensemble have to respect each other's opinion, have to accept their partners as equals. That is the basis a musician needs to express clearly his personal statement on the instrument while the others have to listen carefully. This music forum for the Old City intends to connect people through the language of music and to found a big, sounding community in East Jerusalem.

It so happened that the home base for the festival was at the Austrian Hospice where we were, also, housed for the 'Journey to Jerusalem: Hospitable Memories' exhibit and lecture series. While we were hanging the exhibit, we began to hear the most plaintive and powerfully passionate lamenting and celebrating – emotional pouring forth – of music from a piano one floor below. Finally, wanting to see who was playing such incredible music, one of our group went downstairs and came back dumbfounded. The musician was not only fourteen, but the music we were listening to was his own compositions and improvisations! We all went down to hear him. And there began a most moving experience during that particular time in Jerusalem. The young boy playing was a Palestinian Christian who lived in Haifa, traveling to Jerusalem, during the week, for his music lessons and going to Ramallah to play the organ in the Anglican Church on Sundays.

The Curator of the exhibit is, besides being an archeologist, a Roman Catholic priest. One night when The Rev. Dr Carney Gavin was celebrating the Eucharist on the balcony off the end of the corridor on the floor that held the exhibit and our rooms, this young man approached us. We invited him to join us, which he did. Some days later, he and I were visiting and he asked me if I believed in miracles. I said, 'I do'. He told me, 'Miracles happen in Jerusalem'.

When I asked what he meant, he told me when Gavin put the eucharistic bread into his hand he felt an electric shock. He said he had a second 'miracle' when I put my hand on his shoulder, after he had given us a private recital of his own compositions. (He had a visible cramping of his shoulder, which relaxed when I applied some Healing Touch techniques to the area.) Of course the 'miracle' was this young man and the others – first Austrian and European adults and Palestinian children, later including Israeli Jewish children who were able to afford music classes outside of 'Sounding', but were equally qualified for the program through their musical talent.

The musicians, young and older, became the incarnational mix – a portrait – of the miracle of the possible. This 'possible' was seen and heard in both the individuals, their interactions, their speech and most of all in the music they all loved and shared and performed. It was proof that the arts and music can move people beyond their expectations of themselves and others and beyond the expectations others hold out for them. The music, itself, is proof of this as well – the composers touched into a place within themselves that formed notes of music that spoke to and from the heart of creation's place of peace, brought these many years later into the City of Peace.

Unfortunately, this festival gathering that was sponsored by the Austrian government and sanctioned by the Israeli government – having been presented to and approved by the authorities well in advance of the actual concert series, was not held in a bubble protected from the violence that occurs in Israel/Palestine. As I mentioned, the concerts primarily were performed in the Old City of Jerusalem in such places as the Franciscan Church's Courtyard; the American Colony Hotel's Pascha Room, the Armenian Patriarchy, the Austrian Hospice, the Jerusalem Music Center, the Lutheran Church of the Redeemer's Courtyard and the Ecole Biblique's Arcade Courtyard. Three concerts were held outside of Jerusalem, in Bethlehem at the Edward Said Conservatory of Music; in Nablus and in the Al Kamandjati Music Center in Ramallah. As I mentioned, the Israeli government had approved the concert series and was well aware of the locations of each of the concerts and that children of all ages were participating in the festival.

Midway through the concert in Ramallah, the concert was interrupted by shouting and shooting, on the street side of the wall of the building where the concert took place. People inside the concert hall could hear the moans of those shot. The IDF had shot a suspected terrorist and others who were unfortunate enough to be in the vicinity. Then as witnesses at the concert, who had gone to see what was happening outside saw, a soldier approached the 'terrorist', who was lying on the ground wounded. The soldier walked up to him and shot him point blank, killing him. The concert was canceled at this point.

The youngest children had not been taken to the concert because of concerns about Ramallah and the unpredictable nature of the area. Those children and Austrian and European musicians and concert goers who did attend the concert were traumatized, particularly the ones who saw the killing of the wounded person. Toward the end of the festival, the Ramallah concert was concluded in the Austrian Hospice. Once again, violence interrupted this concert. As was mentioned in the earlier chapter on Settlers, settlers attacked a Christian deacon walking on the Via Dolorosa. Not realizing what the source of the noise was, the concert continued, but afterward, the evening's musical celebration was dampened by this new outburst of unprovoked hatred.

'Sounding Jerusalem', like many other artistic, musical and dramatic gatherings of like-minded people, offers a note of hope, even in the worst of situations. But how sad that the very children to whom the founders of the festival hoped to give a brief break from the violence were denied a complete two weeks of solace in their sanctuary of music. And, one might ask, what happened to the soldier who killed the 'terrorist'? As in most such cases – nothing that we were able to find out. The Israeli occupation appears to go on without the oversight and legal restrictions required by international law.

Tragedy Behind the Theology

After the 1948 War, 880,000 acres of previously 'Arab-owned land was taken over by the Israeli Custodian of Absentee Property' (Najjar 1992: 27). Between 1948 and 1953, 370 new Israeli Jewish settlements were built on Palestinian land designated as 'absentee' property. In addition, 10,000 Palestinian businesses were taken over or destroyed and 95% of the olive groves that Israel now holds were taken from Palestinian owners (Najjar 1992: 27). Those 'absent' or away for personal or business reasons, or at school, were displaced during the emergence of the State of Israel. These people were not allowed to reenter the country. Confiscated land, demolished houses, a people living in their own Diaspora, has created an atmosphere of desperation and despair for the Palestinians and for many Israelis, themselves.

Between 1948 and 1999, 444 Palestinian villages were destroyed (Abu-El-Assal 1999: 162), bulldozed, removed, depopulated – absorbed into the landscape. They are remembered in Palestinian history, in folk songs and in the grieving hearts and memories of those still living. There is a pain and a brokenness of spirit that is hard for those of us who have never experienced such a magnitude of loss to comprehend. It is not just the loss of home – of house and all the personal possessions inside – it is the loss of one's heritage and one's inheritance: house and ground, heirlooms, personal little and big items, plus the loss of place – of town, with its schools, places of worship, stores – all the places where memories are made and life is lived. Only after natural disasters, like hurricanes, can we imagine such a loss of homes and personal property, but that is only part of it, because nature does not remove the land upon which houses stood. This seems to be abhorrent behavior that only humans are capable of.

On a lesser, singular, more personal scale the same destruction is presently taking place. This is the wanton destruction of homes, done in the name of 'security', done in the name of reprisal for an act of violence committed by a family member or by someone suspected of being a 'terrorist'. This goes against international laws, it goes against what should be the common sense of any human being. It is an extreme example of corporate punishment – making everyone in the family suffer to punish a suspected or known individual. Can one even begin to imagine what our cities would look like if every suspected and every convicted person who had committed a violent act had his/her home bulldozed and his/her parents/family's home destroyed? Even imagining the destruction of the home, then one must envision being homeless, without clothing, food, shelter, medicine – anything one might reasonably expect to have in a 'normal' living environment.

Perhaps, then, one might begin – just begin – to feel some of the pain and suffering and hopelessness that has led some Muslims to join the jihad martyrs and has led more than some Christians to flee the area, to leave their homeland for another land where they can attempt to rebuild a home and a life. Ironically, many come to the United States. I say ironically, because it is U.S. built Caterpillar bulldozers and the U.S. funded Israeli military and U.S. arms which have destroyed and continue to destroy the homes and the lives of the Palestinian people.

And now an American martyr, along with others martyred, has made a town – a house – one life – speak for the many. Rachel Corrie was born on 10 April 1979 in Olympia, Washington. She died at age twenty-three, in Rafah in the Gaza Strip, in Israel/Palestine, on 16 March 2003. In her brief twenty-three years, Rachel made a statement in the life she lived, in the death she encountered and in the words she wrote. Like many young women, Rachel kept diaries and journals. Some of her written material has been used in the play, 'My Name is Rachel Corrie'. A powerful play, banned off-Broadway for its message which in actuality helped spread the message, much as 'Banned in Boston' used to ensure a play would have a hit season when it went to New York.

Rachel was one of three children born to Craig and Cindy Corrie, Sarah and Christopher being her elder siblings. Rachel attended Capital High School and Evergreen State College, both in Olympia, Washington. She was a senior at Evergreen when she died. Evidently enthusiastic about dance and drama as well as peace and poetry – the pictures shown of her at the Celebration of her life brought the fullness of her life into focus: dancing in a tutu, walking about as a dove of peace in the Earth Day procession, being a child – a young woman – a person whose life was full of family and friends – a volunteer in a strange land with a universal purpose: peace and justice.

In the fall of 2002, Rachel Corrie wrote these words, words which were included in the Celebration of her life:

> 'We are all born and someday we'll all die. Most likely to some degree alone. Our aloneness in this world is, maybe not anymore, a thing to mourn. Maybe it is a thing that has to do with freedom. What if our aloneness isn't a tragedy. Tragic passing of love affairs and causes and communities and peer groups. What if our aloneness is what allows us to speak the truth without being afraid? What if our aloneness is what allows us to adventure – to experience the world as a dynamic presence – as a changeable interactive thing?'

For a woman from Olympia, the larger world of Israel/Palestine and the work she was involved in as a volunteer with the International Solidarity Movement (ISM), could have seemed overwhelming, but she thrived in spite of the various difficulties inherent in her work. Perhaps her hometown, the state capitol that still has a small town feel about it, located on Puget Sound, with water and trees and views of Mt. Rainier and the Olympic Mountains and a contested passion among the inhabitants of the area for the environment, be one an environmentalist or a person who lives and works off of the environment, was not all that different under the surface, than Gaza. Evergreen State College is known as a progressive environmental institution, which rather suited Rachel who was an expressive lover of the environment – hiking frequently – and passionate about social justice issues. She, with her class, gave a press conference on world hunger when she was in the fifth grade. In the seventh grade she was part of a student walkout supporting striking teachers. It should not be surprising then, that Rachel as a young woman was outspoken, passionate and focused on those whom she considered were being treated unfairly or unjustly. With all of her rhetoric and writing, she had a humble sense of reality and a sense of humor that appeared, as in this excerpt from her writings:

> 'This realization that I will live my life
>
> in this world
>
> where I have privileges.
>
> I can't cool boiling waters in Russia.
>
> I can't be Picasso.
>
> I can't be Jesus.
>
> I can't save the planet single-handedly.
>
> I can wash dishes'.

> Staged reading of excerpts from 'My Name is Rachel Corrie', (16 March 2006, Portland, Oregon.)

American citizen Rachel Corrie was bulldozed to death in Rafah while trying to protect a home about to be razed. As was mentioned earlier, she was there with the ISM. They were trying to protect homes owned by Palestinians from being demolished, living with families in homes that might be targeted for demolition, standing in solidarity with the people of Rafah. The ISM members were obvious and easily recognized in their bright red/orange vests. I have seen the footage of the film taken at the time Rachel was bulldozed to death. She was standing on a tall rise of previously bulldozed earth, in front of the home the Israelis were preparing to bulldoze, other ISM members nearby. She was looking directly into the eyes of the Israeli soldier as she called out to him on a bullhorn to stop the destruction. Looking right at Corrie, the driver of the bulldozer drove ahead, over her, and then – with people screaming at him to stop – he reversed and drove over her again. Cradled in the arms of her friends, her last words were, 'My back is broken'.

As Craig and Cindy Corrie have said, not only was her back broken, but the beauty and the innocence of Rachel and her friends, as well as the lives of her family were broken and shifted and changed forever. To see the reality of what happened is to see an ugliness that should not be imagined, yet is lived out, humans against humans. The soldier driving the bulldozer claimed he did not see Corrie. The Israeli government found no wrongdoing. The United States' government refused to investigate. The lie and the horror and the ongoing seemingly unrestricted violence against Palestinians, in particular, continues.

Since their daughter's death, Craig and Cindy Corrie have devoted their lives to Rachel's causes: peace and justice in Israel/ Palestine, as well as to finding ways to let the truth of their daughter's death be known and recognized in the official/political realms of the United States and Israel. Craig Corrie was formerly an executive in the insurance industry and Cindy Corrie was a former educator, school and community volunteer. Both have left a comfortable, small town existence to stand up for things they knew little about before their daughter's experiences in Israel/ Palestine and her ensuing death. Out of a place of grief they have come as strong voices for truth and justice as they move about the country and the world. They have established the Rachel Corrie Memorial Fund and the Rachel Corrie Foundation for Peace and Justice.

Years ago when I was teaching children in Cambridge, MA, I used a book, *The Wump World*, to help instill a sense of environmental responsibility in the minds and actions of my young students. In *The Wump World*, aliens come to earth with their behemoth machines, their smoking, noxious factories, their asphalt, concrete, clear cutting approach to earth. The Wumps, fuzzy four-legged earth-creatures, disappear into caves and crevasses, as their beautiful, sustaining planet is destroyed. When all has been ravaged, savaged, torn, rendered, wrecked and used up, the aliens depart. The Wumps gradually come out to behold what had been, as no longer being.

Rachel Corrie lived and died in such a world, but she is not the only non-Palestinian or non-Israeli to die in such a place. That sense of desolation – that sense of mindless destruction – that sense of hopelessness struck me, as I watched the British documentary, 'Killing Zone'. In 'Killing Zone', a British team of journalists went into Gaza, focusing on Rafah (the town of Rachel's death) – a town that has been cut in half: one half being in Egypt and the other half remaining in Gaza. This is also the town where two British citizens were shot by the IDF: James Miller, a British HBO cameraman, was killed while approaching the IDF. He was in a group who were waving white flags, identifying themselves as journalists. The IDF had been observing the group that day, and was aware of their presence. Tom Hurndall, a British ISM activist, was shot while trying to pull two children out of the way of gunfire. He died, after having remained in a coma for months. These three non-Palestinian and non-Israeli deaths, as horrific as they are, are minute microcosms of the wounding and the dying that takes place daily in the lives of the Palestinians and, to a lesser extent, the Israelis. As of 2007, roughly 300 Palestinians have been killed for each Israeli.

Aside from the physical brutality – the blood stained stones and streets and sand and earth and walls of Rafah – aside from the psychological brutality – the nightly, continuous dusk to dawn shelling by the IDF, bullet holes in homes and buildings evidencing the passing of the night – aside from the shootings by day in the streets and homes and the United Nations' school building and school yard – aside from all of this, is the wreckage of the world of Rafah, the infrastructure, the architectural structures, the edifices that made up the city. What the IDF had erected as a fence between one half of Rafah and the other, is now a wall. What had been a densely populated and housed urban wall-to-wall town of houses and businesses, is now a strip of desolation separated by another kind of wall. For three meters, on the Gaza side of the wall, houses have been bulldozed. Why? For reasons of security. The only house remaining was the one which Rachel Corrie died protecting. Within a year following her death, the house was bulldozed when the family, who owned the house, was away.

The home was owned and lived in by Samah and Khaled Nasrallah and their three daughters. He worked as an accountant with Palestinian Airlines and she was completing her certification to be a teacher. As with many other home owners in the area, they are long time residents, known and respected – not 'terrorists'. When they returned to their home, they found not a shred of their home or belongings – the area scraped clear of anything reminiscent of them or the Rachel Corrie event. But memory is stronger than any physical reminders. All the other homes in the same area have been pushed down – apart – but rather than scraping them into a flat surface, the pieces have been left to lie in jagged fragments of another time, reminiscent of scenes from 'Planet of the Apes', or of our own country's 9/11 before the clean up in New York City.

The United States-supplied Caterpillar bulldozers are the behemoths of the *Wump World* made real for the people of Palestine. The sheer horror of these machines – giant blades raised – machine gun turrets in place – all armored – darkly moving on their destructive, invincible path defies imagination. And yet this is a reality that is far too real. People from the ISM, in red/orange vests, loudspeakers at hand, calling out for a cessation to the ongoing destruction of homes of people innocent of any crimes – placing their lives on the line, as they face down the machines of death, and Palestinian youths throwing rocks and stones seem to me to be the biblical 'David's' of today.

Everyone should see this movie, 'Killing Zone'. Words do not describe the horror of seeing these weapons of mass destruction in operation, as they knock down homes owned for generations or other homes recently built and still mortgaged and being paid for by the owners. How would any of us respond if our homes were so treated, if we were living nightly under a barrage of bullets, if all we held dear – family, friends, possessions were subject to unannounced destruction – to death? One asks how suicide bombers can do what they do? In such a climate of hopelessness, desperate, unthinkable decisions are made and actions take place. Life can feel like it is of no value in a place like Rafah. Faith, alone, offers hope and for some, that faith – that hope – comes in a death voluntarily given, rather than waiting and living in the fear that one's life will be involuntarily taken.

I do not support suicide bombers, nor do I support the escalating violence on both the Israeli Jewish and the Palestinian Muslim sides.

I do, however, understand how one's utter sense of loss and blindness to any potential, positive future can lead one to become violent. As with South and Central America – those like Torres and Guevara choose the path of change in an explosive righteous wrath and those like Romero and the many others in Liberation Theology choose the path of reason, living prayerful, powerful, outspoken lives of peace. To die as a warrior or to die as a peacemaker, one will ultimately die. To live as one at peace, in a land of peace is the goal and the objective. How one gets there is forever a question posed, to be grappled with and answered from the depths of one's true self. Those using violent means do not in the end win. Bulldozing homes is both a personal and a corporate matter, but history shows that no people occupied remained so forever and that no people occupying kept their hold on an area forever. Encircling cities and towns – cutting off their electricity, water, sewage, phone system and enforcing excessively restrictive curfews – limiting access or excluding inhabitants from access to fields, employment, medical and hospital services – sealing off, isolating and then shooting, strafing, bulldozing homes and those individuals contained within the circle of military confinement, does not make for a positive, peaceful environment.

I think of any city or town in America and how our citizens would react, especially given the tone of the National Rifle Association (NRA). It takes an amazingly strong person to not attempt to fight strength with strength, but rather to continue to fight with logic and faith and a determined hope for the other's change of heart. That's what many are doing, keeping their heart in the midst of this heartless time. That's what faith-based people are doing, but especially the Christians who, while they can name many martyrs – those who have died – can not name any who have responded in kind, fighting, killing and abusing the other – the one called 'enemy' or 'terrorist' or 'neighbor'.

I turn now to a story of a man whose family roots in Palestine go back many centuries. Josif and his brother have a shop on the Via Dolorosa, called the Christ Prison Shop (because it is near the place that Jesus purportedly was held before his crucifixion). The shop features icons, as well as other items of interest – some new and many of an archeological nature. People from St. George's College – people from all over the world – shop at the Christ Prison Shop. There are pictures on the walls of the many famous and everyday people who have been customers in the shop. They shop there because Josif is a very moral and ethical person whose honesty has ensured repeat customers. I met Josif on my first trip to Israel/ Palestine, when my friend, Dick Toll, took me with him to meet the brothers and look around the place as Toll shopped for items to take home to Portland, Oregon. On subsequent trips, I, too, have taken people to the shop on via Dolorosa. I am fond of the brothers and appreciate their knowledge and their hospitality. One almost never enters a shop in the Old City without being offered a cup of the traditional mint tea – brewed with fresh mint – or a glass of Coke or another soft drink.

While at the Austrian Hospice, I went to the shop, which it turned out was only a few doors down the street from where we were staying. When Josif and I started talking, I asked where his brother was and Josif told me that he had died about a year and a half ago. And then Josif told me that he, himself, had just had a stroke, only a few weeks before my arrival at his store. Josif and his brother had started the shop some fifty years before. When his brother died, Josif said, he was broken-hearted, grief stricken and then he, himself, had a stroke. He was taken to the largest hospital in Jerusalem, Hadassa, where as it turned out the director of the hospice had also been taken when she broke her back. She said the medical treatment was excellent, the humane treatment abysmal. She is an Austrian Christian. Josif is a Palestinian Muslim. The hospital is in the Israeli Jewish section of Jerusalem. In Josif's case, he was in the hospital for less than a day when the results of the recent Israeli election became known.

According to Josif, after the elections, thirty politicians had heart attacks or stress reactions that appeared to be heart attacks. Josif was told he had to leave the hospital because they needed his bed for the incoming politicians. He refused. He was completely paralyzed down his right side. The hospital staff insisted that Josif leave. They told him, as Josif recalled the experience, that he could return in a few days, but for the time being he had to go to another place as there was no room for him. Josif continued to refuse to leave unless they could place him in another hospital. Finally, he was ousted from the hospital – simply put out the front door and told to go home until they had room. Josif began a long, approximately ten mile, walk home. As he tried to walk, holding onto the walls and sides of buildings, he said he called upon God to take his life. He felt he had nothing to live for as he tried to walk, stumbling, falling, crawling, clinging to objects to get up and trying again to walk again, falling again, calling out to God. Finally, many, many hours later Josif arrived at his home. He realized he was walking better, that he was much stronger and that he was not falling.

Josif's doctor told him, later, that with the kind of stroke he had (which was evidently located in his neck and in his head) only one in a thousand patients lives. He, Josif, lives. He is still numb down one side, but each day he is stronger. He is presently receiving the medical treatment he was earlier denied, including physical therapy. He is a man who praises God, exults in his own personal miracle of life. As the young musician discussed earlier said, 'miracles happen in Jerusalem'. Josif feels God wanted him to live, and so he intends to live his life out in continued praise and thanksgiving. No one I know knew whether Josif was a Christian or a Muslim. It has never mattered, to me, what he believed because I believed in him as a person, and I still do.

Given his amazing healing experience I was curious, so I asked him about his religious affiliation. He told me he is a Muslim whose family goes back to the original families in Jerusalem. He has lived and he continues to live his faith out in his work and in his personal and family life and in his worshipping life at the mosque. He holds no resentment toward those at the hospital who pushed him out, for without that experience he would never have had the subsequent experience of healing that happened. As he told me the story of his falling and attempting to walk his way home from the hospital, I could not escape comparing Josif's experience to the earlier such walk Jesus made on his own Way of the Cross.

There is no death, thank God, in this experience of tragedy, but there is great tragedy in the disparagement between humanitarian healing services as they are offered to Israeli Jews or to Palestinians – to international citizens or to Palestinians, be they Muslim or Christian. This great tragedy of disservice harms any and all who live in Israel/Palestine, for it is a dehumanizing discredit to those who are in the healing profession, as well as a demoralizing experience for the common persons who may some day be patients. Josif's story is unique, one hopes, but other such experiences indicate Josif is not alone in his hospital/medical treatment. The many documented stories of Palestinians held at Israeli check points while they gave birth or were in need of immediate medical attention are unfortunately not unique. Rather they are outlandish and against what the people – be they Israeli or Palestinian – believe in and desire for themselves and one another. The greatest tragedy, perhaps, in this ongoing sad story of the rupture between brother and sister Semites, is how trust and common courtesy and good will has been erased by fear. This is true on both sides of the issues – on both sides of the wall – on both sides of the unresolved two state situation.

Conclusion

After reading and writing my way through the scriptural, historical, theological and all so human story of Israel/Palestine, I feel that it will take some one person, or group, to act as a catalyst for change, as it will take representatives from all groups to bring about change. A spark can ignite the passions for peace, but it will take a collaborative shift in the will of all the people, or at least in the will of those with enough power to enforce the changes necessary on all the people. It will take a listening, a praying, a sharing between members of the Abrahamic feuding family. It will take persons of great humility, wisdom, patience, compassion and perseverance. It will take an Oscar Romero, a Desmond Tutu, a Nelson Mandela, a Mohandas Gandhi, a Catherine of Siena, an Indira Gandhi, or an Ivone Gebara – persons of deep spiritual knowing whatever their faith base – persons willing to allow the spirit to shift them from a place of the known to a place of the unknown. It will take persons confident in the powerful grace of God and it will take persons fearless in the face of all things physically and emotionally fearsome. Who will emerge as these much needed leaders? Whom will the opposition – on all sides – allow to be free, to live, to lead and to turn prophetic ideals into tangible, physical realities?

I still believe the remaining fragment of the indigenous Christian Church in Israel/Palestine holds the greatest hope of providing such a prophetic voice and person, in part, because it has the least power within the region and therefore the least to lose. Given the circumstance at this time in 2008, the indigenous Christian Church has its very survival to lose, but taking leadership will embolden the people and give them a way to survive. I am hoping for the willingness of the church to act upon its faith in boldness and courage. I also feel that the policies and practices of the greater Christian Church in Israel/Palestine, which includes U.S. based fundamentalist, evangelical and Zionist Christian groups, offer some of the greatest threats to the peace process. When The Rev. Jerry Falwell spoke to Bob Simon, in 2003, on a CBS segment, 'Zion's Christian Soldiers', Falwell said, 'There are seventy million of us... If there is one thing that brings us together quickly, its whenever we begin to detect our government becoming a little anti-Israel'. Previous to this, in 1998, Falwell had promised Israel's Benjamin Netanyahu he would, '...mobilize evangelical churches to oppose steps involving territorial concessions to the Palestinians'. The response from evangelical pastors and theologians in Palestine to this latter statement, according to Sherri Muzhor in *The Jordan Times* on 3 July 2003, was, 'Our task of sharing the love of Christ in this region is becoming increasingly difficult as our brothers and sisters in the West openly express sentiments and endorse policies that produce greater injustice and aggression against Palestinian Christians and Muslims'. These two diverse statements exhibit a growing divide that exists within the greater Christian Church. Just as in South and Central America, the polities of literalists and liberationists are in conflict in Israel/Palestine to the disadvantage of both the Israelis and the Palestinians.

In addition, ideological, theological and political differences between the resident denominations in Israel/Palestine and a sense most of these denominations have of private ownership of places sacred, creates an air of tension and discord. Even the most peace-centered of denominations has its own partisan parochial practices which are hurtful to their own churches, the larger body of Christian churches and the peace process, itself. Finally, God and men have continually – as recorded by men in the various scriptures – forged relationships which have eroded the broader relationships within the Abrahamic family.

There is time for change, but not much. There is a need for change, and it must be dramatic. With the ever-escalating war in Iraq, which has moved from a war of 'liberation' to a war polarizing the Western and Arab cultures and the primarily Christian and Muslim faiths (while making the Israelis feel more vulnerable), the situation in Israel/Palestine is even more volatile. With a few gigantic, almost myth-like exceptions, the men of Israel/Palestine have not been able to bring about peace. They seem entrenched in the rhetoric, policies and practices of the past. What I feel Israel/Palestine needs is an infusion of fresh new ideas, or a new look at the old ideas allowing for the clarity a new vision – a new way of being – can bring. It is this creative and often unexpected and unpredicted movement of spirit that can move the respective states into finding and implementing a reasonable and acceptable and suitable solution. South Africa is the most comparable modern example of a land and a people who made a major shift from an unjust to a more just balance of power, with accountability and forgiveness built into the healing process that followed. In this land of Israel/Palestine – this land with a transforming and transfiguring history of hope, there is, also, room for the unexpected guest of God's providence. After all, this is not only the land of Abraham, Ishmael, Isaac Jacob and Esau; it is as well the land of Esther, Hannah, Deborah, Mary the mother of Jesus, Mary Magdalene, and Martha and all the others who were women prophets or women of faith who lived beyond the constricting borders of their era's expectations. Is it not time to let men and women lead together, as Jesus allowed men and women to work together with him in creating and living out a new model of life?

All will not be pleased if the status quo changes. The risk that change might bring discomfort to a few is far less than the risk that the present lack of change in attitude or action is presently bringing to Israel/Palestine. The children deserve a future free of post traumatic stress and all the illnesses and disorders and body-breaking-soul-wrenching-psyche-destroying terrors that come from the reality of warfare. The land of *here*, rather than the land of *wherever*, is the land the Israeli Jews and the Palestinian Muslims and Christians crave for and deserve. The children need adults to break from their ancient modes of thinking and do something truly revolutionary – revolutionary in the understanding that a revolution for change can bring about the positive results needed without additional destruction or adversarial actions. It will take more than a few brave women and men to speak and to act to move their world forward, with international support and protection to bring about a truly new Jerusalem – a new age of enlightenment. Unfortunately, since 1948, one person and one idea after another has been gunned down. When passions are so high and emotions so unpredictable, it takes incredible faith and willingness to serve one's people and the cause of freedom for all. As some have been killed, or died, or been imprisoned for their beliefs and actions – Jews, Muslims and Christians – other people of vision have arisen. There is hope in this continual resurrection – this continual re-birthing of people of goodwill and vision – of people willing to step forward into a place lacking any solid footing or guaranteed outcome.

As an Episcopalian/Anglican, I look to our retired bishop, Riah Hanna Abu El-Assal, and to our present bishop in Jerusalem, Suheil Dawani; to Naim Stifan Ateek, our Episcopal/Anglican priest/ founder of Sabeel; and Hanan Mikhail Ashrawi, our Episcopal/ Anglican woman in a political role dominated by men. As a Christian, I look toward Elias Chacour, Archbishop of the Melkite Church, Jean Zaru, Quaker and Sabeel Board Member and Mitri Raheb, Lutheran pastor. As a person of hope, I look toward Israeli/ Palestinian persons other than those mentioned in the body of this book: Dr Haidar Abdel-Shafi, Founder and Director of the Red Crescent Society of Gaza; Yehezkel Landau, Co-director of Open House, a center for Jewish-Arab reconciliation and coexistence in Ramle, Israel; Rabbi Michael Lerner, Founder of the Tikkun Community and Gila Svirsky, Founding member of Women in Black. These people represent all the people of good faith who choose to live in their faith in the hopes of finding a solution that will perhaps not satisfy all, but will ensure that safety and reason for all will ultimately prevail. As a person who believes in the power of Liberation Theology, I look ultimately to the common, everyday people to lead, to become leaders, to emerge victorious with a workable and livable plan for peace.

In our own Episcopal Church of the United States of America, we recently consecrated a new Presiding Bishop, Katharine Jefferts Schori. We have only had women priests and bishops in the Episcopal Church within the last quarter century. This is still seen as a relatively new and often difficult – or celebratory – change within the structure of the church, depending on one's theological or personal perspective. Those of us women who have remained in the service of Christ within the framework of the church have not always done so with ease or without challenges or threats. Some parts of the Episcopal Church have been rent asunder as individual churches have left to become part of another Anglican communion – usually under the auspices of a bishop outside of the United States.

This unfortunate schism began after women's ordination and has continued. On the other hand, people have joined the Episcopal Church because of women's ordination and our church's various stands for justice and equality. The Rt. Rev. Katharine Jefferts Schori is the first woman to serve as Presiding Bishop. This has brought about more cries against what some see as an overly progressive and liberal stance for the church. In fact, while our new Presiding Bishop does stand for equality and justice issues that offend some, she is the most balanced, centered, calm person who could be envisioned for this time and these issues. She is a person of faith. No matter what one might think about what she believes, it is hard to imagine that what she believes and what she proclaims comes from something other than a deep spiritual place of truth and grace and hope. She is not judgmental or vindictive. She offers an open hand to all in what I see as the true intention and personhood of Christ.

And so, along that line of thinking, it seems the Episcopal Diocese of Jerusalem could consider allowing women to be ordained – breaking down one more barrier, as Jesus broke down so many barriers in his lifetime. I pick out the Episcopal Diocese of Jerusalem because it is my denomination. It is the most likely indigenous denomination, that does not already ordain women, to ordain women – if not now, in the near future. And why push for the ordination of women in the church in Israel/Palestine? Because our Presiding Bishop has shown she is able to converse with the most conservative of bishops and prelates and archbishops, bringing a new voice, a new understanding, a new compassion and a new face to the church. Why not allow those strong women within the Palestinian Christian community who are, already, doing so much to bring about peace and harmony and salvation to the area, bring their own fresh voice of strength to the table of those ordained, with the men ordained, as they look to the future of the church and Israel/Palestine?

When I went to Israel/Palestine, in 1998, the Dean of St. George's College asked me to celebrate the Eucharist for our study group. Because the diocese did not – and still does not – allow women ordained to function as such in the diocese, I was invited into the Roman Catholic convent next to the Church of the Holy Nativity, where I celebrated the mass for our group and for the congregation present. It was a first for that particular Roman Catholic church. I was, as it turned out, the second woman to celebrate in the diocese, The Rev. Carol Anderson, Rector of All Saints' Church, Beverly Hills, California, having preceded me as celebrant a few weeks earlier, in another location of Israel/Palestine.

It was amazing – the overwhelmingly positive response of the women in the convent, the response of those in the congregation and, following the service, the response of a Roman Catholic priest in the Church of the Holy Nativity (when he saw me in my clergy collar). The following Sunday, at the reception held by the Episcopal cathedral's Arab congregation for our visiting group at St. George's Cathedral, when the women of the congregation learned I was ordained, they clustered about me. They were thrilled. They were delighted. They were curious and accepting and most affirming. When I see what the women are doing outside of the church's ordination framework, I am compelled to ask why not give full voice, full sacramental rites to women within the ordination framework of the church?

I am cognizant of the problems this could bring with relations within the indigenous Christian community, especially the Orthodox Church. I am aware, as well, of the support and acceptance I have received from my brother ministers within the more patriarchal, hierarchical and conservative wings of the church: Protestant, Roman Catholic and Orthodox. If Hanan Ashrawi can break down the barriers of the world political, why not give the same opportunity – and support – to Palestinian Christian women who feel called to serve as one ordained within the Diocese of Jerusalem? Ordained or lay – supported or not – the voices and faces and insights of women must meet equally, with men, at the table of opportunity. A new land – a new nation – or two new nations on one land – will need as much leadership, pastoral care, educated directives, ecumenical and interfaith understanding as it can muster.

Since men have not yet solved the problems, I suggest they allow women to move into the process – opening the door, rather than forcing the women to battle down the door or wedge it open and sneak into the process toward peace. In a war zone – in a time of war – there is need for all people, men and women, elderly and young, to be participants in the work toward peace.

It came to me in a service at the monastery of the Society of St. John the Evangelist, in Cambridge, Massachusetts, that from contemplation comes action and from action comes change. This is not a new or extraordinary concept, but put into practice it could be both.

Contemplation: First, we need to join our Palestinian Christian family in prayer, not only in a Sunday morning prayer-notation that mentions the Palestinian Christians, but in significant prayer time – special vigils, times set apart to hold them in our intentions and in God's arms of light and love.

Action: Not only should we be with them – our Palestinian Christians – in prayer, but they should be with us in ways that make them visible in our churches. We need reminders that they exist, as they need reminders that we know they exist. Peace candles – lit at each service – photos of churches and members of congregations, children's pen pal programs, adopt or support-a-family, or a church or a group, or a hospital – or a way, some way, of adopting new understandings and building new relationships with Palestinian Christians are all ways that the Episcopal Diocese of Olympia, and others, are attempting to make these crucial links between individuals and congregations. We need to join our Palestinian Christian brothers and sisters in ways that make them real – in prayerful, educational, experiential ways, real ways of learning to know them and giving them, in turn, an opportunity to know us. We can offer summer camps for children – children who are losing their very childhood; we can go and be part of our individual denominational projects, of Sabeel's witnessing, of secular peace groups. We can go and we can listen and watch and learn and then return to speak our truth. And, finally, we can bring people to us – for a respite is in order for all the people, especially the priests and the peace workers in Israel/Palestine.

There is a great need for us to bring in delegations for peace, from all the mainline churches, flooding Israel/Palestine with a presence that is supportive of our sister and brother Christians in Israel/Palestine. The religious Zionist Jews and Zionist Christians, in this country, are doing this now, and very successfully. We need to have a counter voice of wisdom and experience and grace that can be heard throughout the United States. We need to galvanize our people, here, to support our baptismal people, there – not in opposition to another group or religion, but in support of a dying faith in the land of our common birth. All of this, contemplation, action and change-making must absolutely be done with the Palestinian Christian Churches, under their direction, with their input as to what would and will work for them, in a cooperative, collaborative and collegial way. The idea is to support them, to reveal them to our world, to know them as they wish to be known.

The idea is not to colonize the churches, turning one oppression into another, but to be with them in solidarity.

Because we are the ones – in the United States – who are supporting the Israeli government and their practices with ten million dollars a day and other additional assistance, we are responsible to those receiving the brunt of our 'gifts'. As American citizens, we are called to be responsible for the actions our government makes on our behalf, with our tax money. We must be pro-active, not only reactive. Each of the three actions, be they active or passive, remains with us as a sign of our judgment and our decision making.

As Naim Ateek believes, '…the true God is a God of justice, truth and peace for all peoples, a God who calls all peoples into relations of justice and peace with one another' (Ateek 1997: 187). We as Christians have the right and the responsibility to help our Palestinian Christians be what they are in a way that is neither tribalistic, legalistic nor oppositional. We have the right and the responsibility to see that they can come to their peace table as one equal in the sight of the power brokers as well as in the sight of God. Ultimately, whatever we do, hope comes out of the people of Israel/Palestine. As with South and Central America, the Christians of Palestine teach us about our faith as they live it out in a land of desperation that is overshadowed by a cloud of the unknown. They are reminders to us that hope comes as faith comes, from the heart. It may take a laying down of arms – a national day of Palestinian nonviolent protest – a visible sign of a determination to live in peace and not responsive violence, it may take a drastic and dramatic event, but the time will come when peace can and peace will reign. May it be in our lifetimes!

BIBLIOGRAPHY

Abu-El-Assal, Riah, *Caught In Between: The Extraordinary Story of an Arab Palestinian Christian Israeli* (London: Holy Trinity Church, 1999).

Abu-Jaber, Diana, *The Oregonian* (Portland, OR: November 4, 1901).

Aburish, Said K., *The Forgotten Faithful: The Christians of the Holy Land* (London: Quartet Books, 1993).

Alter, Robert, *The Art of Biblical Narrative* (New York, Basic Books, 1981).

Arc, Thomas L., *Israeli Peace, Palestinian Justice: Liberation Theology and the Peace Process* (Atlanta, GA: Clarity Press, 1994).

Aruri, Naseer, *The Obstruction of Peace: The United States, Israel and the Palestinians* (Monroe, ME: Common Courage Press, 1995).

Ashrawi, Hanan, *This Side of Peace: A Personal Account* (New York: Simon and Schuster, 1995).

Armstrong, Karen, *A History of God, The 4,000-Year Quest of Judaism, Christianity and Islam* (New York: Ballantine Books, 1994).

_____ *The Battle for God* (New York: Ballantine Books, 2001).

_____ *Jerusalem: One City, Three Faiths* (New York: Ballantine Books, 1997).

Ateek, Naim, Marc H. Ellis and Rosemary Radford Ruether (eds.), *Faith and the Intifada: Palestinian Christian Voices* (Maryknoll, KY: Orbis Books, 1992).

Armstrong, Karen, and Michael Prior (eds.), *Holy Land, Hollow Jubilee: God, Justice and the Palestinians* (London: Melisende, 1999).

_____ Cedar Duaybis and Marla Schrader (eds.), *Jerusalem, What Makes For Peace! A Palestinian Christian Contribution to Peacemaking* (London: Melisende, 1997).

_____ *Justice and Only Justice: A Palestinian Theology of Liberation* (Maryknoll, NY: Orbis Books, 1989).

_____ *Toward a Strategy for the Episcopal Church in Israel With Special Focus On The Political Situation: Analysis and Prospect* (D.Min. Thesis, San Francisco Theological Seminary, 1982).

Barry, Tom, *Roots of Rebellion: Land and Hunger in Central America* (Boston, MA: South End Press, 1987).

Bayer, Charles, *A Guide to Liberation Theology for Middle Class Congregations* (St. Louis, MO: CBP Press, 1986).

Benvenisti, Meron, *Intimate Enemies: Jews and Arabs in a Shared Land* (Berkeley: University of California Press, 1995).

Berrigan, Daniel, *No Bars to Manhood* (Garden City, NY: Doubleday, 1970).

Berryman, Phillip, *Cry of the Earth, Cry of the Poor* (Maryknoll, NY: Orbis Books, 1997).

_____ translator. *Feet-on-the-Ground-Theology* (Maryknoll, NY: Orbis Books, 1987a).

_____ *Liberation Theology, Essential Facts About the Revolutionary Religious Movement in Latin America and Beyond* (New York: Pantheon Books, 1987b).

_____ *Stubborn Hope: Religion, Politics and Revolution in Central America* (Maryknoll, NY: Orbis Books, l994).

Birch, Bruce C., *Let Justice Roll Down: The Old Testament, Ethics, & Christian Life* (Louisville, KY: Westminster/John Knox Press, 1991).

Boff, Leonardo, O.F.M., *Ecclesiogenesis: The Base Communities Reinvent the Church* (Maryknoll, NY: Orbis Books, 1977).

_____ *The Theology of Captivity* (Vozes, Brazil: Ceropolis, 1980).

_____ *When Theology Listens to the Poor* (San Francisco, CA: Harper and Row, 1984).

_____ *Church: Charism and Power: Liberation Theology and the Institutional Church* (New York, Crossroads, 1985).

_____ *Jesus Christ Liberator* (Maryknoll, NY: Orbis Books, 1986 [1972]).

_____ *The Maternal Face of God* (San Francisco, CA: Harper & Row, 1987).

Boff, Clodovis, *Theology and Praxis: Epitemological Foundations* (Maryknoll, NY: Orbis Books, 1978).

_____ *Feet-On-The-Ground-Theology, A Brazilian Journey* (Trans. Phillip Berryman; Maryknoll, New York: Orbis Books, 1987).

Boff, Leonardo and Clodovis Boff, *Introducing Liberation Theology* (Maryhill, NY : Orbis Books, 1987).

Bonds, Joy et al. *Our Roots Are Still Alive: The Story of the Palestinian People* (Institute for Independent Social Journalism, New York: Peoples Press, 1977).

Brettler, Marc Zvi, *The Creation of History in Ancient Israel* (New York: Routledge, 1995).

Bright, John, *The Authority of the Old Testament* (Nashville, TN: Abingdon Press, 1967).

Brockman, James R., *The Word Remains: A Life of Oscar Romero* (Maryknoll, NY: Orbis Books, l982).

Bruggeman, Walter, *The Land: Place as Gift, Promise, and Challenge in Biblical Faith* (Philadelphia, PA: Fortress Press, 1977).

Burdick, John, (ed.), *The Church at the Grassroots in Latin America: Perspectives on Thirty Years of Activism* (Westport, CN: Praeger, 2000).

Carter, Jimmy, *Palestine Peace Not Apartheid* (New York: Simon & Schuster, 2006).

Chacour, Elias, *Blood Brothers* (Tarrytown, NY: Fleming H. Revell, 1984).

_____ *We Belong to the Land* (Chicago, IL: University of Notre Dame Press, 2001).

Chakmakjian, Hagop A., *In Quest of Justice and Peace in the Middle East: The Palestinian Conflict in Biblical Perspective* (New York: Vantage Press, l980).

Collins, Larry, and Dominique LaPierre, *O Jerusalem* (New York: Simon and Schuster, 1972).

Coote, Robert and Mary, *Power, Politics and The Making of the Bible* (Minneapolis, MN: Fortress Press, 1990).

Cone, James, H., *A Black Theology of Liberation* (Philadelphia, PA: Lippincott, 1970).

_____ *Speaking the Truth: Ecumenism, Liberation and Black Theology* (Grand Rapids, MI: W.B. Eerdmans Publishing Company, 1986).

Chua, Amy, *World on Fire, How Exporting Free Market Democracy Breeds Ethnic Hatred and Global Instability* (New York, Doubleday, 2003).

Cross, Frank Moore, 'Justice: Perspectives from the Prophetic Tradition' in James L. Mays and David L. Peterson (eds.), *Prophecy in Israel* (Philadelphia, PA: Fortress Press, 1987).

Ellis, Marc, H., *Toward a Jewish Theology of Liberation* (Maryknoll, NY: Orbis Books, 1987).

_____ *Unholy Alliance: Religion and Atrocity in Our Time* (Minneapolis, MN: Fortress Press, 1997).

_____ *O Jerusalem! The Contested Future of the Jewish Covenant* (Minneapolis, MN: Fortress Press, 1999).

Fabella, Virginia, and Sergio Torres (eds.), *Irruption of the Third World: Challenge to Theology: Papers from the Fifth International Conference of the Ecumenical Association of the Third World* (Maryknoll, NY: Orbis Books, 1983).

Friedman, Thomas, *From Beirut to Jerusalem* (New York: Anchor, 1991).

Gebara, Ivone, *Longing for Running Water: Ecofeminism and Liberation* (Minneapolis, MN: Fortress Press, 1999).

Gottwald, Norman K., *The Tribes of Yahweh: A Sociology of the Religion of Liberated Israel, 1250-1050 B.C.* (Maryknoll, NY: Orbis Books, 1979).

Gutierrez, Gustavo, *A Spirituality of Liberation* (Maryknoll, NY: Orbis Books, 1972).

_____ *A Theology of Liberation* (Maryknoll, NY: Orbis Books, 1973).

_____ *We Drink from Our Own Wells: The Spiritual Journey of a People* (Maryknoll, NY: Orbis Books, 1984).

Habel, Norman C., *Literary Criticism of the Old Testament* (Philadelphia, PA: Fortress Press, 1971).

Harkabi, Yehoshafat, *Israel's Fateful Hour* (New York: Harper and Row, 1986).

Haling, G.R., and Abdul-Kader A. Shareef (eds.), *Approaches to the Qur'an* (London: Routledge, 1993).

Heller, Mark A. and Sari Nusseibeh, *No Trumpets, No Drums: A Two-state Settlement of the Israeli Palestinian Conflict* (New York: Hill and Wang, 1991).

Hilterman, Joost R., *Behind the Intifada: Labor and Women's Movements in the Occupied Territories* (Princeton, NJ: Princeton University Press, 1991).

Holy Bible, New Revised Standard Version, with Apocrypha (New York: Oxford University Press, 1989).

Holy Qur'an (trans M.H. Shakir, New York: Tahrike Tarsile Qur'an, Inc., 1985).

Hourani, Albert, *A History of the Arab Peoples* (New York: Wagner Books Edition, 1991).

Kellerman, Abaron, *Society and Settlement: Jewish Land of Israel in the Twentieth Century* (Albany, NY: State University of New York Press, 1993).

Lacquer, Walter, and Danny Rubin, *The Israel-Arab Reader* (East Rutherford: Pelican, 1987).

Lange, Martin and Reinhold Iblacker (eds.), *Witnesses of Hope* (Maryknoll, NY: Orbis Books, 1981).

Lernoux, Penny, *Cry of the People: The Struggle for Human Rights in Latin America: The Catholic Church in Conflict with U.S. Policy* (New York: Penguin Books, 1982).

Lewis, Janet Lahr, 'Archbishop Elias Chacour', Cornerstone Magazine. Issue 40, Spring 2006.

Lockman, Zachary and Joel Beinin. *Intifada: The Palestinian Uprising Against the Israeli Occupation* (Boston, MA: South End Press, 1989).

Lueders, Arnold J., *The Islamic Sacred Book in The Light of The Christian Scriptures* (Pasadene, CA: Southern California Bible College, 1950).

Mays, James L., and David L. Peterson (eds.), *Prophecy in Israel* (Philadelphia, PA: Fortress Press, 1987).

Mehdi, Mohammed Taki, *Peace in the Middle East* (New York: New World Press, 1967).

Murphy-O'Connor, Jerome, *The Holy Land, The Indispensable Archaeological Guide For Travellers* (Oxford: Oxford University Press, 1992).

Najjar, Orayb Aref, *Portraits of Palestinian Women* (Salt Lake City, UT: University of Utah Press, 1992).

Neher, Andre, *Moses and the Vocation of the Jewish People* (Irene Marinoff trans., New York: Harper Torchbooks, l959).

Nouwen, Henri, *The Wounded Healer, Ministry in Contemporary Society* (Garden City, NY: Doubleday, 1972).

_____ *Gracias! A Latin American Journal* (San Francisco, CA: Harper & Row, l983).

_____ *Love In a Fearful Land: A Guatemalan Story* (Notre Dame, IN: Ave Maria Press, 1985).

Peters, Rudolph, *Jihad in Classical and Modern Islam: A Reader* (Princeton, NJ: Princeton University Press, 1996).

Pneuman, Mary, 'The Rev. Canon Naim Ateek Preaches at St. Thomas' Medina', *The Episcopal Voice*, Vol. 87, No. 5, (June 2001) p. 5.

Prior, Michael, *The Bible and Colonialism, A Moral Critique* (Sheffield, UK: Sheffield Academic Press, l999).

_____ *Western Scholarship and The History of Palestine* (London, UK: Fox Communications and Publications, 1998).

Quigley, J., *Palestine and Israel: A Challenge to Justice* (Durham, NC: Duke University Press, 1990).

Raheb, Mitri, *Bethlehem Besieged, Stories of Hope in Times of Trouble* (Minneapolis, MN: Fortress Press, 2004).

_____ *I Am a Palestinian Christian* (Minneapolis, MN: Fortress Press, l995).

Rambo, Lewis R., 'Reflections on Conflict in Israel and the West Bank', *Pacific Theological Review, Reflections for Ministry Today*, Vol. XXI, No.1. (Fall 1987).

Rantisi, Audeh, *Blessed Are The Peacemakers: A Palestinian Christian in the Occupied West Bank* (Grand Rapids, MI: Zondervan Books, 1990).

Rosenwasser, Penny, *Voices From a Promised Land: Palestinian and Israeli Peace Activists Speak Their Hearts* (Willimantic: Curbstone Press, 1992).

Rowland, Christopher (ed.), *The Cambridge Companion to Liberation Theology* (Cambridge, UK: Cambridge University Press, 1999).

Ruether, Rosemary Radford, *The Wrath of Jonah, The Crisis of Religious Nationalism in the Israeli-Palestinian Conflict* (San Francisco: Harper, 1989).

Sabeel Position Paper, *The Jerusalem Sabeel Document, Principles For A Just Peace in Palestine-Israel* (Jerusalem: Sabeel Ecumenical Liberation Theology Center, 2001).

Said, Edward, *After The Last Sky: Palestinian Lives* (New York: Pantheon Books, 1986).

_____ *Covering Islam* (New York: Vintage Books, 1997).

_____ *The End of the Peace Process: Oslo and After* (New York: Pantheon Press, 2000).

_____ *Peace and Its Discontents: Essays on Palestine in the Middle East Peace Process* (New York: Vintage Press, 1993).

_____ *The Politics of Dispossession* (New York: Knopf, 1995).

_____ *The Question of Palestine* (New York: Vintage, 1992).

Sarwar, Ghulam, *Islam, Beliefs and Teachings*, The Muslim Educational Trust, (Nottingham, UK: Edwin Packer & Johnson Ltd, 1989).

Shafir, Gershon, *Land, Labor and the Origins of the Israeli-Palestinian Conflict* (Berkeley, CA: University of California Press, 1996).

Shehadeh, Raja, *The Third Way: A Journal of Life in the West Bank* (New York: Quartet Books, 1982).

Sigmund, Paul E., *Liberation Theology at the Crossroads: Democracy or Revolution?* (New York: Oxford University Press, 1990).

Sizer, Stephen, 'The Origins of Christian Zionism', *Cornerstone Magazine*, Issue 31, Winter 2003.

Smith, Pamela Ann, *Palestine and the Palestinians, 1876–1983* (New York: St. Martin's Press, 1984).

Smith-Christopher, Daniel (ed.), *Text & Experience: Towards a Cultural Exegesis of the Bible* (Sheffield, UK: Sheffield Academic Press, 1995).

Sobrino, Jon, S.J., *Christology at the Crossroads* (Maryknoll, NY: Orbis Books, 1982 [1978]).

_____ 'Fullness of Life, The Martyrs Give Us Love', written for the 20th anniversary of the martyrdom of the four US Churchwomen, 2001.

_____ *Spirituality of Liberation, Toward Political Holiness* (Maryknoll, NY: Orbis Books, 1989).

Strum, Phillippa, *The Women are Marching: The Second Sex and the Palestinian Revolution* (Chicago: Lawrence Hill Books, 1992).

Wagner, Donald E., *Dying in the Land of Promise, Palestine and Palestinian Christianity from Pentecost to 2000* (London, UK: Melisende, 2000).

Wallace, Jim, 'Against Impossible Odds', Sojourners Magazine, September/October, 2001.

Whitelam, Keith W., *The Invention of Ancient Israel: The Silencing of Palestinian History* (London: Routledge, 1996).

Zaru, Jean, *A Christian Palestinian Life: Faith and Struggle* (Jerusalem: Sabeel, 2004).

_____ *Overcoming Direct and Structural Violence: Truth and Peace-Keeping in the Palestinian Experience* (Jerusalem: Sabeel, 2004).

General Index

SCRIPTURE INDEX

Printed in the United States
130780LV00001BA/4/P

9 781845 533809